THE BIRTH OF WESTERN PAINTING

Plate I

Detail from

THE RAISING OF LAZARUS

in the

PANTANASSA AT MISTRA

(*See note to Plate* 34)

THE BIRTH
OF
WESTERN PAINTING

A History of Colour, Form, and Iconography,
illustrated from the Paintings
of MISTRA *and* MOUNT ATHOS,
of Giotto and Duccio,
and of EL GRECO

by

ROBERT BYRON

and

DAVID TALBOT RICE

WITH 94 PLATES

REPRINTED BY
HACKER ART BOOKS
NEW YORK
1968

FIRST PUBLISHED
1930

Printed in the United States of America

THIS monograph, a mere suggestion of the problems that await solution before the history of European culture can properly be written, is the outcome of a joint enterprise conceived at the end of 1926. The text and notes are by Robert Byron. The bulk of the illustrations is the work of David Talbot Rice. But the book's double authorship consists in more than the binding together of letterpress and pictures. For in the first place neither author would have undertaken it by himself. And in the second, having once begun it, the responsibility of each to the other compelled its fulfilment.

THE authors wish to record their sense of obligation and gratitude to Professor Gabriel Millet. Without his previous researches, extending over thirty or forty years, the subject could scarcely have been approached in detail. On all occasions he has been ready with advice, and has permitted access to the unique collection of photographs in the *Ecole des Hautes Etudes*. Finally, his willingness that others should share the fruits of a scholar's life has made it possible to reproduce numerous plates, indicated in the list of illustrations, from the two monumental portfolios, which, above all else, contributed to prepare the ground here covered: *Monuments byzantins de Mistra,* published in 1910, and *Monuments de l'Athos, I. Les Peintures,* published in 1927. To the publishers of these works, the Librairie Ernest Leroux, of 28, Rue Bonaparte, Paris, VIe, an equal tribute of thanks is offered.

ACKNOWLEDGMENTS are due to the *Burlington Magazine, the London Mercury,* and the *New Statesman,* for permission to reproduce the substance of articles.

CONTENTS

vii

CONTENTS

CONTENTS

LIST OF ILLUSTRATIONS

xi

Notes giving full details of place, date, school, artist, and iconographic precedent and meaning, so far as they are known, will be found opposite each picture.

" . . . preguntando yo á Dominico Greco el año 1611,
cuál era más difícil, el debujo ó el colorido? me responde
que el colorido. Y no es tan de maravillar como oirle
hablar con tan poco aprecio de Micael Angel (siendo el
padre de la pintura) diciendo que era un buen hombre y
que no supo pintar."

" . . . on asking Dominico Greco in the year 1611,
which is the more difficult, drawing or colour, he
replies, colour. And this was not so extraordinary as
to hear him express so little appreciation of Michael
Angelo (despite his being the father of painting) and say
that he was a good man, but that he could not paint."

PACHECO : *El Arte de la Pintura.*

THE BIRTH OF WESTERN PAINTING

CHAPTER 1

THE TRADITION OF INTERPRETATIONAL ART

THE universe is eternal, and man, with all substance, bestrides the temporal dimension. In his heart there is a goal: eternity is bounded by perfection. To say that man has attained this or that far towards perfection is not sense; there can be no fractions of infinity. Nevertheless, he shall be perfect; not only he, but by chance some animal may reach perfection before him; and all animals, all semi-animals, all plants, all life, shall have realised their greatness, sought the goal, and come to it, before time is measured. Thus the constancy of things, like the needle of a compass, is discovered pointing always to the end of that which has no end. This is the Reality of the universe.

Of this constancy, man, when he became man, was soon aware. God arose, and gods. But the temporal definition intruded, and led to the belief that individuals shall only attain the common goal when they are gone hence and the flesh is dust. Mystics, however, set themselves to reach communion with Reality in the present. And that, transposed from pure contemplation to the realm of activity, is art. The language of art is familiar form:

thereby are expressed the quest of man and the intrinsic excellence of the world in assisting it. Many perceive the quest and admit the excellence. But it is the particular mark of the artist that he is able, in a manner ultimately comprehensible to others, to interpret the emotions evoked by the perception.

Times have been when artists have fallen to accepting the natural world without inquiry and reproducing it. Such was the misfortune of Antiquity and, with the exception of the French impressionists, of Europe from the sixteenth to the nineteenth centuries. The twentieth preens itself on its evasion of this blind alley. And the painter is braced to the escape. The eye is now the least of his weapons, and the form of terrestrial object takes a hundred shapes and patterns according to its emotional significance. Yet the laboriously evolved rules for the representation of three dimensions in two do not lend themselves easily to reform. And it is mainly on colour that the painter relies for his new effects. A painter is by definition one who employs colour in his method. Yet a moment's thought reveals how few are those who have carried the use of it to more than decoration or the achievement of sculptural or perspective illusion. Even in the works of those that have, there is visible an exaggerated harmony, a blending of each colour-compartment to superfluous amity with its neighbour. But in modern times, a new principle has arisen. Just as the bare machinery of the human intellect is now revealed in literature; as the reader is made to explore the psychological foundations of each event and action like a visitor to a motor-works beginning his inspection with the smelting of crude ore; so the elements of the palette are clarified and placed side by side in clean opponent fields, where they exist not as part of one unbroken tonic harmony, but independently, by virtue of their own reactions to those adjacent, as the eye travels over the canvas. In the first confusion of this process, some artists, like Manet, tended towards the loss of all form; others, like Picasso, towards excessive formalisation. These extremes are now in liquidation. For, despite the apparent novelty of its method, the ultimate fruition of modern painting is not a mystery wholly without precedent for its solution. There is one spiritual ancestor who sought what the present seeks, and whose attainment the present is still far from having surpassed. This is El Greco.

Different artists occupy different place in the estimation of different generations. The Victorians enjoyed Guido Reni and Domenichino; the pinnacles of their esteem were reserved for the Sistine Madonna and the Venus of Milo. And just as this knowledge of them is clue to their whole mentality, so is the painting of Greco to that of the twentieth century. A future age, having escaped altogether the confinements of representational art, may, for all we know, come to regard Greco as we regard Raphael. But for us, and in relation to us, he is always relevant and always great, great not only as a painter but as a man, one to whom the vision of his world's Reality was vouchsafed and who pursued it independently of mental fashion, a cosmic figure, sustained in his own life by a profound conviction of his own magnitude. On his canvasses, the whole gamut of emotions provoked by landscape, allegory, or sitter, are co-ordinated in the expression of a grand philosophy, of the intrinsic, mystical seed of perfection contained in all terrestrial phenomena and the artist's debt thereto in his communing.

Of all the artists in our cognisance, El Greco relied most completely on colour. That, not even his most ardent detractors can deny. He created form simply by the play of colour and by no other means. "Light and shade," "distance," "recession" were alien to the vocabulary of his thought. The St. Maurice, which, for those who accept the precepts of modern art, is incomparably the greatest painting in the world, was never drawn. It was conceived in terms of colour and written in them without more ado. Meier-Graefe, in *The Spanish Journey,* describes the impossibility of copying a part only of its enormous expanse, owing to the difficulties not only of reproducing any of the colours without their fellows, but of reaching a conclusion as to what, in isolated reality, are the colours that have been employed. "It is just as possible," he writes, "to think of this picture in different colours, as to think of Faust written in a different metre."

Thus it is, that no painting by El Greco can admit, in the smallest degree, of reproduction, and that those who have never been to Spain can form but the barest idea of what he was capable.

Much has been written, in the last quarter of a century, on the subject of this man. Señor Cossio, his original enthusiast, followed several monographs with a monumental volume of research in 1908. And in the same year, Herr Julius Meier-Graefe discovered him to Northern Europe in *Die Spanische Reise,* since translated into English. Studies have followed in all languages. And one and all have sought to explain the circumstances that produced this lonely artist, who stands seemingly outside any known trend of cultural development. Previous to his advent, Spaniards had borrowed a Flemish manner for their painting;

hard, cruel primitives, significant of a chivalry worn to free-booting in the winter of the Middle Ages, infused with no sap of the Italian Renascence, and distinguished for no virtue of colour-ing save the ordinary map-like sequences of contemporary manu-scripts, alone survive. Into this arid sphere was precipitated an artist whose technique was radically different, not only from any-thing that could be found in Spain, but from any in Western Europe. It were as though an angel had come out of heaven. But this was a man. And writers have submitted numerous theories concerning the mould in which his genius was originally cast.

First in the formative process they have put Venice, whither the artist sailed as a young man from his native island of Crete. They have pointed the resemblance between his early pictures, such as the Christ in the Temple, and those of Tintoretto; they have analysed the palette of Titian to compare with his own. Simul-taneously they have omitted to ask themselves what had created the distinction between Venetian art and that of the rest of Italy. They have not thought of the civilisation that bore Venice and still gives her that complexion of strange unfamiliarity which is her charm. They have spoken of Tintoretto without St. Mark's. They have avoided reference to Murano or the Virgin of Torcello. Crete, they say, was a Venetian dominion and had been for three centuries. The young islander, with the Turk enthroned in his natural capital on the Bosporus, and the greater part of his people reduced to savagery, gravitated, in his search for a career, to Venice, where a school of Cretan artists was already long estab-lished. And there learned an art, which, after a sojourn in Rome when Michael Angelo's decoration of the Sistine Chapel was barely thirty years old, he carried to Toledo.   Only ignorance can excuse so absurd an hypothesis.   The St. Maurice, commissioned immediately after his arrival in Spain, was learned neither in Venice nor Rome, as anyone with a rudimentary knowledge of Italian painting can immediately perceive.   No painting native to either town exhibits the smallest trace of the main principles underlying its execution.

Yet another approach to the problem has been added by the recent study of the baroque, the art of the counter-Reformation and the Catholic mystics, born, according to Mr. Sacheverell Sitwell, of the demand for self-expression on the part of the great southern towns.   But Mr. Sitwell is chiefly concerned to show what true intellectual worth El Greco might have infused into this barren movement, had he secured the allegiance which those who came after denied him and only we have paid. Others have identified his mysticism with the Jesuit crusade; have derived his clouds and rays from the plaster atmospherics of Catholic altars; and have confounded his light with the spurious drama of the chiaroscuro as popularised by Caravaggio and Ribera.   Seriously to postulate the evolution of the most profound realism that art has known from these mummings is no more plausible than the ascription to Lenin of the ideals of the Holy Alliance.

Scarcely had El Greco, at the beginning of the twentieth century, been hailed from the supercilious oblivion of ten generations—"*Domenico Theotocopuli . . . who painted horrors at the Escorial*," ran the succinct notice of Chambers' biographical dictionary in 1899—than the critics, exhausted by the patent futility of these explanations, turned doctors.   Hesitating at the dementia which they inwardly favoured, but which no detail of the artist's life could be found to corroborate, they enunciated a theory of ocular defect and pronounced astigmatism responsible for the increasingly strange forms disclosed by each rescued canvas. Taking lenses ground to the correction of astigmatism, they photographed the paintings both with and without them; the results were placed side by side to display the admirable normality of the glass; but the critics forgot, during this labour of science, that the monuments of another art were still extant in Eastern Europe, produced over a course of seven centuries by hundreds and thousands of astigmatics, from which the same test might evoke similar results; and they forgot also to apply it to the struggling painters of the Paris cafés. Of the function of El Greco's colour they said nothing. For who has ever made the elements of the spectrum dependent on the muscular degrees of ocular focus?

Though but the forerunner of a whole bulk of literature, the most understanding study of El Greco has remained that of Herr Meier-Graefe, which was made accessible to English readers, under the title of *The Spanish Journey,* in 1926. And he has avoided committal to these untenable proposals. Already, in 1908, a critic of international repute, and esteemed particularly as the mouthpiece of the impressionists, he emphasises in his book not only the discovery of the one true precursor of modern art in a land where he had only sought Velasquez, but the extraordinary failure of any previous school of painting to account for his antecedents. The following passages, borrowed haphazard from the random collection of a diarist's impressions and letters, illustrate the baffled astonishment that pervades the whole volume:

"Let us analyse: Where does he come from? We do not know."

"A foundling who hailed neither from Venice nor Rome."

"The mystery of El Greco which exists but once in the history of the world depends upon the incomprehensible fact that the storm which was to come after him, the storm in which we live, was let loose by him for himself and he became its master."

"He discovered a realm of new possibilities. . . . There is a greater difference between him and Titian, his master, than between him and Renoir and Cézanne. . . . It is an immense thought that the work of one single human being could reveal the highest cultural aspirations of millennia—one can say without exaggeration—from Pheidias to the present moment. No attribute sufficiently honours him."

". . . as it were an altogether new Greek tradition."

It was a Greek tradition, but not a new one, as Herr Meier-Graefe has since discovered. In his *Pyramide und Tempel,* published after a visit to Daphni near Athens in 1927, he writes: "These mosaics show not only the past . . . but point also in an absolutely recognisable and sometimes astonishing manner to the great Greek master of the sixteenth century."

Herr Meier-Graefe was by no means the first to display an inkling into Greco's true artistic antecedents. As early as 1880 Don Pedro de Madrazzo was talking of the Byzantine character of Greco's pictures, in the *Almanaque de la Illustracion Española y Americana.* And Señor Cossio, in 1906, was already able to summarise a number of Byzantine hypotheses put forward by others. Sentenach, writing in 1912, points the affinity of the "hieratic compositions of Mount Athos"; Melida, in 1915, of the "small heads, short waists and long legs" of the Byzantine mosaics in Italy. Monsieur Bertaux, in the *Revue de l'Art Ancien et Moderne* two years earlier, had been alive to features of iconography common to both. Sir Charles Holmes, in the *Burlington Magazine* of 1924, compared Greco's Agony in the Garden in the National Gallery with a Cretan panel; and Señor Emilio Villar has continued the expansion of Greco's Byzantinism in his book *El Greco en España,* published in Madrid in 1928. But what is so profoundly odd is that, instead of these fortuitous comparisons, no attempt should ever have been made towards a scientific co-ordination of Greco's art with the schools of Byzantine painting contemporary with, and immediately preceding, the artist's lifetime. Mosaics of four centuries or a thousand years before, together with occasional miniatures, may give a clue; but how can they provide the solid evidence which everyone has been seeking for a quarter of a century, and continues to seek? Yet that evidence exists, and is not even particularly inaccessible. Let anyone go to the Escurial and Toledo with the Byzantine frescoes of the fourteenth, fifteenth, and sixteenth centuries at Mistra and Mount Athos fresh in his mind, and El Greco's immediate origins, which have puzzled the foremost critics of Europe into the most absurd statements, will become perfectly plain. Perhaps someone has already done so. If so, he has remained unfortunately silent.

The affinity between Byzantine and modern art is no longer disputed. Only its recognition has elevated the former, after centuries' contempt as a mere degradation of the Antique, to an important place in the general survey of European culture. With this recognition, however, the lesson is regarded as learnt.

An actual link is presumed to be missing. And manuals of Byzantine art, having approached its inception from the period of Hellenistic transition, from, in fact, the classical standpoint, either stop short or lose interest at the precise moment when the real evolutionary significance of their subject is about to become manifest. They note the Renascence of Platonic studies witnessed by Constantinople in the eleventh century; they discern, as they think, a corresponding reversion to Hellenic naturalism in art; following the destruction of the Empire by the Latin crusaders in 1204, and its restoration in 1261, they praise the mosaics of the Kahrié mosque in Stambul; they spare a sentence to Mistra, a word to Athos, and a reference to the Balkans; and they imply that, in reality, the monuments of Greek art subsequent to 1204 provide no more than a curious and pathetic epilogue to the whole, thus bringing their pages to a close with suitable regret. Modern writers have never, therefore, discovered the greatest of all Byzantine memorials, and the link between the glorious middle period of Byzantine art which they extol and their own contemporaries: the paintings of El Greco, created more than a century after the fall of Constantinople to the Turk in 1453.

The sack of that city in 1204; the annexation of Levantine trade by the Venetians and Genoese; together with the encroachments of the Turkish Sultanates in Asia Minor and the Latin feudatories of the Morea, had reduced the Greek Empire of the Palæologi to a condition of poverty as bare as its previous wealth had been spectacular. The universal craft of mosaic was consequently, with few exceptions, displaced by that of painting. Henceforth, the facts of cardinal import are that, despite the depression and ultimate disappearance of Constantinople as a

cultural centre, Greek painters, culminating in a school traditionally termed Cretan, were engaged on the production of a
spontaneous art, excluding foreign influence, underivative, and
allowing a freer degree of individual interpretation than is usually
believed, up till the middle of the sixteenth century; that El
Greco was born in Crete in 1541; and that these later Byzantine
frescoes exhibit exactly that principle of conception of form in
terms of colour which is the basis of all Greco's Spanish pictures
and of painting in the twentieth century. This identity would
long have been plain to the very tyros of artistic study had the
surviving works of the last Byzantines been more familiar.

The link is supplied. But if "the Greek" was a Byzantine,
it yet remains to discover what elements in Byzantine art produced him, and what, in fact, gave that art a character so infinitely removed from that of any other, that it continued unsympathetic to the West of Europe long after the popularisation of
more alien cultures from the Far East. Again, it is with a philosophy that the secret lies, or rather, if the two be different, with
a religion. The inquiry sweeps us back into the thunderous
orbit of the Hebrew Jehovah.

Byzantine art came into being with Constantine's official
recognition of Christianity as the religion of the Empire, and
his transference of its capital to Byzantium in 330. The Roman
world was already Hellenised; its centre was now implanted in
the Greek lands. The Greeks, acquainted with the mysteries
of Oriental building and decoration, became the chief custodians
of the new religion, alike of its dogma and its art. The year
537, in the reign of Justinian, witnessed the completion of St.

Sophia, a climax of religious architecture surpassed in no land or age. But any mosaics of the sixth and seventh centuries that the great church may contain are hidden. To examine the representational art of the period in the sphere of mural ornament, it is necessary to turn to Salonica, Ravenna and Rome; for Greek artists were in Italy and taught the Italians their crafts and iconography. Such decoration as that of St. George at Salonica or St. Constanza at Rome may be discounted as of purely pagan inspiration. More important subjects, in other words, Christian figures, appear in St. Demetrius at Salonica, in St. Pudenziana, S. Maria Maggiore and numerous other churches at Rome, and in St. Apollinare in Classe, St. Apollinare Nuovo, St. Vitale, and the mausoleum of Galla Placidia, at Ravenna. In this first phase of Byzantine art, two main features are noticeable. One is the survival of what may conveniently be termed the type of the Fayum portraits, of faces crudely outlined, large and meaningless eyes, and drapery denoted by uninteresting and excessively conventionalised lines; the other, the use of symbols, lambs, crosses, and palms, and the symbolic, uncomfortably dramatic land- and sky-scapes of the older oriental religions. Portrayal of Christ, save as a child, is exceptional. The scenes of his human life are almost wholly absent. The art of the time felt itself unable to approach a model of such holiness; as indeed it was.

In the Eastern provinces, however, different forces were at work. The elements of the Trinity might be fixed by negation; absence of statement might be the only true companion of boundless, cosmic sanctity. But what sort of attraction could this impersonality exercise on the common folk, unconversant with the philosophic mysteries? A didactic school of art arose, that those who could not read, might see, the events of the Gospels and the form of Christ in his human adventures. But in the whole unfathomable sea of symbols, popular oriental realism, Hellenistic facility, and finally didactic iconography, that ebbed and flowed in Christian art from the fourth to the eighth centuries, the major quality of Byzantine art in the middle period was lacking. The will to philosophic expression was there; the means were not. Yet in the Macedonian era of the tenth century, a superb emotional compromise between material representation and the intangible magnitude of the Deity had been achieved. The interval, between 726 and 834, had witnessed the iconoclast controversy. And it was by the intellectual reactions of that movement that the transformation was wrought.

Historians have conducted only the most superficial research into the origins of that missionary enterprise which was launched on Constantinople in 726, which provoked rebellion in Italy and Greece, which laid the foundations of the Great Schism of 1054, and which threatened to relegate European art to a limbo of decorative futility. To the majority it has seemed but the culminating aberration of four centuries' theological and Christological controversy, and its movers, though endowed with outstanding political ability, as surely the victims of religious derangement as the lady who but lately slept in her bonnet for fear that Christ's second coming should surprise the vanity of her tresses. The Hebrew God, whose enormous implication of human guilt not even the galaxies of the celestial court, the angels and archangels, the saints and apostles, nor the Queen-Mother herself, could disguise, now ruled the world. And it is only necessary to recall the biblical prohibitions of idolatry, the catechism in which childhood is faced with a problem calculated to deter the profoundest intellect, to envisage the Jewish attitude towards any kind of representation of Jehovah whatsoever.   Nor had the Jews the monopoly of this feeling.   A pagan iconoclast literature exists, produced by the intellectual temper of the second century A.D.   The hollowness of the Hellenic tradition had become apparent in the West before the advent of Christianity.   The Christian Church, it is true, sanctioned art from its inception; but its hesitations are manifest in the use of symbols to denote the central figures of the Trinity; and history reveals a thin stream of iconoclast opinion running through the period prior to the great onslaught of the eighth century.   Meanwhile, the original Judaism, whence Christianity derived, was spreading Eastwards.   Islam was its bastard.   Its dominion was felt from the bottom of Arabia to territories that are now Russia.   And just as the revival of Old Testament reading later contributed to form the extreme elements of the Reformation, so in those days contact with the Jewish prejudice against any attempt to state the majesty of God in terrestrial terms gave rise to an Eastern campaign against idolatry, which found supporters among the Paulician Protestants of Armenia, and simultaneously provoked a reaction among orthodox Moslems in favour of the letter of Mahomedan teaching and the wholesale prohibition of all representational art.   The strength of the Byzantines lay in Asia Minor.   And thence hailed the iconoclast Emperors, inspired by a fanatic but magnificent ideal to preserve intact the ineffable holiness of the God of Israel.

Success was denied them and art survived.   But in the attempt they laid in Constantinople the foundation of European painting and created an ideal of representation which El Greco, its last exponent, failed to implant in the West, and which only the French artists of the nineteenth century, unconscious of the tradition behind them, revived. Gone were the sheep and fruit-bearing palms; vanished the dwarfish caricatures of Eastern illuminators; broken the earthen fetters of Antiquity. Just as the Orthodox Church had been tempered in the contest, so a fugitive art had gained new character in adversity. A fresh and homogeneous trend of cultural aspiration was in train. If God might be painted after all, not only in innocence or majesty, but in the commonplace and degradation of earthly life, then painting should be worthy and attempt the highest. A mystical renunciation of the transient phenomena of earth for the universal in-being of Reality was henceforth its creed, enshrined in a fixed iconography, whose rigid apportionment of subject and space alone could put intelligible bounds to so immeasurable an aim. This was the outcome of the iconoclast controversy, which Professor Bréhier, the only writer who has approached this crisis in European culture with comprehension, sums in the following words: "The outstanding characteristic of Byzantine iconography, as constituted after the controversy over the pictures, is the rigid and systematic arrangement of the compositions. The theological point of view is no longer the same as in previous epochs; it is no longer a question of affirming Trinitarian or Christological dogmas which no one disputes; the purpose of art henceforth is to render visible the mysteries of the supra-natural world for the benefit of the believer; the pictures have the same object as the Liturgy; they possess the same sacramental character and form the requisite setting for the mystery of the Eucharist. Art, therefore, represents the immutable, that which is; it takes no account of contingencies, of ephemeral incidents; being outside time, it bears no relation to history. The facts of the Gospel are not interesting for themselves, but for the mystery of which they are the symbol. The supreme purpose of art is to present the believer with all the truths which he must accept, and with all the beings with whom he must attain communion through prayer."[1]

Of particular significance in this process of development, having regard to later events, was the emergence, with the new iconography, of new colour, and its immediate adaptation from mere design to the expression of form. The exercise of contrasting colour-fields, for which Byzantine art was henceforth to be distinguished, and which, from now on, was to be the chief instrument in the advance of formal interpretation necessitated by the condonation of God's portrayal in human semblance, must have derived, since it did not exist before, from the psychological assimilation of the iconoclast ideal. It may be inquired, whence came the actual tints of the colours used, the claret reds, silvery greens, and honey yellows; to which, perhaps, the landscape of the Greek lands makes reply. But one fact is indisputable, to which the history of art offers no parallel. Simultaneously with the inflexible austerity of the iconoclast enterprise, there came to Byzantine art a taste for materials of fabulous luxury, and, moreover, the wealth to gratify it. There resulted from this extraordinary coincidence an extreme splendour, which still bewilders the senses in the few buildings such as St. Mark's at Venice or the monastery church of St. Luke of Stiris where

[1] *L'Art chrétien* (see Bibliography), p. 136.

the *décor* has survived complete. And the essence of the bewilderment, like the nausea induced by the electric splendour of modern stage production, derives from colour effects over an area unequalled in human experience outside landscape. The circumstance of marble panelling and mosaic vault, together with enamels and stuffs of which the world has still to produce the equal, conspired still further in the development of the Byzantine colour sense.

During the eleventh and twelfth centuries, two distinct intellectual currents were busy, which were ultimately to converge and give Byzantine art its final complexion. The art of splendid mysticism described above was essentially the product of Constantinople. There the iconoclast forces had been loosed; and there alone, since the expansion of Islam, was the tradition of Antiquity preserved, with its impeccable sense of proportion and anatomy, on which alone the interpretations of emotional art can successfully be based. Not only the spirit, but the books were there as well. And with the revival of Platonic studies by the Patriarch Photius in the ninth century and Psellos the Hellenist in the eleventh, there came about an intellectual transformation, which was the forerunner of the Italian Renascence in the fifteenth. There ensued, in art, not, as is generally stated, a reversion to Hellenic naturalism, but a gentler, more humane depiction of the celestial types, such as may be observed in the Christ of the Romanus ivory in the Cabinet des Médailles. A similar modification, romanticism it might almost be called, was at work in the provinces and Patriarchates under the rule of Moslems, and subsequently of crusaders. For the common people, the Byzantine Christ Pantocrator was become altogether too fearful and remote;

2

and his mother, the popular medium of intercession, too much a queen enthroned. The Cappadocian school of illustrators, recruited from the monks and so, largely, from the people themselves, also responded to this other demand for increased humanisation, particularly by the enlargement of the cycles of the Passion and Crucifixion, with all their dolorous incidents from the capture in the garden to the mother grieving over the body of her son. These motives spread, not only throughout the Greek lands, but to Italy, carried thither by the Byzantine artists of Sicily and Calabria, by the traffic in Byzantine icons, and by the returning pilgrims from the Holy Land. In keeping with this double trend of emphasis on the dignity of human experience, generated alike in the capital and the provinces, there arose in the twelfth century a new and gentler mysticism, bound up with the divinity of human suffering, which permeated all classes of society and gave the Byzantine state the peculiar theocratic aspect of its latter years. The new spirit, like the new iconography, was communicated to Italy. And thence came St. Francis, and after him, Dante. Thus it is, that artists such as Giotto and the masters of Mistra, who could have had no sort of connection with one another's works and who were wholly divorced from a common cultural centre, achieved paintings, not even contemporary in date, whose identity, both in iconography and spirit, must astound the most casual observer.

In the comparison of these two, the short-lived Giottesque school, and the three centuries of Byzantine painting that succeeded the restoration of the Empire in 1261, colour again offers the predominant distinction, and illustrates how, had the Eastern Empire survived in the fulness of its wealth and dominion, El Greco would have occupied, instead of his pinnacle, but one place among a hundred such great painters between Albania and the Euphrates. Professor Gabriel Millet, after a life's research, has divided later Byzantine painters into two schools: the Macedonian and the Cretan. The former was at work on Mount Athos in the first quarter of the fourteenth century, where its supreme examples are the great scenes of the Crucifixion and the Entry into Jerusalem in the monastery church of Vatopedi. An extraordinary dignity, the very triumph of sorrow, but for the despairing grief of the watching women at the foot of the Cross, pervades the one; a disquiet, presage of impending disaster, the other. But the colours, dark blue and cold whitish-grey, interspersed with touches of red and green, though suited to their sombre occasions, are not in themselves the instrument of emotional form. Nor is this the case in the church of the Protaton at Caryes, the capital of Athos, where the same school worked; here, in the savage expression of the actors, seems to linger a trace of the old Cappadocian crudity. It is plain that this school, which flourished also in Serbia, had forsaken the ancient tradition, had introduced dolour not only into its themes, but into its colour and form like the Italians. With the Cretan painters—traditionally so-called on the Holy Mountain—this was not the case. Both Cretans and Macedonians had accepted the prevalent humanisation, had striven to capture more of the sympathy of the beholder. But the Macedonians had gone the way of the West and lost their light in the process.

El Greco's St. Maurice, a gigantic canvas, is as badly hung in the Escurial as any picture could be. The room is bathed in the obscurity of a winter's afternoon; the picture itself is relegated to the darkest corner of it; among its companions, two Roger van der Weydens reach the summit of incongruity. Yet these surroundings constitute, in fact, a far more advantageous setting than the altar of blood-coloured pillars for which it was originally designed, or the pretentious backing and chattering mob of a well-lit gallery. For this painting is independent of earthly provision. It has its own light. With the glimmer of some inexorable jewel, it slowly removes the beholder from his surroundings into itself. It embraces wholly his consciousness. Whereas the examination of the surrounding pictures demands continued optical perseverance. Such a luminosity differs from the warm drama of Rembrandt as a diamond from a pearl. Its achievement can only be come at, and that probably but once or twice in the history of the world, by the most profound exercise of the principles of colour relation. And it is precisely this quality of light, though in a lesser degree, which the Cretan painters have perpetuated in the churches of the Pantanassa and Peribleptos at Mistra, and at Xenophontos and St. Paul's on Mount Athos; which they have attained by fields of pure colour; and with which they have clothed the familiar incidents in a radiance astonishing to eyes trained in the harmonious precepts and domesticated iconography of Western painting. Here is none of the nursery preoccupation with birds and daisies that moved the founders of the Italian Renascence. If the Gospel story must be human, and the beholder grieve or triumph with its incident, let him do so magnificently, with his whole soul. Every discordant plane must swell the tide of his emotion.

This, then, was the tradition: the symbolic art of early Christianity, reformed by the Judaic ideal of iconoclasm to discard its symbols for a yet more symbolic interpretation of the human form itself; the emergence of the modern principle of colour relation, accentuated by the splendour of the artist's materials; the humanisation of this art through the simultaneous revival of Platonic study and the popular demand for a greater comfort than a mere day of judgment; and, in this form, the preservation of the old colour by the Cretan school of painters; this was the tradition which, ere its flame had departed, was communicated to Domenicos Theotocopoulos and smouldered within him while he assumed the conventions of Italy, probed the secrets of the human build, and disguised his own conceit beneath the partially sympathetic palettes of Titian and Tintoretto.

About 1577 he reaches Toledo. Suddenly, confined no longer by the iconography of his native Church or the conventions of revived Antiquity, he is free to loose his secret, to give it, not a second prison of naturalism, but freedom, absolute and opposed by no engrained culture in the country of his adoption. The colour of the Pantanassa at Mistra promptly appears in the Divestment, his first great picture on Spanish soil, painted for the sacristy of Toledo Cathedral, where it still hangs. Immediately, he proceeds to the St. Maurice. Philip II. disapproves it. He retreats to the Burial of Count Orgaz. He settles at Toledo, a semi-oriental city, set in a landscape whose form and colour not even the Greek lands can rival. His personality becomes a legend, and his paintings, as he grows old, seem to call from its depths the whole history of his race. Then Velasquez takes timidly of his brushwork and his colour, and founds a national school.

For those who have visited neither Madrid nor Toledo, a personal experience may serve to indicate the universality of

Greco's art, the greatness of him not as a painter alone, but as a man and a philosopher. The writer, pondering his writer's ambitions as he walked the encircling hills of the latter town, knew suddenly that Greco had taught him, as no other man had ever done, what can be made of the symbols of human understanding. The instruments of language and colour, of grammar and brush, became suddenly inseparable. Only the purpose of art was apparent—to express, through beauty, the purpose of man. It seemed, for one transient moment, as though not only any artist, but any human being whatsoever, engaged in any high aim, might model his work on Greco's. The illusion passed. But there remained a new and deeper knowledge of that single quest which is at the bottom of all true art and thought.

Such is the thesis which it is intended to expand. Proof lies with the paintings themselves. Here it is hoped, chiefly, to analyse the psychological conditions that produced them. To illustrate these, a certain space must be devoted to the development of East Christian iconography. But this book can make no claim to fulfil the functions of an iconographic manual. Nor is it concerned, save incidentally, with any province of art save that of the fresco-painter. Emphasis is laid on colour, because that, being the essential agent of Byzantine, El Greco's, and Modern painting, is their chief link; and because writers on the art of the mediæval Levant have largely ignored its significance. But it is no part of the authors' intention to pose as apostles of a novel and scientific principle of colour relation. They have simply borrowed the lessons of modern art and transferred them to a field hitherto monopolised by the archæologist.

The illustrations are taken chiefly from Mistra and Mount Athos. Than the paintings of the former, it may be said that no more beautiful examples of Byzantine art have yet been discovered. But it has been suggested that next in merit may properly come the cycles of the Slav churches painted by Greek artists in Serbia and Russia. This is possible. Nevertheless, it is primarily on Mount Athos that a first reconnoitre in the subject should be made; for there may be studied the whole development of later Byzantine painting in the works of both schools, from the beginning of the fourteenth to the end of the sixteenth centuries; and there only, with the exception of a few paintings in the Meteora monasteries, have survived the cycles of the later Cretan painters who were the direct forbears of El Greco. Each place was a centre of Greek life: Mistra the capital of a Despotat which out-lasted the Byzantine Empire by eight years; and Athos, the last refuge of the Byzantine mystical spirit, which it has continued to be to this day.

The reader may regret that the illustrations are not coloured; that the size of the paintings is but vaguely indicated in the text, if at all; and that many of the photographs contain blemishes which seem due to the carelessness of the operator, rather than, as is in reality the case, to the bad condition of the plaster or the proximity of an inaccessible window. He is asked to remember, however, that the enterprise was a private one, financed by no institution of learning; that the time of its participants was limited; and that the actual technical difficulties of the photography had already taxed the numerous experts in that science accompanying Professor Millet during his protracted sojourns at Mistra and on the Holy Mountain. The kindness of the latter has allowed us to reproduce many of his results beside our own. Photographs can add no force to the argument of colour relation. But they can, perhaps, demonstrate that there flourished in the Greek lands from the fourteenth to the sixteenth centuries a vigorous and beautiful school of painting, which has received consideration neither as a separate cultural manifestation nor as an evolutionary link; and that, behind it, lay the impulse of a great and ancient religious philosophy.

CHAPTER 2

THE BEGINNINGS OF INTERPRETATION

I. An Examination of the Existing Monuments to show the Change Produced in Byzantine Art by the Iconoclast Controversy

IT must be admitted that, of the numerous European cultures whose monuments our taste considers great, Byzantine representational art was the first to discover that principle of interpreting, instead of reproducing, perceived phenomena, which in our time has come to underlie all artistic expression. But Byzantine art is not, as its casual acquaintances are inclined to suppose, a cultural entity which pursued its hieratic way unchanged or unmodified from the fourth to the sixteenth centuries of the Christian era. Many reactions to political and psychological conditions may be distinguished in it. Particularly, between the eighth and tenth centuries, there was wrought a fundamental transformation; and it was only subsequently to that time that the qualities which evoke our peculiar admiration became apparent. In place of the Hellenistic tradition, on the one hand, vainly striving to adapt itself to the uncompromising demands of greater spiritual forces than had originally produced it; and of the didactic tradition of monkish illustrators on the other; there now arose a novel method of interpreting visible objects, which was capable, thenceforth, of sustained and consistent development down to the sixteenth century. Comparison between the

25

monuments of the fifth to the seventh centuries and those of the tenth and eleventh will reveal how radical the change that was wrought.

The difference may be summarised in three main categories: Composition, Form, and Colour.

In their compositions and iconography, the artists of the earlier period betray the devices which their art was obliged to adopt in dealing with a subject outside its scope. The figures are not composed; they are ranked, like ninepins. In the portraits of Justinian and Theodora with their attendants in St. Vitale at Ravenna; in the long friezes of male and female saints in St. Apollinare Nuovo at the same town; in the Virgin at Parenzo (see Plate 3. i), flanked by stiff lines of local dignitaries; in all these mosaics of the sixth century; in those of St. Demetrius between the prefect Leo and a bishop in his church at Salonica (see Plate 5. i), of the Virgin and saints in the oratory of St. Venantius at the Lateran, in the paintings of the same subject in the cemetery of Commodilla, and of Christ enthroned among his apostles in S. Maria Antiqua at Rome; these dating from the seventh; the same fear of naturalism, instead of its conquest, finds expression, and seeks refuge not in the interpretation of the human form, but in its reduction to a mere symbol, to a unit in a flat and purely, if magnificently, ornamental design. In many cases, symbols were actually employed; not merely the birds, beasts, and architecture, of pleasant Iranian or Pompeian decoration as exemplified in St. George at Salonica; but those best calculated to state the hypotheses of the new religion. The fish was used for its acrostic value by the earliest Christian communities. To this were now added sheep and the Shepherd, a

Mazdaic as well as a biblical theme according to Strzygowski, which may be observed in the apse of St. Apollinare in Classe (sixth century) and in the Mausoleum of Galla Placidia (see Plate 2. i), both at Ravenna. Peacocks were introduced, since their flesh was incorruptible. And the old Hellenistic and Oriental landscapes, pastoral and dramatic, were continued to depict the glories of the world to come, as in St. Constanza (fourth century) and SS. Cosmas and Damian at Rome. Some of the earliest mosaics, dating from the fifth century, have retained their Hellenistic facility. These, such as the Good Shepherds in the Mausoleum of Galla Placidia (see Plate 2. i) and St. Apollinare Nuovo at Ravenna are simply the products of a debased secular art and have no real connection with the paramount religion. A happier example of this earlier period is the circular mosaic in the dome of the Orthodox Baptistery at Ravenna (early fifth century); but how great the eventual improvement in grouping and in the elimination of superfluous detail is revealed by comparison with the dome of St. Sophia at Salonica, where a similar composition was executed in the middle of the eleventh century.

Passing the period of the iconoclast controversy, when the transformation already mentioned came about, the methods of filling a given space have so altered that comparison between the same subjects is only occasionally possible. The stiff rows of saints and prelates are divorced from the central figures of the Gospel story, and are preserved only as dados; while, even in these, the figures are isolated from one another by marked variations of posture. The main compositions have become essentially scenic and derive their unity from a pattern of light and shade. The change may be observed on comparing the sixth century Virgin at Parenzo (see Plate 3. i) with the late ninth century Panaghia (Virgin) Angeloktistos at Chiti in Cyprus (see Plate 3. ii).   In the latter, the two attendant angels infuse their centrepiece with a celestial rhythm which is wholly foreign to the static rigidity of the other.   From now on, moreover, the scenes of Christ's earthly life are the artist's main preoccupation.   These had already been introduced by crude popular illustrators, and from their hands have survived chiefly in miniatures; though an exceptional mural cycle, exhibiting a series of cramped and dwarfish figures, is to be found among the mosaics of St. Apollinare Nuovo at Ravenna (sixth century).   Other examples, painted before 741, are preserved in S. Maria Antiqua at Rome. These, while exhibiting some affinity with the provincial art of Cappadocia in the tenth century, bear none towards the decorative and emotional scenes which began to fill the churches at the centre of the Greek Empire about the same period.   To compare the crucifixion of S. Maria Antiqua with the mosaic of the same subject at Daphni is to epitomise the enormous divergencies of which Byzantine art was capable before and after the iconoclast controversy.

With regard to form, the distinction between the two periods is both facial and bodily.   In the earlier, the type of the Fayum portraits, staring eyes, heavily outlined nose and eyebrows, and fleshy, high-coloured cheeks, persist, and may be observed in the faces of Justinian and Theodora at Ravenna (sixth century), in the Virgin at Parenzo (see Plate 3. i) and its accompanying Annunciation, in the surviving mosaics of St. Demetrius at Salonica, and in the solitary Panaghia in the apse of St. Sophia in the same town.   This latter dates from the end of the eighth century, and must be compared with the delicate, spiritualised head of the same figure in the church of the Koimisis at Nicæa, executed not more than half a century later. Both Salonica and Nicæa were within the cultural orbit of Constantinople; and the difference between the two heads illustrates how novel was the reaction of art to the iconoclast movement. Thenceforth, within that orbit, the type of the Fayum portrait disappears. Even the technique of the mosaicist is reformed, by the hitherto unprecedented use of cubes of varying sizes to produce the same textural effect as large and small brushes. The human face is now built, in various planes, instead of out-lined, as though in poker-work. In sculpture, a similar trans-formation took place, as is shown in the two ivories of St. John the Baptist on Plate 4. The first, taken from the sixth cen-tury chair of Maximian at Ravenna, is coarsely moulded in the naturalistic tradition of Antiquity; the second, dating from the eleventh, displays a supremely sensitive and dignified inter-pretation of the human face in that most difficult medium, bas-relief. Only in the further provinces, and in Italy, the Hellen-istic-Alexandrine tradition, now become wholly didactic and absorbed in what is commonly known as the Cappadocian school, was preserved by the monks to play a part in the iconographic expansion of the thirteenth to the fifteenth centuries.

In body and drapery, the change wrought by the eighth and ninth centuries was equally significant. In the first mosaics of the earlier period, such as the dome of the Orthodox Baptistery at Ravenna, the Good Shepherd in the Mausoleum of Galla Placidia (both fifth century), and the scenes from the life of Christ in St. Apollinare Nuovo (sixth century), something of the Hellenistic precept of anatomy is retained by purely linear means.

But in the majority of the pre-iconoclast mosaics and paintings, there is no anatomy at all; the drapery might conceal either a body or a scarecrow; it hangs in rigid folds, not undecorative, but allowing no interpretation of human form or movement. And the folds themselves are but sadly suggested, by a method less wholly linear perhaps, but scarcely to be dignified by the terms light and shade. Turning from these, such as the St. Demetrius on Plate 5. i, to the late ninth century Panaghia Angeloktistos on Plate 3. ii, or, to take an extreme example, the Christ descending into Hell at the monastery of St. Luke of Stiris (eleventh century; see Plate 5. ii), the reader can gauge the extent of the metamorphosis. In the Panaghia, the drapery is now constructed of tones, that of the centre figure being in-spired, despite its would-be immobility, by a sweeping harmony compatible with the activities of the angels, and bringing rhythmic unity to the whole composition. The Christ of St. Luke's ex-hibits the same principles in a violent mood characteristic of the Cretan painters and El Greco four and five centuries later. The light and shade are achieved by angry tones; lines are employed to accentuate the rhythm of the various planes; while the drapery of the subsidiary figures not only expresses their mental experi-ences of the moment, but contributes to the importance of the central figure; so that the whole scene fits easily into its archi-tectural semicircle. From now on, the Byzantine artist was con-cerned, not so much with the human anatomy, as with the human movement. This was the medium of his composition, and this which his drapery sought to express. If, as at Daphni, or in the fourteenth century mosque of the Kahrié at Constantinople, he desired quiet—as indeed he always did in the case of his central and holiest figures—this was attained, not by the imposition of impervious vestments, but by movement restrained; so that though the body were even motionless, its clothing was still fluttered in the rhythm of the composition and the tempo demanded by the portrayal of great events.

Colour followed suit.   Instead of a haphazard sequence of large divisions like the countries on a map, it became now, by a system of close interplay, the foremost instrument of that super-lative interior light which El Greco communicated to the know-ledge of the West.   Where formerly the tunic was of one shade, the mantle of another, and the folds denoted only by darker lines, there now came into force the principle of tones reacting organi-cally to their neighbours in the interests, not of decoration, but of form.   Scenes, bodies, faces show the same change.   In the Mausoleum of Galla Placidia, or the apse of St. Sophia at Salonica (fifth and eighth centuries), the colour effect, though magnificent, is simple: sapphire and gold, gold and chocolate. At Daphni or St. Luke's of Stiris, the spectator is confronted by all the combinations and semi-tones of the palette ranged upon a principle of contrast, which is carried from the largest area to the smallest.   The draperies, passed rapidly in review, exhibit the play of colour in the composition; the planes of the draperies similar alternations, which give an effect, infinitely profound, of light and shadow and movement; and in the planes, various tones, crimson and coral, purple of grapes and Prussian blue, are at work to produce a textural meaning unfamiliar to the artists of the previous age.   This finer interplay attains its highest value in the faces.   The head of the Christ in the apse of St. Pudenziana at Rome (402-417), one of the least crude of the earlier period, exhibits cubes of the same size as those employed in the clouds behind; the flesh is of an earthy tint, sparsely interspersed with vermilion squares; the lines of the nose and eyes are heavily indicated in brown. There are no contrasts; the whole composition is grand in the extreme; but the author was no more a colourist than Michael Angelo. Turn to the eleventh century mosaics of St. George and St. Demetrius in the church of Xenophontos on Mount Athos, the finest examples of mosaic technique in existence. Here, the cubes are of three different sizes, those of the faces being the smallest. "Placed in lines of tiny blocks, firm and regular, the colours range from shadow of deepest sepia, through olive-green, to scarlet, pink, and at last . . . to lines of pure white miraculously worked down the outline of the nose and round the corners of the eyes. While in places, to express, not a depression, but a quality of the skin, minute patches of brilliant blue are introduced."[1] This was the technique that rendered possible the transition from mosaic to painting after the fourth crusade, and enabled painting to take the luminous colours of mosaic with it.

The monuments thus quoted to illustrate the change in the vision of the Byzantine artist that arrived between the eighth and tenth centuries are but a small proportion of those that might serve this purpose. But the most scrupulous examination of all those that have survived from before the iconoclast controversy cannot reveal any of those fundamental principles on which Byzantine art of the middle and later periods was to be based.[2]

[1] From *The Station*, by Robert Byron, p. 182. This passage was written in front of the mosaic in question.

[2] The regulation of iconography, in which the change played a considerable part, will be discussed later.

In the sphere of representational art, the ninth and tenth centuries witnessed the birth of an organic cultural manifestation, no longer derivative, and as fully implanted with the seed of independent life as a youth embarking on a career without the assistance of dead parents. Such is the ignorance of the present age with regard to the precedents for its own artistic revolution that some inquiry may be justified into the political and psychological circumstances which ultimately gave Byzantine art its individual complexion, and enabled it, a century after the extinction of its cultural centre, to produce El Greco.

II. The Ignominy Implicit in Representational Art

"Thou shalt not make unto thee any graven image, or any likeness of any thing that is in heaven above, or that is in the earth beneath, or that is in the water under the earth : thou shalt not bow down thyself to them, nor serve them : for I the Lord thy God am a jealous God. . . ." By means of the second commandment, the reiterated and violent injunctions of the Old Testament prophets, and the awful calamities that pursued those who disregarded these prohibitions, the illiterate infant is confronted, in its earliest lessons, with a problem so intricate and obscure that no comprehensive summary or explanation of it has ever been written. The natural result is that, in the mind of the adult, the problem very soon ceases to exist at all. To what purpose is the memory burdened with these complicated anathemas against idols that no one ever thinks to erect? With what aim are the young menaced with examinations and lured with prizes in order to encourage the knowledge of this inex-

3

plicable sin and the retributions that overtook its devotees?   In the minds of children, similar questions attach to the teaching of algebra and Latin; these, in time, are resolved.   But the educational value to be derived from this peculiar twist of the Jewish conscience retains its pristine mystery through the whole span of life, numbered for ever among the aberrations of pedagogues and clergy.   The Jews, apparently, reverted to idols as other men to drink; and since Christ was a Jew, we, children of a Christian state, must perforce exhibit a respectful attention to that people's idiosyncracies.   That is the explanation.   The fact that this problem may reasonably be brought to illuminate one of the fundamental impulses of the human taste is not considered.

Let it be imagined that in our day a new Messiah has come; that the spirit of the universe, be it a mathematical entity or a voice on the wind, has again entered human form, trod England instead of Palestine, and gone; that, in so doing, He has succeeded, posthumously, in bringing consciousness to the spark of communion with an external Reality which is innate in every man, and which it is the avowed purpose of the so-called rational intellect to render dormant; that, in fact, not only the masses, but the greatest minds and executives of the land have again discovered an ideal to take precedence in holiness even of country and honour; picture this eventuality; and then conceive the effect of tidings that an authentic photograph of this new God, to whose worship a whole planet has subscribed, of this Man, beside whose life that of Christ is but the career of an injudicious social reformer, has lately come to light in a Brixton lodging-house, depicting Him in a sailor suit after the pattern of his Britannic Majesty's navy, against a background of artificial foliage, and supported at

the elbow by an artificial log; suppose, moreover, that this intelligence is followed by the discovery of others : of a daguerreotype of His mother, in poke bonnet and paisley shawl, fondly dandling the Infant Deity and gently placing in Its mouth a rubber sucker; of a family group including the husband, a working plumber with sartorial ambitions, whose lack of means has precluded his divorce; and finally of a snapshot from a local paper taken several decades later, in which the Focus of a highly spiritualised monotheism may be observed opening a sale of art needle-work, accompanied by a band of humble, though since exalted, followers; conjure these events and ponder their outcome.   In the new religion, it may be imagined that, if the trend of progress in the old be continued, all forms of worship tending to the localisation of God, including the severest and emptiest of churches, have been uncompromisingly prohibited by the express command of the Founder Himself.   Following the discovery of the photographs, a problem of stupendous import is in train : What shall be done with them, and where shall they be deposited?   Two parties arise : on the one hand the cultured religious purists, who press for their immediate destruction as threatening to revive all the fetishism, superstition, and congregational imbecilities, from which the world has only lately been freed; on the other, the enormous and hysterical masses, who fasten upon these material tokens of their God with animal hunger.   It seems as though, in the English parliament, the purists will carry the day.   The United States, fortress of mob-superstition, declare war.   The purists accept the challenge.   And the world is made desolate. . . .
Or, suppose again that the photographs had never existed; but that, to satisfy the cravings of industrial barbarism, artists are

at work on a badge for the new fraternity, a gibbet, instrument
of the God's earthly death, geometrically formalised; that this
activity is followed by the manufacture of actual portraits adorned
with the round collar which was the mark of ministry in the
old pagan cult, Christianity; and that these, in their turn, are
expanded into actual scences from the life in Brixton, culminating in the final arrest and trial, with the Lord Chief Justice's
sapient comments inscribed below.   Is it hard to visualise the disgust with which the purists must view these practices, and the
measures, resulting in the disruption of state and society, with
which they will seek to repress them?   History tells of similar
happenings.   We, to understand those happenings, must place
ourselves and our world in similar circumstances, must remember
that the time has always been, and the time will surely come
again, when only a new religion can galvanise life into the
moribund frame of Reason and custom on which all societies
are founded.   We must recall that which we now hold sacred;
that which we might hold yet more sacred; and then our own
feelings towards the annexation of that sacredness by the devices
of representational art, and the consequent imprisonment of the
ineffable in churches and shrines.   This done, the second commandment and the Old Testament controversies, together with
their reflections in Christianity, become psychologically intelligible.

The argument has strayed far from "art" in its confined
sense.   It will stray further.   It must become religious; because
art was now to become, for the first time in European history,
a product of the emotions; and in the Byzantine Empire all
emotions were ultimately connected with God.   A great secular

art in that sphere is not conceivable. Art, to be great art, must absorb the artist's whole personality, must leave nothing even to God; when every man is already God's servant, only by service to God also will it be great. During four centuries, Christian art had been laboriously breaking free of the Antique tradition; the iconoclast controversy contributed the final rupture of this bond, gave European art its first true greatness, and by failing, saved art. Yet, though the matter of the argument be extra-rational, the argument itself is not. From the religious point of view, the localisation of God in temples, pictures, and sacramental food, is justified by its beneficial attraction for the masses; hence, in our time, the revival of Roman Catholic practices, resulting from the sudden elevation of the people and the consequent degradation of everything else. Art, however, and the large view of history on which the understanding of art is based, can take no account of a detachment dictated by temporary exigencies. Judged æsthetically, the iconoclast impulse of the eighth century was a momentous and fortunate occurrence.

The peculiarity of Iconoclasm, as distinct from other manifestations of "Protestantism," was that its effort was directed against art; and that it was in this sphere that its chief effect was felt. The achievement of Christ, stated as a broad generalisation, had been the popularisation throughout Europe and the Levant of Jewish monotheism, and the displacement, by that means, of the miscellaneous cults of which the Mediterranean peoples, for all their philosophies, were the prey. No sooner had Christianity obtained universal acceptance, than this achievement was menaced: by art. The Hellenistic mode of representation was more photographic than any photographs in a Brixton lodging-house; and its function, in the popular estimation, was that of the camera—the provision of souvenirs. Symbols and symbolic representation proved a vain refuge;[1] the popular demand for "human interest" was not to be withstood then, more than it is now. Each picture and each bust became simply one more interruption of man's commerce with his God. The logic of the case was plain. And when political circumstances called to the East Roman throne a dynasty of religious purists, they proceeded forthwith to an attack on all religious art, and therefore, as far as posterity was concerned, on all art. Art won; but was reformed in the process and stamped thenceforward with a character of rigid compromise. Symbols were discarded, and a safer refuge found in true interpretation. The iconodule defence of pictures for their mystic significance as vehicles of the sacred was assimilated to probe still deeper into the reality of visible object. And the process was assisted by the boundless wealth and magnificence of taste that now came to the Empire. Strzygowski has written: "Non-representational art is not more backward or more primitive than representational; it is simply different. . . . To personify or anthropomorphise all and everything is to attempt the opening of every door with the master key 'Man.' . . . It is clear enough that the present generation has deliberately turned against representation." It is clear enough of that other, Byzantine, generation also. Art is now become the vehicle of all great human ideas. In the eighth and ninth centuries it was likewise transformed from their companion into their servant.

[1] As early as 681 the Council of Constantinople stated that the figure of Christ was preferable to the lamb.

III. The Tradition of Idolatry and Defence of Religious Art

It has been the custom of historians to regard the iconoclast controversy as an outcome of religious lunacy only less explicable than the Christological disputes of the fourth and fifth centuries. They readily admit that precedent is to be found in the Bible; but, as has been shown, the passages in that book pertaining to idols are considered by them and their readers to augment rather than diminish the obscurity of the problem. Nor does it occur to either that other precedents are to be found; that other races beside the Jews were troubled by an iconoclast conscience. The materials are sparse. But such as have survived illustrate the persistence in all ages, and under all conditions, of the opposition to purely reproductional art, and of the arguments fabricated, consciously and unconsciously, to counteract this opposition.

If the history of the movement begins in the Bible, it is the Bible that reveals, equally, how strong and persistent was the instinct of the most fundamentally monotheistic people in history towards the grosser forms of localisation. The very fear of idols exhibited by the Old Testament chroniclers implies a belief in the efficacy of the demons supposed to inhabit them. And though the chroniclers seek to conceal it, it is clear that until a comparatively recent period in Jewish history, about the fifth century B.C., idolatrous worship was continuous. Even Moses, who overthrew the Golden Calf, designed something suspiciously like a hollow idol in the ephod with its jewelled appurtenances. Nor, as is customarily taken for granted, was the prejudice against representational art absolute: Were not the ends of the mercy seat of the ark formed of cherubims whose faces are expressly mentioned? And were not the curtains of the ark woven with the same celestial creatures? (Exodus, xxv., xxvi., xxviii.). Jehu, despite his holocaust of Baal-worshippers, gave his allegiance to the golden calves of Jeroboam, thereby provoking no recorded protest from Elisha, who had nominated him for the throne (2 Kings x.); Isaiah (ii.) talks of a land full of idols; Jeremiah (xliv.) inveighs against their prevalence. Moses had been disavowed by King Hezekiah, who "removed the high places"—objecting, presumably, to any outward forms of worship whatever—"and brake the images, and cut down the groves and brake in pieces the brasen serpent that Moses had made; for unto those days the children of Israel did burn incense to it" (2 Kings, xviii.). Nevertheless, the heresy continued. Ezekiel tells how even the Levites had formerly ministered to idols. But this does not prevent him from prescribing a certain measure of decorative art in his ordinance of the temple: "so that a palm tree was between a cherub and a cherub; and every cherub had two faces; so that the face of a man was toward the palm tree on the one side, and the face of a young lion toward the palm tree on the other" (xli.). Here were monsters worthy of the Philistines. At length came the Hellenistic age, and with it the expansion of Greek naturalism to the furthest confines of Asia. Jews at Carthage and Rome decorated their cemeteries in the fashion of the day; and their coins have survived impressed with the image of Noah. Thus it is apparent that among the people most wholly concerned with the spiritual danger of art, the instinct towards representation was never altogether stifled; a fact which illustrates the magni-

tude of the task that lay before the iconoclast Emperors in dealing with the histrionic and naturally anthropomorphic Greeks.

In the classical world, as will be seen later, the iconoclast impulse was at work long before the propagation of Christianity,
and provoked a literature aiming at the reasoned defence of
statues as the proper instruments of communion with God—
thus foreshadowing that of the iconodules in the eighth and
ninth centuries. Plato had already expounded the theory that
in honouring statues, "though lifeless, we believe that our reverence is agreeable to the living gods, and brings us favours of
them." The Stoics and Seneca were of two minds on the subject; but the attitude of the latter was sufficiently favourable to
induce the censure of St. Augustine: "Philosophy had taught
him not to be superstitious with regard to nature; but laws and
customs held him fast as far as society was concerned." The
position adopted by Plutarch was also dubious: in some passages
he condemns all forms of localisation; in others, regret for the
crumbling of all faith before the prevalent scepticism leads him
to invoke the popular demonology, that religion may be saved
from total extinction. He favoured the simplicity of the early
Greek fetish in preference to the elaborate shrines of his time.
And he notes, with some aptitude, that the Egyptians have
created in the Sphinx a symbol of the mystery attaching to other
symbols. Celsus, in the second century A.D., advised against the
disregarding of lesser gods, particularly those of the state; and
he blamed the Christians for their impiety: "If the idols are
nothing, what is so dreadful in attending a sacred feast?" Maxi-
mus of Tyre, also of the second century, having himself seen
the lesser gods, explained that, while they have no need of statues,

the latter serve as a convenient symbol of their presence; just as the Persians use fire; the Egyptians beasts; and the Celts a sacred oak.   Finally, in the third century, the great mystic Plotinus, whose life's business was the evocation of the Almighty, regarded statues as an essential help in that matter.   "The universal Soul . . ." he wrote, "can easily be made present in every object disposed to receive its action and to participate, in some degree, in its power."

While these apologies illustrate the function of art as a utilitarian religious adjunct, that of Dio Chrysostom, in the second century A.D., treats the matter from a more æsthetic point of view. After lauding nature as the source of divine experience, the Stoic orator turns his panegyric to Pheidias' statue of Zeus; to which Pheidias, arraigned as it were on a charge of idolatry, makes the following reply: "No sculptor or painter can portray pure thought and spirit alone.   But since the being inhabited by reason is familiar to us, it is that to which we have recourse, and we invest God with the human body as being the vessel of thought and Reason. . . .   To object that it were better to place before the human eye neither statue nor image of the gods, on the ground that we must direct our gaze solely towards heavenly things, is surely impossible.   Every being endowed with Reason adores those things on high, believing that he sees the auspicious deities from afar.   But thanks to the impulse which urges us towards God, every man is infused with an irresistible longing to worship and serve him at close quarters . . . to offer him garlands and sacrifices. . . .   As for the features of my statue, no one, not even a fool, could compare them with those of a man. . . .   Its human likeness is designed to show, in symbolic manner, the

relation between men and gods.   The gentleness and kindness
which it emanates tell of a friendly god, a god of suppliants. . . .
It is this that I have sought to achieve by means of my art, since
I am unable to express it in words."   Thus, by a sophisticated
process of reasoning intended to cover the plainly uneasy conscience of six centuries later, is the sculptor made the unwitting
apologist of the incurable anthropomorphism of Antiquity.   "A
friendly god"—there may be virtue in such an entity; but the
conception, like that of those parsons and schoolmasters who envisage Christ as the prototype of Lord Baden-Powell, is essentially
non-religious.   The tone of the whole speech gives the impression
that, though its author may have had some inkling into the
spiritual potentiality of art, the sculpture in question, which he,
and possibly even we, could not but have admired,[1] was of such
an overpowering, idealised, and exquisite earthiness as to stifle
altogether any idea of how art in itself might attain this elevation.
The logic of Antiquity had produced a reasoned justification of
art as a spiritual intermediary in an attempt to preserve some
kind of ordered religion in the growing philosophic chaos; for,
in the eyes of Antiquity, religion was impossible without symbols;
and the increasingly abstract character of religious speculation
was growing less and less content with bald representations or
idealisations of the human form.   But the art of Antiquity, the
rotten Hellenistic art of the Roman Empire, based on the so-called
inspiration of nature, lacked the innate capacity to rise to its new
responsibility.   The influence of Pheidias was still too strong.
Not even Christianity was sufficient to bring about the necessary

---

[1] The extraordinary human appeal of this particular statue is recorded by
Livy and Quintilian also.

change—to invent an art which, instead of merely focussing, should interpret, the emotions. Only in the eighth and ninth centuries did the reflection in Constantinople of an anti-representational and anti-Hellenistic revolt on the part of the Semites and Arabs throughout the Near East prove strong enough to engineer this transformation.

Beneath the more or less elevated philosophy of art as the instrument of religious communion thus adumbrated by the writers of later Antiquity, there flourished a popular and non-intellectual demonology, which was also focussed on statues and material symbols. Some, like the Artemis of Ephesus or the Zeus-Ammon of Egypt, were of human semblance; others took the form of phalluses, columns, steles and pyramids; others, like the thunderbolt of Athena at Athens or the white stone of Hercules at Hyettos, were content, simply, with the shapes of nature. Sometimes they were robed in gorgeous vestments; sometimes borne in progress by their priests. Of those that made signs and performed miracles, Ælian, in the third century, drew up a list, in order to confound the sceptic Epicureans. Relics formed a separate cult. The lance of Achilles, the arm of Diomed, the sceptre of Agamemnon, were all preserved and honoured like any god. Christianity had no sooner become the state religion of the Empire than it absorbed these practices, and with them, a deep-seated incentive to representation. Another factor in the preservation of artistic symbols under the new religion, was the Roman imperial cult, which Constantine I. the Great, by proclaiming himself vice-regent of Christ's Father, astutely fortified. This visible investiture of the ruler with the sanctity of the state persisted through the whole of Byzantine history, and has found supreme expression from the pen of Constantine VII. Porphyrogenitus. "When we exhibit this order and harmony in the imperial power," wrote the Emperor of his pontifical court, "we represent in miniature the order and rhythm with which the Creator has infused the universe." In the first centuries of the Christian Empire, the army continued to anoint and worship the images of the Cæsars, as had been done under the Antonines. For many years, a wooden statue of Constantine was paraded through the streets of his city on the day of its foundation. Until the reign of Constantine V. (740-775) statues of the Emperors, of which one still survives at Barletta, were erected on accession, and laurelled busts in wax were despatched to all parts of the Empire. And Codrinus records, at the end of the fourteenth century, that in a Christmas procession, the icon of the Emperor received the same honour as those of the saints. Here again was Christianity fully acquiescent in a custom of representation which was almost avowedly idolatrous.

The popular mythology inherited by the new religion, together with the survival of the imperial cult, immediately tended to obscure the original monotheistic conception. Writes Harnack in volume iv. of his *History of Dogma*: "To live in the sphere of pure and impure spirits, to be visited, refreshed and strengthened by the former, to be tempted and assailed by the latter, was soon held to be a sign of a heroic Christianity. . . . The one God, whom the people had never understood, threatened to disappear, even in the views of refined theologians, behind the . . . complicated intermediaries who appeared more tangible and therefore more trustworthy. . . . The cultured Christian . . . would rather picture the fulness and variety of mortal life than dwell for ever on the desolate and terrifying thought of the One, who was so incomprehensible that not even his being could be conceived." Even with the demons still openly pagan, the earliest Christian writers were unable to deny their force. "If it is they who animate the images of the sanctuary," wrote Athenagoras in the second century, "all the more reason to execrate the statues. . . . Fallen angels . . . vagrant and rebellious demi-gods, it is they who lure men and hold them to the service of idols." Tatian accepted their existence, despite their patent inferiority; St. Augustine likewise. Tertullian blamed the artist for providing them with bodies. Then, gradually, their importance[1] was overshadowed by the cult of the saints. The shrine became the lodging of the relic, the grisly mortal fragment linked with death and therefore with the start of true life. In the fourth century, the suppression of the Nestorian heresy at the Council of Chalcedon rendered Christ's incarnation, the very fact of his flesh, the central dogma of the Church; and the significance of Mary, the ponderous queen of motherhood, was correspondingly increased, to obscure still further Jewish conception of the One. Simultaneously emerged the doctrine of transsubstantiation, typifying the whole "cycle of material things that could be seen, heard, tasted, smelt and touched." In these developments in Christianity was preserved still as wide a field for art as had ever been provided by the gods of Olympus or the aerial spirits of the pagan Empire.

Apologists, in plain terms, of a Christian art, were soon forth-

---

[1] They continued to form a secondary hierarchy. Psellos, in the eleventh century, wrote a treatise on demonology, in which he admits their bodies, those of the angels being immaterial, those of the demons material but invisible.

coming.   One of the Hermetic writers, about the second century, had already enunciated the mystical defence that was later to become prominent: "It is not the gold, the silver, the wood, nor the stone that we adore; for we also know that it is only inanimate matter, the work of mortal man: but the spirit residing therein; it is this that we call God."   The doctrine of the Neoplatonists, that the function of art was not merely to teach, but to provide the outward symbols of the supra-terrestrial, was similarly expanded by Denys the Areopagite.   St. Basil (329-379) maintained that the efficacy of the gospel depended as much on its representation as its letter; and in his panegyric on the martyr Barlaam, he cried: "Come help me, famous painters of heroic deeds; enhance with your art the imperfect portrait of this general; illuminate with colour the victorious athlete that I have depicted with so little lustre. . . .   And portray also, in your picture, him who presides at contests and awards the crown, the Christ Agonothetes."   The tears of St. Gregory of Nyssa (331-395), which had remained pent during the recital of the incident where Abraham is about to sacrifice his son, were unloosed for the picture of it.   St. Cyril, the unscrupulous Patriarch of Alexandria (d. 444), likewise wept before the delineation of a young Christian martyred in the amphitheatre. By degrees whole cycles of ecclesiastical art arose.   In the first half of the fifth century, the prefect Olympiodorus of Constantinople wrote to St. Nilus of Sinai begging his approval of a scheme of church decoration consisting of birds, beasts, and hunting-scenes.   "I can only reply," wrote the saint, "that no one but a babe or a suckling would wish to pervert the eyes of the faithful with such trivialities as you describe. . . .

It is not unfitting to decorate both sides of the holy temple, by the hands of the finest painters, with scenes from the Old and New Testaments, that the man who is ignorant of writing and unable to read the Holy Writ may observe the painting and gain knowledge of the fathers of all virtue, who served the true God; and that he may thus be roused to emulate them." In the sixth century, Leontius, bishop of Neapolis in Cyprus, delivered the opinion that "the pictures are books, always open, which are explained and venerated in the churches in order to recall, by visible means, God himself, and to adore him through the saints and their works." Then, at length, Pope Gregory I. the Great (540-604), in his letter to Serenus, bishop of Marseilles, uttered his famous dictum and compromise, which has endured ever since as the text of Roman Catholic observance: "In forbidding the adoration of pictures, you deserve commendation; but in destroying them, you are to blame." In his eyes, also, they were the only gospel of the illiterate.

The above quotations are corroborated by many other patristic passages; and they illustrate, first how the tradition of religious art in later Antiquity was absorbed by Christianity, and secondly how that tradition was then deliberately expanded by some of the greatest minds of the new religion. But their tenor engenders the suspicion that they were actually the outcome of latent controversy; they betray, by their very being, an attitude of defence. The immediate forces that launched the iconoclast reform upon the Greek Empire were yet, in the sixth century, scarcely discernible. But the psychological impulse underlying that movement may also be traced from the remotest periods of Hebrew and classical history.

IV. THE TRADITION OF ICONOCLASM AND THE CENSURE OF ART

The Old Testament polemic against idolatry, though patent from the earliest times and politically prominent in the days of the Kings, only attained that intensity of feeling which later distinguished the Jewish religion, after the Captivity.   In Isaiah (xliv.), the whole theory of sacred representation is demolished with satire that would have done credit to Juvenal: "The smith with the tongs both worketh in the coals and fashioneth it with hammers, and worketh it with the strength of his arms. . . .   The carpenter stretcheth out his rule; he marketh it out with a line; he fitteth it with planes, and he marketh it out with the compass, and maketh it after the figure of a man, according to the beauty of a man; that it may remain in the house.   He heweth him down cedars, and taketh the cypress and the oak, which he strengtheneth for himself among the trees of the forest: he planteth an ash and the rain doth nourish it.   Then shall it be for a man to burn: for he will take thereof and warm himself; yea, he kindleth it and baketh bread; yea, he maketh a god and worshippeth it; he maketh it a graven image and falleth down thereto.   He burneth part thereof in the fire; with part thereof he eateth flesh; he roasteth roast, and is satisfied; yea, he warmeth himself, and saith, Aha, I am warm, I have seen the fire: and the residue thereof he maketh a god, even his graven image: he falleth down unto it, and worshippeth it, and prayeth unto it, and saith, Deliver me, for thou art my God."

Long after, these thunderings are echoed in a voice of more refined and philosophical intelligence.   St. Paul writes to the

4

Romans (i., 20-23): "For the invisible things of him from the creation of the world are clearly seen, being understood by the things that are made, even his eternal power and Godhead; so that they are without excuse: because that, when they knew God, they glorified him not as God, neither were thankful; but . . . changed the glory of the incorruptible God into an image made like to corruptible man, and to birds and four-footed beasts and creeping things."   The writer's purpose was to deliver a homily on morality.   But in saying that the invisible must be understood through the already visible, instead of through a formula of anthropomorphic invention, he was enunciating the truth which is the basis of all great art, and which, in European art, was only brought to light by the iconoclast attack of eight centuries later.   This idea is expanded by Sir William Ramsay: "We must clearly understand at the outset, both the intensity of Paul's hatred for idolatry, and the reason and nature of that hatred. . . .   Since the only reality in the world is God, any serious error about the nature of God—*i.e.,* any idolatry—must distort our conception of the world and external nature. . . .   Paul abhorred idolatry as the enemy of mankind."   Nor were St. Paul's admonitions confined to the Romans.   "Forasmuch then," he told the men of Athens (Acts xvii.), "as we are the offspring of God, we ought not to think that the Godhead is like unto gold, or silver, or stone, graven by art and man's device.   And the times of this ignorance God winked at; but now commandeth all men everywhere to repent."

Meanwhile the Romans had reached Jersusalem; and Pompey, hastening through the famous temple, was arrested in his profanity at the Holy of Holies by: emptiness.[1] In deference to the popular sentiment against representation, subsequent generals forwent the usual custom of carrying the sacred effigies of the Emperors through the streets of the conquered capital. And special coins were struck for Jewish use without the impress of the sovereign's head. Absorbed within the Roman Empire, and threatened with its uniform Hellenistic culture, the chosen race now strove to preserve its individuality by unflinching loyalty to the God so persistently denied in the past, and by strenuous opposition to all depiction of the human form. Yet, though robbed of material freedom, the influence of that race on the outside world was by no means at an end, and by no means transmitted through Christ alone. As early as the third century B.C., Aristobulus had attempted the first harmonisation of Judaic and Greek philosophy. But his effort was surpassed by that of Philo, himself a Jew almost contemporary with Christ, who on one occasion formed part of an embassy from Alexandria to Rome to protest against the enforced worship of Caligula. To him posterity is indebted for the first genuine philosophic statement of religious faith. And in his view, not only was the conception of God in terms of man an impiety vaster than the ocean; but all works of art, irrespective of significance, were incompatible with true belief. "Seeing these much esteemed works of calligraphers, of sculptors, and of other craftsmen, in forms inanimate, in paintings and statues . . . among these things, nothing, as I said, has been held worthy of commendation in the sight of God."

[1] This discovery, in a shrine so widely advertised, provoked the derision of the ancient world. The idea of religion without symbols was one which that world could not grasp.

Here is the first considered enunciation of that sweeping proscription of all art, which the Jews later bequeathed to Islam, and whose psychological effect was mainly responsible for the controversy of the eighth and ninth centuries.

With the exception of a few isolated movements in early Christianity, it is generally supposed that, until the expansion of Islam, the impulse against representational art remained a monopoly of the Hebrews and the Semitic nomads adjacent to them. This was not the case. The arguments of iconoclasm may have derived equally from a whole succession of thought in the classical world.

Xenophanes, the parent of Greek monotheism (540-500 B.C.), inveighed against the representation of gods as men; animals, he argued, would likewise depict them as animals, were they able. Pythagoras, his contemporary, viewed statues with similar contempt; for him, the expression of God's being was best attempted by mathematics.   Euripides (480-406 B.C.) was moved to ask in public, What building made of man could contain the body of God?   The cynics were avowed enemies, not only of cults, but of all art; Diogenes, their foremost philosopher (412-323 B.C.), is reported to have heaped a wooden Hercules on his fire with the words: "Come, accomplish thy thirteenth labour by helping me cook my dish of lentils."   The Stoics, with their practical eye to the interest and weakness of the common man, hesitated to give free rein to their scorn.   But the scorn was growing. Strabo (b. 64 B.C.) lauded Moses for his condemnation of images.   And Plutarch (A.D. 46-c. 120), despite similar utilitarian doubts (see page 41), maintained that to worship the gods in stone was to deny them, the inevitable result being their con-

ception in human form.   Lucian (125-180) employed shafts of
frank irreligion, picturing the gods assembling in precedence of
material value, the Egyptian ones of precious metal in front, and
all the deities of good Greek stone behind.   For the classical
world, the argument had become merely destructive in the hands
of sceptics and satirists.   But others were at hand to resume it on
a more solemn basis.   For these it was no question of laughter,
but of the day of judgement.

The earliest surviving Christian attacks on representational
symbols, outside the New Testament, are those of Aristides and
Justin Martyr in the second century.   Tatian, a disciple of
the latter, condemned all sculpture, as such, and compiled a
list of monuments in that form, each commemorating a sinner.
In the third century, St. Clement of Alexandria likewise loosed
his pen against art for its own sake: its development, in his
opinion, must vary with the errors that enslave men.   The demons
he repudiates altogether: "Makers of gods worship neither gods
nor spirits, in my opinion, but the world and art."   Art, in fact,
from being merely suspect, is becoming intrinsically wicked.
Athenagoras, in the second century, allowed that it was more
deceitful and empty than an actual source of corruption.   But
Origen, in the third, and Eusebius the historian, in the fourth,
scorned the symbolist defence of it (see pages 41-44) as a despicable sophism.   In the opinion of the latter, the miracles of the
statues were achieved by conjuring: "And why," he wrote,
"is it necessary to borrow the human body in order to present
or previsualise the Divine Wisdom?"   To worship likenesses
of Jesus Christ or of the apostles Peter and Paul was, in his
words, "a custom of the Gentiles."   St. Augustine (353-430),

while unable to deny the demons, was no less definite in his anathemas.

It was not long before the polemic moved from words to actions. By the Spanish council of Elvira in the early fourth century, all church decoration was expressly forbidden; and it was ruled that "there must be no pictures in the church, that the walls should have no images of that which is revered and worshipped." At the end of the same century, according to iconoclast tradition,[1] St. Epiphanius of Cyprus openly tore in pieces a stuff bearing the effigy of Christ or a saint, invoking the Scriptures to support his action. A hundred years later, Xenaias, prior to his elevation to the Monophysite see of Hierapolis in Phrygia, denounced any depiction of the Virgin and saints. In the sixth century, Antioch was the scene of formidable riots against the pictures; and at Edessa the miraculous icon of Christ was stoned by the troops. About the same time, a painted crucifixion at Narbonne provoked such indignation as to oblige its being veiled. Finally, in 599, the policy of bishop Serenus of Marseilles in actually destroying all the pictures and images in the city elicited the remonstrance from Pope Gregory I. the Great already quoted on page 48.

[1] This incident is probably founded on fact, though contained in a letter purporting to come from Epiphanius himself and almost certainly manufactured by the iconoclast party at the time of the controversy.

V. The General Impulse to Religious Purism throughout
the Near East and its Effect in Constantinople

The position, therefore, at the opening of the seventh century,
was as follows: In defence of art were ranged, first the popular
mythology of spirits and demi-gods, now translated from pagan
demons into angels and saints, and demanding, as of yore, the
provision of material, if only painted, bodies; and secondly, the
exponents of the symbolic value of artistic representation as a
convenient means of localisation of, and communion with, God—
these latter fortified by the permanent emphasis on Christ's human
attributes and adventures that resulted from the councils of the
fifth century.   Against art stood the whole later Jewish tradition
of the now prevalent monotheistic religion; a tenuous, but unbroken current of Antique philosophy; and finally a growing
body of influential opinion among the early Christian prelates
and writers, who saw an intolerable menace in the inevitable
tendency of art to anthropomorphise the otherwise unqualified
God and his manifestations.   Already, from Phrygia to Spain,
consciences had been troubled, and words translated into actions.

Such a state of affairs, in which art, manifested in terms of
those objects to which the human eye is accustomed, was regarded
as nothing less than a sin against the Holy Ghost, is only intelligible to the mind of the twentieth century (for which art,
in the absence of religion, provides the residue of hope), when
the prevailing character of the art in question is considered.   Suppose, again, the Brixton Messiah: our allegiance might be
strengthened by a portrait from Van Gogh; but scarcely by one
from Alma Tadema.   The philosophers of the time might invent

the theory of symbolic significance; but the Hellenistic ideal of representation, the engrained, debased, and commonplace naturalism of a millennium, was incapable of achieving it.   Hence the excessive rarity of the Greek type of Christ, and the prompt substitution of the Semitic.   The germ of the interpretational method was suggested psychologically by the very difference between the single Christian conception of Reality and all the heterogeneous vapourings of Antiquity.   But suggestion was not enough to rescue the art of Antiquity from the bottom of its pit, as has been shown by examination of the extant monuments.   The course of cultural evolution was at a standstill.   Art, by its debasement, was proving an impediment to man's spiritual ascension, and had forfeited man's respect.   Only a physical shock could save it.   And a physical shock it received.   In 717 Leo III. the Isaurian ascended the throne of Constantinople.   And in 726 the first edict was uttered against all the holy pictures of the Greek Empire.

Viewed in proportion to their historical effect, the actual causes which led to the espousal by the Emperor Leo and a powerful military party of the hitherto relatively unimportant opposition to sacred art have remained strangely obscure.   The spectacle of a succession of sovereigns, politically astute, magnificent in war, and no less remarkable for their administrative reforms, deliberately setting the axe of religious purism to the roots of popular belief; risking not only personal loss, but the disruption of the whole Empire; and adopting this course without the remotest chance of any compensatory political advantage; is profoundly mysterious; and places the iconoclast controversy on a plane apart from all the other movements of religious reform in history.   The evidence allows only one explanation: a psychological wave of self-assertion on the part of the fundamentally anti-representational tradition of the Near and Middle East against the still pervasive Hellenism.   This is more than a mere hypothesis, as simultaneous developments in Islam indicate.   And the immediate source of this self-assertion, and of Islam itself, was undoubtedly Judaic.

The conditions of mind that led to the triumph of Christianity, far from putting the final thorn to the crown of Jewish humiliation, were, in fact, also responsible for a considerable expansion in Jewish missionary enterprise.   St. John Chrysostom (347-407) records that, in his native town of Antioch, Christian ladies were wont to attend the synagogues, and that Christian litigants preferred to submit their disputes to the Jewish courts.   Until about 620 the Jewish kingdom of Homeritis flourished in the Arabian desert; one of its rulers was the first to lay a carpet in the Caaba at Mecca; and many Arab tribes preserved their Judaic rites after its extinction by the Abyssinians.   In the first quarter of the eighth century, exactly synchronising with similar purist movements, and doubtless due to the same impulse of feeling, there arose in Judaism the Karaite heresy, which sought to revive the old Sadducean protestantism, the direct inspiration from the written word, in face of the hieratic Rabbinism that had displaced it.   With particular emphasis, it was reaffirmed that "God is without form and in every sense One."   Later in the century, the Turcoman tribe of the Khazars, inhabiting a territory near the Caspian, were converted to Judaism; and though religious toleration was practised, adherence to that religion was a necessary condition of royal succession.   At the beginning of the ninth century, a sect of Greeks following the Mosaic rite was reported from the district of Upper Phrygia, whence hailed the iconoclast Emperor Michael II. the Amorian. And a certain significance attaches to the fact that the famous Bagratid dynasty of Armenia later strove to prove itself of Jewish descent.

Apart, however, from their political effect, the Jews, wherever their numbers were sufficient, were always ready to engage on theological ground. According to Anastasius Sinaita, Patriarch of Antioch (d. 609), they were wont to blame the Christians that, contrary to the word of God forbidding the worship of anything fashioned by the hands of man, they made and adored crosses and icons. Leontius, bishop of Neapolis in Cyprus in the early seventh century, has testified to the savagery of their contempt for Christian practices : they tore down icons and trod them in ditches; they caricatured those of the Passion; such as they could not reach, they stoned; no less violent was their hatred of the cross. The Frankish bishop, Arculf, while in Jerusalem, saw a man, who was doubtless a Jew, seize a bas-relief of the Virgin and hurl it down a lavatory. Little credit can be attached to the Orthodox legends purporting to prove actual communication between the first Isaurian Emperors and the Jews. But there is no doubt that the iconoclast activity of that people was particularly marked in the period immediately preceding the outbreak in Christianity.

The beginning of the seventh century saw the foundation of Islam and the national birth of the Arabs. The original intention of Mahomet had been probably to harmonise his faith with that of the Judaised Arabs of Medina, among whom he had sojourned after his expulsion from Mecca. But though he afterwards repudiated them, it was the letter of Mosaic observance, and the fusion of civil and religious life, that subsequently gave his faith its peculiar character; the Mahomedan conquests, in Jewish eyes, provided a welcome exchange from Christian rule. Marked exception was taken by the Prophet or his immediate followers to the Christian practice of Mariolatry, and certain passages in the Koran were written expressly to disavow it. Nor was Mahomet's horror of idolatry less pronounced.

But the attitude of Islam towards representational art in general has been widely distorted. The Koran contains but the faintest condemnation even of statues; and Mahomet, though he threw down the idols of Mecca, talked complacently enough of the sacred pictures that his wives had seen in Abyssinia, and is even reported to have rescued an icon of the Virgin from the holocaust at the Caaba. Stuffs woven with beasts and men gave him no offence; his infant wife, Ayesha, was permitted her dolls. The fanatical prohibition of all representational art, through which the painter became the byword of earth and the black sheep of hell, was a later development, and one which must have resulted, in the opinion of Sir Thomas Arnold, both from contact with Judaism and reaction against Hellenistic naturalism. The significant fact is that it arose with the Traditions of the Prophet, written at the end of the seventh century, and openly derived from the Talmud; and that it was therefore, to all intents and purposes, contemporary with the outbreak of the Karaite purist revival in Judaism, and the iconoclast protestantism in Christianity. The existence of a homogeneous spiritual impulse at work among the peoples of the Near East, irrespective of creed, is thus corroborated.

The immediate outcome of the impulse in Islam was the formulation of definite theological argument against representation. Whereas the Greek iconodule defence was that, since Christ became man, he could be depicted, the Mahomedan maintained that it was sinful to represent man at all; for in so doing the artist was intruding on the functions of God. In actual fact, numerous schools of representational art did develop in Islam[1]: examples survive in Spain; the mechanical tree of the Caliphs of Bagdad was flanked by phalanxes of mounted knights, which also moved; the Fatimid court of Egypt was adorned with all manner of works of art; coins exist bearing the impress of the early Caliphs robed like Byzantine Emperors; while the variety of Persian miniatures scarcely needs mention. The outstanding point is that the anti-representational impulse was neither co-incident with the foundation of Islam, nor a permanent impulse; but that it had its origin, and enjoyed its strongest effect, simultaneously with the iconoclast controversy in Christianity.[2] Towards the end of the seventh century, the Caliph Omar II. inaugurated a forcible movement against art, which appears to have been continued by his successor Yezid in the eighth; each, according to Byzantine historians, was directly inspired by Jews. Both in the mosques, and in all Christian churches in Mahomedan territory, religious paintings were either destroyed or hid.

[1] Their existence or non-existence had no connection with the Shi'ite heresy, as is often stated.

[2] It is a curious, and perhaps noteworthy, coincidence that, of the two surviving examples of Islamic representational art from the early period, the frescoes of the palace of Kusejr 'Amra date from between 705 and 715, and those of Samarra from between 847 and 861, the gap between them thus marking almost the exact limits of the iconoclast controversy in the Orthodox Church.

"On the outbreak of iconoclasm," writes Strzygowski, "the forces which had been developing an art averse to Hellenism shook the foundations laid by Church and court." That art was anti-representational. The non-Christian and the Orthodox Christian origins of the movement have been examined. It remains to trace the impulse, through the Christian heresies, to the very seat of the outbreak. The Emperor Leo III., who promulgated the first official Christian edict against religious pictures in 726, was born at Germanicia in Syria. But the post whence he ascended the throne was the generalship of the Anatolic theme. That theme included a large part of the ancient province of Phrygia and was limited, on the east, by Lesser Armenia.

Strzygowski has conducted an exhaustive analysis into the pre-Christian anti-representational religions of the hinterland of Asia Minor and the adjacent East; and it is to an original Mazdaic tradition that he ascribes the prejudice of the Armenian national Church, founded about 300, against anthropomorphic art. The existence of that prejudice is proved by a body of evidence. The council of Chalcedon, whereby the Incarnation was emphasised in perpetuity for the Orthodox and Catholic West, was officially repudiated by the Armenian Church. And as early as the sixth century, a party had already arisen to condemn the veneration of pictures. In the seventh, an Armenian historian referred to the icon-lovers as a "sect." The Patriarch Wahan (968-970) was deposed on account of his substitution of pictures for the cross. And in the twelfth and thirteenth centuries, Armenian Patriarchs were still defending themselves against the reproaches of the Byzantine sovereigns for their hostility to pictures.

Meanwhile, bearing yet further testimony to the wave of

religious purism that overtook the Near and Middle East in the
seventh and eighth centuries, there came about a revival of the
old adoptionist Christianity of the early Church, which held that
Christ's divinity dated not from his entry into Mary's womb,
but from his infusion with the Holy Ghost at the time of Baptism.[1]
This doctrine now gave rise to a definite sect known as the
Paulicians, who denied the original divinity of Christ, the virginity
of his mother, and the intercession of the saints.　In 1837, con-
fessions extorted at the instance of the Russian authorities of
Alexandropol disclosed that its latter converts had been instructed
"not to worship things made with hands, that is to say the images
of the saints and the cross."　In fact, for iconolatry, the Paulicians
merely substituted anthropolatry, believing that the divine spirit
entered their elders, as they held it to have done Christ.　But
towards sacred art and symbols their attitude was definite enough.

It is not surprising, therefore, holding in mind the spread of
Judaism, and the purist revivals in that religion, in Islam, and
in Armenian Christianity, to discover that, in the period of Leo's
micrasiatic sojourn, an avowedly iconoclast party was already in
existence within the Orthodox Church itself.　Its central figure

[1] It was not until the fourth century that Christmas day displaced the
feast of the Baptism, celebrated on January 4th, as the foremost festival of
the Church.　The survivals of this phase in Christianity are summarised in
F. C. Conybeare: *The Key of Truth,* Oxford, 1898.　It has been traced in
Spain, Burgundy, Bavaria and the Balkans, to which latter it was translated
by the forcible colonisation of the Danube frontier, in the eighth and tenth
centuries, with Armenian and Paulician captives.　It became there known as
Bogomilism, and was observed by Lady Mary Wortley-Montagu at Philippo-
polis in 1717.　Bede hints that it was once prevalent in England and Wales.
Preserved by the Cathars of Lyons and Languedoc, it doubtless contributed
to the hysterical sects of the early Reformation.　In England it is now represented by the Anabaptists.

was bishop Constantius of Nacolia in Phrygia; and though the metropolitans of his diocese and the archbishop John of Synnada provided opposition to his measures, the Syrian renegade Beser, bishop Thomas of Claudiopolis, and archbishop Theodosius of Ephesus, are named among his sympathisers.   It is not unreasonable to suppose that Leo, before his accession to the throne, was in communication with these prelates.

Attempts have been made by writers on the subject to derive the opinions of the iconoclast emperors directly from either the Jews or the Paulicians.   This can scarcely have been the case. Both Jews and Paulicians abhorred the cross.   The iconoclasts, on the other hand, made a cult of it.   They falsified the letter of St. Nilus quoted on pages 47-48 to advocate its monopoly of ecclesiastical decoration.   Michael III. the Drunkard complained in 824 that the iconodules, during their interval of power, had removed the cross from the churches.   And inscriptions exist in Cappadocia still further proving the devotion to this symbol —a devotion which was also prominent in the Armenian national Church.   A certain affinity between the iconoclasts and the Jews and Paulicians there undoubtedly was, which was emphasised, in the popular mind, by the extremes of Constantine V. Copronymus, who denied the divinity of Christ, the cult of the Virgin, the efficacy of relics, and the title of "saint" to martyrs and their churches; while his views on infant baptism, the pet aversion of adoptionist theology, are illustrated by a surname derived from the popular belief that, with prophetic significance, he had dirtied his own font in a manner not uncommon to babies.   He however far surpassed his party in unorthodoxy.   Similarly Michael II. the Amorian observed the Jewish Sabbath and was not prepared to deny the contingency of Judas' redemption.   Leo III., on the other hand, proscribed the Jews.   And Leo V. persecuted the Paulicians. It seemed certain that the iconoclast enterprise owed its immediate origins not to outside influences, but to a definite party within the Greek Church, which caught the ear of a future Emperor; and which was the outcome of a very widespread movement.   To identify that enterprise, as has been attempted, with a policy of depressing the Church for secular purposes, is ridiculous.   This would have necessitated no attack on pictures, and none of the disastrous popular discontent that ensued.   Such a policy was afterwards pursued only by the very pillars of Orthodoxy, Nicephorus II. Phocas and Isaac I. Comnenus.

The history of the controversy in the Eastern Empire may be shortly summarised.   Following the first edict of Leo III. in 726, there were riots in Constantinople, a rebellion in Greece, the assertion of administrative independence on the part of Venice and Ravenna, the despatch of a formidable expedition against the Pope, which was wrecked in the Adriatic, and the forfeiture by the latter of his ecclesiastical jurisdiction in southern Italy and Illyria.   Leo was succeeded in 740 by his son Constantine V., whose council of 754 passed the following decree: "We declare unanimously . . . that there shall be rejected and removed and cursed out of the Christian Church every likeness which is made out of any material whatever by the *evil art of painters*.   Whoever in future dares to make such a thing or to venerate it, or to set it up in a church or in a private house, or possesses it in secret, shall, if bishop, priest, or deacon, be deposed, if monk or layman, anathematised and become liable to be tried by the secular laws as an adversary of God."   Constantine's persecution of the monks led to an enormous influx of Greek refugees into southern Italy. But his son Leo IV. the Chazar was more tolerant.   And eventually, in 787, the latter's widow Irene had the sacred pictures restored at the seventh Œcumenical Council of Nicæa.   This was attended by 350 bishops, after a previous council, convoked in Constantinople, had been forcibly dispelled by the iconoclast soldiery.

The council of Nicæa was a council of reform.   It was realised that the iconoclasts had a measure of right on their side; and that if they were to be successfully opposed, many abuses of the Church and of monastic life must be eliminated.   Concerning the pictures, however, its victory was only temporary.   A military rebellion in 813 brought to the throne another iconoclast Emperor, Leo V., who immediately convoked a committee, which "he lodged and fed like pigs," in order to prepare a work against the icons.   The monks were again dispersed; works of art destroyed.   On Christmas day, 820, the assassination of Leo led to the accession of Michael II. the Amorian, who was succeeded in 826 by his son Theophilus.   The latter was given to dispensing justice in person; monks, whose subordination had become intolerable, were occasionally punished; and two of their number were branded on the forehead with satirical verses composed by the Emperor himself.   Theophilus' encouragement of the secular arts made his court, modelled on that of the Caliphs of Bagdad, renowned for its magnificence. On his death in 842, Theodora, his widow, again restored the icons, this time in perpetuity.   Such was the chagrin of the learned Patriarch, John the Grammarian, that, rather than participate in a public discussion on the subject, he pretended to cut open his stomach.

VI. The Eventual Reformation of Art

The details of the dispute in Constantinople reveal both the length to which the cult of icons had been carried by the Greeks, and the mystic justification of symbolism which was provoked in their defence.

It was not until the fourth and fifth centuries that the miraculous attributes of pagan statues and fetishes were transferred to pictures. St. Basil then admitted his veneration; and there came into existence a class of pictures known as the ἀχειροποίητοι, "non-handmade." Of these, the most famous was the Virgin of Edessa, which not only averted the Persian invaders, but actually led Heraclius to Ctesiphon in search of the true Cross.[1] Numerous others of the same subject, and also one from the hand of St. Luke, were revered in Constantinople, and were accorded a place in every important public function. Prostration to them became the universal habit; kisses were showered upon them; incense was burned before them; monks donated them the hairs from their tonsures; their colours were scraped from off them and mixed with the sacraments; till at last they were even made to stand godparents to the children of the devout. The abuses were manifold and patent; the arguments of attack obvious, and theologically sustained by passages from the Old and New Testaments of which some have already been quoted. The ordinary iconoclast disputed neither God's incarnation in Christ, nor the cult of Virgin and saints. But he did maintain that to re-embody those beings, now celestial,

[1] A more recent example, painted by the angels in 1860, is preserved in the Rumanian skiti of the Prodrome on Mount Athos.

in material elements, constituted an unwarrantable interpolation of earthly symbols between God and man.   Those symbols might, and did, survive.   But it was inevitable that the fierce contention of 150 years, intimately connected with the fundamental spiritual axioms of the Christian, the Jewish and the Mahomedan religions, should leave its impress on their character.   The chief outcome of the controversy was the formulation of a rigid iconography, which sufficed to prevent, once and for all, any backsliding towards meaningless naturalism.   The picture, the human representation, was designed henceforth as an illustration of Reality and as a vehicle of the deepest human emotions.   The puerile concept of reproduction had finally disappeared.   In this elevation of art to its highest function, though at the price of the artist's freedom, the iconodule defence, raised by the controversy to a high philosophic level, also played a part.

The iconodule argument was based on the threefold assumption of the pictures' miraculous properties, of their instructive value to the illiterate, and of their symbolic value.   It is the emphasis on the latter which concerns the subsequent development of art.   In the romance of Barlaam and Joseph, that extraordinary Christian transposition of the life of Buddha dating from the seventh century, it had already been maintained that the veneration accorded an icon attained, in fact, to the icon's original. This was the chief iconodule contention: that pictures, like statues to Plotinus, were an effective means of communication with the extra-terrestrial universe. Theodore of Studium (A.D. 759-826), in applauding the action of the Spatharius John in making an icon of St. Demetrius godfather to his child, was applauding the invocation of the saint himself to this function, and regarded the picture, since the saint was not at hand, as a legitimate substitute. This view was adopted henceforth as the basis of the Orthodox attitude towards representational art. In the *Guide to Painting,* compiled by Denys, monk of Fourna of Agrapha, from a sixteenth-century source, it is again set forth, and so explicitly as to show how deeply engrained in the Greek Church was the fear of an always potential iconoclast conscience. "We have learnt, not only from the holy fathers, but even from the apostles, and, I dare say it, from Christ himself . . . how the sacred pictures must be done. We depict Christ in human form by means of painting, because he appeared on earth holding converse with men and because he was made mortal man, like us, save for sin. In the same way we depict the eternal Father as an old man, because thus was he seen by Daniel (ch. vii.). (This is a development; Theodore of Studium expressly stated that it would be impious to portray God himself.) We depict the Holy Ghost as a dove, because thus was it seen in Jordan. We depict also the features of the holy Virgin and of all the saints, and we reverence them with respect, but we do not adore them. Thus we do not say that such and such a painted portrait is Christ or the holy Virgin, or an actual saint; but, when we make homage of veneration to the picture, we refer that homage to the prototype which the picture represents for us. When, for example, the picture that we salute and kiss represents Christ, the respect in which we hold the image we refer to Christ himself, son of God, made man for us. We adore neither the colours nor the art; but the type of Christ, the actual person of Christ, who is in heaven; for, says St. Basil, the honour accorded a picture attains to the model.   Similarly, when we look with respect upon a picture of the holy Virgin, or of some other saint, it is the prototype that we honour.   If we depict them, it is that we may recall their virtues and their works and may exalt our souls towards them.   We act, then, wisely in painting the holy pictures.   Anathema to the libellers and blasphemers!''

Art, following the iconoclast controversy, was recognised as a power.   "Who," asks Theodore of Studium, "having seen an image, a picture, or a statue, and regarded it attentively and in detail, does not preserve in his heart an idea of it . . . whose obsession pursues him even to his home?"   The idea might be good or bad, according to the image; the power was the point. St. John Damascene (A.D. 676-*c.* 760), crying from afar in the monastery of St. Sabbas in Jerusalem, echoed this sentiment: the Church, in representing the works of saints and the life of Christ, was seeking to instil a courage similar to theirs into men.   "When I lack books," he wrote, "or my thoughts are a torture to me like thorns, forbidding the indulgence of reading, then I betake myself to the church, the open refuge of all the soul's ills.   The sweetness of the paintings attracts my attention, holds fast my gaze, like a smiling meadow, and unconsciously bears my soul to God."   "Pictures," he said elsewhere, "are a script[1], concise and easy of interpretation: they speak and are not dumb like the idols of the gentiles; for all writing, read in church, informs

---

[1] According to the Patriarch Nicephorus (ninth century), there had used to exist gospels in which every incident was pictured side by side with the words for the benefit of the illiterate.   This system, as an adjunct to the liturgy instead of the text, was now to be applied to the walls of churches.

us of the sacred incidents." Here, then, was art invested with an emotional authority such as no man had ever before dreamed of; and, at the same time, reduced to a cipher, a mere script in scenes, like a film. The danger of freedom in that anthropomorphic South had been realised. But the South could never dispense with art. Hence arose a compromise, of austere and unearthly magnificence, whereby the artist, in place of reproducing a subject in the exact likeness of his world, was now to reproduce his own emotional reaction to the central and One Factor in his and everyone else's lives.

This was the outcome of the long iconoclast tradition and of the fight in which it was ultimately vanquished. In support of art: the spasmodic reversion of even the Jews to representational devices for the purpose of localising their God; the universal practice of anthropomorphic representation by Antiquity, and its reasoned defence by the later philosophers; culminating in the absorbtion of this practice by Christianity and in its extenuation by Christian apology; In opposition to art: the Old Testament polemic against the devices of representation and localisation, echoed in the New; the iconoclast tradition of numerous early Greek thinkers, inherited and expanded by a growing body of philosophers and satirists under the Roman Empire; and, at length, the first troubling of the Christian conscience; Finally: the spread of Judaism and the rise of Islam; the simultaneous reinforcement of the anti-representational instinct in Judaism, in Islam, and in Christianity, by the wave of religious purism that overtook the Near East in the seventh and eighth centuries; together with the last train of events that led to the identification of the supreme power in the Byzantine state with the resulting party in the Orthodox Church; These are the historical phenomena to which posterity owes the first European discovery of the spiritual responsibility of æsthetics and the elevation of art, both by those concerned to defend it and by those at length obliged to acquiesce in it, to the position of a spiritual intermediary.   Thus was born, among the mediæval Greeks, that mode of artistic interpretation which culminated in El Greco, which was again revived in the nineteenth century, and which now constitutes the first hope of the early industrial era.

CHAPTER 3

THE DEVELOPMENT OF INTERPRETATION

DESPITE the exhaustive literature evoked by them, two problems, still unsolved, continue to obscure the general history of European painting. The first is to discover the exact cultural and intellectual impulse which produced the early Sienese and Florentine artists, as exemplified in Duccio and Giotto. The second, which has already been mentioned, is the origin of El Greco, and, through him, of the whole Spanish school. It has hitherto been customary to link both with the Renascence; to call the first the parent of it, and the second a legacy, shaped by the counter-reformation. In reality, both were the outcome of a single mode of religious thought, and one which, moreover, was actively opposed to the scientific and rational heroics of revived Antiquity. This mode originated in the Greek lands, and there kept Latin materialism at bay, till its last and greatest exponent was gone to Spain, and its culture was extinguished. The circumstances by which the Hellenistic artifice of reproduction was originally displaced, in the eighth and ninth centuries, by the art of interpretation, have been examined in the last chapter. It now remains to observe, first the form in which that art was moulded within the sphere of Constantinople, and secondly the course of its translation to the West. To the process of this occidentation the monuments of Athos and Mistra alone provide the historical clue.

72

I. THE BORROWING OF ISLAMIC SPLENDOUR AND THE DEVELOPMENT OF COLOUR

Before proceeding to the philosophy of the new art, it is essential to imagine the medium in which it was working.

As the iconoclast controversy drew to its close, a new tide of political and intellectual activity was flowing from the East; it was the spring of Islam; the whole world seemed destined to crumple before the armies of the Caliph and to yield him up its secrets—save only the impregnable walls on the Bosporus. The struggle between Greek and Arab, intermittent in its violence, and never again to provide such a menace as called Leo III. the Isaurian to the East Roman throne in 717, had bred mutual respect and intercourse. With the reign of Harun al Raschid in Bagdad (786-809), the Abbassid Caliphate developed an intellectual and material splendour which the tales of the Arabian Nights have rendered familiar all the world over. And the ninth century witnessed the growth of a cultural rivalry between the cities of the Tigris and the Golden Horn. The Empress Theodora, who restored the icons, her brother the Cæsar Bardas, and the able Patriarchs John the Grammarian and Photius, were all of partially Armenian descent; and the honour in which such blood was held is illustrated by Basil the Macedonian's advertising his possession of it for the purpose of reinforcing his claim to the throne. In the West there was only darkness; the light of Charlemagne's court had gone out; and the eyes of the Byzantines were turned to the effulgent East. The East returned the compliment. So absorbed was the Caliph Mamun in geometry—the savants of his court having attained the knowledge of Euclid, but not the theory—that he offered the Emperor Theophilus a sum of gold equivalent in modern purchasing value to £86,000 in return for a visit of Leo the Mathematician. John the Grammarian had already visited Bagdad at the head of an embassy of legendary magnificence; and an Arab plan with which he returned was used as the basis of Theophilus' palace of Bryas in Asia Minor. Photius, also, had been employed as ambassador in the East during his secular career, an experience which contributed to the intellectual liberalism which stamped the circle of which he was the leader, and the Cæsar Bardas the patron; "despite religious barriers," wrote his pupil the Patriarch Nicolas Mysticus, to a Moslem Emir of Crete, "yet wisdom, kindness and the other qualities which adorn human nature attract the affection of those who love fair things;" the Emir's lately deceased father having been so endowed, Photius had therefore loved him.

The most permanent testimony to this invigorating intercourse was to be found in the additions made by Theophilus to the Great Palace of Constantinople. Beside the throne-room of the birds that sang, the lions that roared, and the throne that levitated into the ceiling, all by mechanical devices,[1] we read of a triconch building of two floors, each with three apses, those of the lower being placed between, not beneath, those of the higher, and the whole being roofed with gilded lead or copper. The upper story connected with the hall of the Sigma, which was shaped like half a moon; the lower with the Mysticon, so called from its acoustic transmission of whispers. The whole group was panelled and pillared in variegated marbles. More expert knowledge might

[1] See *The Byzantine Achievement*, by Robert Byron, pp. 224-225.

connect this plan with Armenian buildings such as the churches of Artik or Vagharshapat; but whatever the province of its origin, there is little doubt that this oriental fashion of profuse apse-construction was responsible for the final version of the Greek cross type of church. This, perfected by the Armenian architect of Basil I. the Macedonian in the next era, and never substantially modified, was destined, henceforth, to provide the complicated setting of panels, vaults, and friezes, to which the now equally fixed iconography of the Greek painters and mosaicists was adapted.

Theophilus, whose iconoclastic tenets would seem to have been dictated more by the increasing rationalism of his age than the religious purism of his predecessors in the eighth century, also fostered a form of Eastern secular decoration, and impressed ecclesiastical artists to that end. The hall of the Pearl, supported on eight columns of rose-coloured marble, was adorned with pictures of animals; and the walls of the Kamilas, a palatial summer-house roofed in gold and sustained by six green pillars, exhibited mosaics of fruit-pickers against a gold ground, above a dado of marble panelling. Another house nearby contained similar mosaics of green trees rising into a golden sky; while below it stood an open loggia, called, from its harmonies of porphyry, verde antique, and Carian white, together with a floor like " a flowering meadow," the Musikos : a name which particularly illustrates the Byzantine sensitiveness to the relation of colours.

The incomparable splendour of the Byzantine interior derived originally from the amalgamation of Roman feeling for size and solidity with the Persian conception of absolute and dazzling sovereignty; this amalgamation, refined by Greek sanity of form,

Justinian perfected and enshrined for all time in his church of St. Sophia. Yet, "where sixth-century mosaic is gorgeous in a worldly way with its purples and jewels, the splendour of that of the eleventh and twelfth is unearthly; on a gold background (at Daphni) peppered with cubes of black, sealing-wax red, and other dark shades, stand figures clothed in tones that avoid the primary colours and tend towards the crystalline and amethystine to be expected in Heaven"[1]—tones, as even the architecturally-minded Strzygowski has written, "which seem to clothe a dogma itself in all the hues of a peacock's plumage." This was the corollary of the artistic revolution wrought by the iconoclast controversy. Simultaneously with a now inflexible austerity of form and iconography, in itself an ally of emotional grandeur, there arrived from the East a taste for sheer richness, brilliance of colour, and depth of textural effect (black and red cubes among the gold), which must have transformed any art but one wholly consecrated to the affirmation of religious truth into a mere system of oriental vulgarity, such as the Russian later became. The contrary happened. And Byzantine art attained that one superlative quality which not even its most convinced detractors have ventured to dispute. But mosaic, it may be argued, is not painting; and these remarks may therefore seem inapplicable to the general train of the argument. If the reader, however, will turn to the frontispiece[2] of *Our Lady of Vladimir,* published in Prague by the Seminarium Kondakovianum in 1928 and to be found in the library of the Victoria and Albert Museum, he will find a painting of two heads, which, if not

[1] *Byzantine Art,* by H. Pierce and R. Tyler, London, 1926, p. 47.
[2] A very fine example of colour reproduction.

earlier, was certainly in existence by the first half of the twelfth century, and was originally sent to Russia from Constantinople; and he will then realise how the splendour of the glass cube could be communicated to the brush. This icon, preserving, on the faces, its original paint, stands as a landmark in the cultural history of Europe. "Primitive" in form, it appears, when compared with an Italian work of the fourteenth or fifteenth centuries, as the work of a master beside that of an uncertain copyist. Forming a modelling of such delicacy and meaning as to recall the Mona Lisa, the colours of the Virgin's face range from a brilliant rich vermilion on the lips and at the corners of the eyes, through red on apple-green and then green alone, to eyes and eyebrows of unfathomable, gold purple. Only the nose, and then to its advantage, betrays the touch of the mosaicist, with its single gleaming line of white running from below the bridge to an outward curve at the bottom. The countenance of the child is lighter, pink and green, with touches of primrose yellow between them, and brown shadows. Even to those already versed in the subtleties of technique and colour displayed by Byzantine art in the middle period, the palette of this picture and the artist's mastery of it reveal a completely unexpected genius, ranking with, and above, the already familiar mosaics, ivories, and buildings.

II. THE RISE OF LITURGICAL SYMBOLISM AND OFFICIAL ICONOGRAPHY

The character and purpose of Byzantine art in its post-iconoclastic phases are best understood by comparison with the Gothic cathedrals, those "encyclopædias in stone," of the West. In the latter sphere, the principle of Aristotelian scholastics, that religion must investigate the whole earth, must annex to itself and mould the whole range of human learning, was predominant; and the religious artist was called upon to express every fact, natural, ethical, philosophical, and celestial, of which the limited but slowly broadening ecclesiastical outlook was able to take cognisance. The original didactic impulse behind Christian art was now expanded to regulate the very limits of the human brain and perception. Christ might guard the door; his mother receive the entrant. But it was this world, not theirs, with which the artist was primarily concerned, and which he was obliged to reduce to terms that the Roman Church, with its nose trained to a fundamentally non-religious tradition of Greek thought, considered that Christ and his mother might approve.

In the sphere of Constantinople, following the iconoclast era, precisely the opposite ideal was at work. The iconodule defence had survived; and the concern of the artist was to evoke, through his pictures, not this world, but the other. Both the didactic purpose of relaying the gospel story to the illiterate, and the conception of the effigy as an earthly form inhabited by, or connected with, the celestial reality, were now overshadowed by a greater, sacramental significance: the pictures, like the liturgy, came to present the small history in which the Christian mystery was contained, not simply that the beholder might learn its events as the modern schoolboy draws maps of St. Paul's journeys; but that he might attain, through the reminder of those events, actual communion during life on earth with that firmament of divine arbitration of which the Latin Church taught only the post-human expectation. The spiritual function of art, as forming an integral part of church and service, was only less than that of the consecrated bread and wine. That this elevated purpose should have produced results which have defied the understanding of a rationally-minded posterity is not surprising.

To comprehend this investiture of the whole complex of ecclesiastical ceremony and ornament with symbolic significance, it is essential to recall the elaborate symmetry of Greek church architecture (see Plate 6): the inner and outer nartheces; the nave and the central dome above it; the apse-ended transepts; the impenetrable iconostasis with its single entrance curtained above a pair of low folding doors; the main apse of the chancel flanked by lesser apses, each supporting a tall tubular cupola; and one and all decorated, save where the surrounding wooden stalls prevent, with the prescribed scenes and figures. "The church," said the Patriarch Germanos in the eighth century, "is the sky of earth where resides . . . the celestial God." To St. Symeon of Salonica (c. 1420), the lower portion of the building represented this world; the upper, the other. The altar was simultaneously Christ's tomb and the throne of God. In the opinion of Gregory Palamas (fourteenth century), the church was the burial-place where lay the body of the Lord. "He who hastens to this holy sepulchre . . . shall see the Lord himself with the eyes of his body; for he who looks with faith upon the mystic table and the bread of life set thereon sees the word of God in person become flesh for us and dwelling in us." Similarly the ciborium was placed in conjunction with the altar, in order to epitomise the crucifixion, the burial, and the resurrection of Christ.

No less symbolic was the growing conception of the Liturgy. In the eleventh century Theodore of Andida is found reproaching his congregations for forgetting that the divisions of the service were calculated to recall, not only the crucifixion and resurrection, but the conception, birth, baptism, election of apostles, and miracles in addition; how, he argues, should an historian portray the life of an individual without tracing it from the earliest, without beginning, fullness and end? and the evangelists have provided the necessary facts. Nicolas Cabasilas (fourteenth century) maintained the same view: that which precedes the consecration represented that which preceded Christ's death; that which follows, the descent of the Holy Ghost and the conversion of the peoples. The Liturgy was a guide, not simply of words, but of facts, and even more than facts. "It provides us not only with a spectacle, but with an emotion, our imagination receiving an impression clearer than our eyes." At the moment of the consecration, the divine body was actually perceptible; the procession of the elements to the altar was at once the funeral and triumph of the Deity. An inscription formerly above the altar of the church of the Lavra on Mount Athos carries these ideas to a climax: "Seeing the tribune of the altar of the Lord, stand trembling, O man, and cast down thine eyes, for within is the Christ daily sacrificed, and all the ranks of the holy angels prostrate themselves before him in fear and ritual." The famous painting of the Divine Liturgy from the Peribleptos at Mistra (see Plate 77. i) illustrates the feeling evoked by the ceremony of the consecration among the later Byzantine artists.[1]

---

[1] A conception of symbolism attaching to every province of ecclesiastical art, music, painting, vestments, sculpture and architecture, down to the sand, chalk, and water of the mortar, was elaborated by Durandus (1230-1296) in the true encyclopædic manner of the West. The Crusades had resulted in a great influx of Byzantine literature and ideas. But such a theory as the

Such had become the meaning of outward religious observance for the Greeks.   This tendency to symbolism was apparent not only in the manner and technique of artistic representation, but also in the ordinance of the actual subjects.

Following the iconoclast controversy, a new iconography developed.   Its novelty lay not in the invention of fresh themes, but in the elimination of a number of the older and the systematisation of those that remained.   The Good Shepherd and the vegetable and beastly allegories disappeared.   The pastoral motive was displaced by that of royalty; henceforth, as in a court, each unit in the scheme of decoration played its appointed part and occupied its appointed place.   The central dome was reft by the stupendous frown of the Christ Pantocrator, the sovereign judge (see Plate 12. i, ii), depicted in bust; in the apse sat or stood the queen, his mother (see Plate 13).   Surrounding, the angels assumed the stiff uniforms of ushers to the imperial court;[1] prophets and apostles preserving more traditional draperies, continued the royal entourage.   Beneath all, stood the saints in rank, the ascetics in skins, the military in the Roman kilts and chased breastplates of the Byzantine forces (see Plate 82. i), the great bishops of the early Church in appropriate vestments (see Plate 79), and the hermits or monks in the black habit of their order.   Elsewhere, the life of Christ was divided into twelve great feasts, emphasising chiefly his birth and his death; the miracles, it was plainly stated by Nicolas Cabasilas, had become of secondary importance to

present, expanded to the limits of logical absurdity in eight books, had little effect on the practice of Western artists.

[1] It is curious to observe the incongruous survival of this habit in Giotto's decoration of the upper church at Assisi, the scene being that in which St. Jerome of Assisi examines St. Francis' dead body.

man's spiritual health, when compared with such events as those of the Passion. Annunciation, Nativity, Epiphany, Presentation, Baptism, Transfiguration, Resurrection of Lazarus, Ascension and Pentecost; these were the incidents best calculated to entrain the beholder to intercourse with their hero. In addition, the Last Supper was now and then depicted, and the Communion of the Apostles, with two Christs dispensing it in two kinds from either side of a pillared tabernacle. Intermittent scenes of the Washing of Feet, the Betrayal in the Garden, the Deposition from the Cross, the Descent into Hell, and the Incredulity of Thomas, were also introduced into the regular cycles. A similar series arose to portray the life of the Virgin, culminating, usually over the west door, in her dormition. Finally there appeared the Last Judgement, a confused and ingenuous panorama of punishment and reward, which in the East was quickly banished to narthex or refectory, and in the West awaited the brush of Michael Angelo to reduce it to an ordered composition.

Splendid and luminous mosaics; evocation of the Christian mystery rather than the Christian story; and a royal iconography, laying chief stress on the beginning and end of the Saviour's earthly life; these, the distinctive features of Byzantine art after the iconoclast controversy, have been shortly summarised. But this art of the middle period was an official art, flourishing within the walls or the cultural sphere of Constantinople; and its effect was designed primarily to influence the educated and sophisticated intellects of a capital. For the mass of the population, particularly in Asia, it may well be imagined that religious observance and decoration had assumed a complexion too remote, philosophic, and grandiose, to attract those whose chief demand was for comfort, both in this world and with regard to the next.   And it is certain that, in Asia Minor and Syria, popular modes of celebrating the liturgy, and a popular art, were flourishing simultaneously with the dazzling and inhuman products of Constantinople.   In the eleventh century, upon the revival of Plato and consequent humanisation of thought at the centre (see below), this art moved to Europe; the crudity and ineptitude of its form were revised in the process; but its spirit gave rise to a homogeneous movement, which pervaded the awakening genius of the Italians, and at the same time brought a novel sympathy to painting and mosaic at the centres of Byzantine life.   The interpretational method discovered by iconoclasm was not displaced; but it was to be employed, under the new influence, to evoke the tears or affection of the beholder, rather than his awe and admiration.

III. The Popular Demand for "Human Interest" in Ceremony and in Art

The conception of the liturgy as a symbolic illustration of the cardinal events in Christ's life was one which the ordinary man, literate or not, must have found difficult to grasp; and the habit had arisen, owing to the demand for optical reminder of those events, of introducing actually dramatic interludes into the church services.   At Jerusalem, in the days when the city was still within the Byzantine frontiers, the Patriarch had become the chief actor in the scenes of the Passion: on Holy Thursday he washed the feet of the apostles; on Good Friday, bearing a cross, he was led by a rope attached to his neck to the prison; on Easter day he emerged from the sepulchre with the words, "Hail! Christ is risen." These *rites plastiques,* as Professor Millet calls them, exercised a peculiar effect on early iconography : the Marys appear dressed as deaconesses and holding censers; the Washing of Feet is lit by an Orthodox candelabra. Most particularly, the spectacle of the Patriarch-Christ led by the rope held the imagination of the watching artist, as a vivid illustration of the indignity of the Passion.

At length these tendencies spread to Constantinople. The Patriarch Theophylact, in the tenth century, introduced symbolic dances into the services of St. Sophia; apposite recitations from the apocryphal gospels, more realistic and detailed than the versions of the evangelists, became habitual; set passages of oratory, such as the sermon of George of Nicomedia on the Lament of the Virgin, were declaimed on suitable days. In addition to these unofficial readings, numerous homilies were delivered; many of them, particularly those of the monk James of Kokkinobaphos, of which manuscripts are preserved in the Bibliothèque Nationale and the Vatican, exhibit, both in text and miniature, details which derive neither from the gospels nor the apocryphal gospels, and which can only have drawn their inspiration from the religious drama. At the Annunciation, a regular argument takes place between God and the angel; upon the Visitation of Mary to Elisabeth, St. John delivers a long speech from his mother's womb. There is apparent, moreover, both in conversation and picture, an element of the comic : in one case, Mary is frankly appalled at the probable consequences of the angel Gabriel's appearance; Joseph, she says, will cut off her head if he finds him there, "because the old fellow is jealous." Joseph, on his return, cries that he will kill the rival who has brought dishonour on his venerable head. "Depart," he exhorts the Virgin, "and go find your lover. No longer shall you eat the bread of my table."[1] The backgrounds of the illustrations attaching to these incidents seem to represent a kind of stage scenery, an impression which is corroborated by Luitprand's reference (tenth century) to the *ludi scenici* celebrated by the Greeks. The figures themselves run; the angels fly; there is nothing hieratic. In the twelfth century, the preacher Theophanes Kerameos, speaking of Christ's degradation at the hands of the soldiers, stated in plain terms that the reality of the scene must have far surpassed the official account. "On that day," says Professor Millet, "a new thought came to break the barriers of dogma and liberate the imagination of the artist."

It is easy to see that this tendency to the dramatisation of religious observance was alien to the static and gorgeous official art of the Byzantine capital; and to imagine, therefore, the part that it must have played in the later development and humanisation of Byzantine iconography. Its arrival from the provinces dated from the tenth to the twelfth centuries. Simultaneously came the crusaders, and the same apocryphal gospels and dramatic homilies were translated into Latin and spread over western Europe. Hence originated the Western mystery plays, infinitely bolder in their expansion of authenticated detail, but deriving, without doubt, from Eastern habit and Eastern texts. Particu-

---

[1] Before lamenting the disappearance of such robust humour, the reader should at least be aware of the St. Joseph's orphanage for illegitimate children in outer London.

larly the Passion caught the western eye, and all its incidents were elaborated, thus preparing the ground for that pronounced exaltation of the divinity of suffering, which was to become the outstanding religious motive of the thirteenth and fourteenth centuries.

In 1204 Constantinople fell to the armies of the fourth crusade; and for fifty-seven years the seat of Greek sovereignty was transferred to Nicæa. Under the dynasties of Comnenus and Angelus in the twelfth century the theocratic complexion of the Byzantine state had become increasingly marked; following the restoration of the capital in 1261, it was intensified by the universal detestation of the Latins and their Church, and by the popular opposition to the oft-proposed healing of the schism—a measure which alone could obtain help for the Empire against the advancing Turks. Patriotism took the form of a defence of creed; the monastic influence was all-powerful. The revival of Reason and Science, heralded by Psellos in the eleventh century (see below), was obscured. A wave of mysticism, of which the Hesychasts of Mount Athos, who observed the light of the Transfiguration emerge from their navels, have remained the most famous exponents, overspread the Greek lands. The air was thick with contemplation. The victories of the Turks, the diminution of the Empire till only the capital and the Peloponnese remained, were received with a kind of averted fatalism. Christ and the Virgin endured.

Into such an atmosphere, the popular art of Cappadocia, so-called because its chief monuments survive in that furthest province of Asia Minor, was transported by monks and miniaturists; and was received by the growing demand for the humanisation and expansion of the official iconography. Certain scenes from the Christian story, which had been discarded in the sphere of Constantinople after the iconoclast controversy, still survived in the rock churches of Asia, and may be seen to this day; their date is fixed in or about the reign of Nicephorus Phocas (963-969). Here, at Toqale Kilisseh, Qaranleq Kilisseh, Tchareqle Kilisseh, and Qeledjar, the Passion had already been elaborated into numerous scenes such as the Betrayal in the Garden, the Road to Calvary, the Putting Up to the Cross and the Taking Down, and the Lament of the Virgin over her son's body. From photographs, these frescoes appear but a debased survival of the crude Hellenistic art of the East, with huge staring heads dwarfing small though active bodies; of their colours, save from personal observation, it is useless to speak; though the artists would seem, if judged by the coloured plates in M. de Jerphanion's albums, to have been wholly ignorant of that principle of colour reaction which was the outstanding feature of the official art. In technique, therefore, the infusion of monastic art had no influence; it was absorbed in a better. But its part in the introduction of new themes, and in the elaboration of the Passion and of the suffering of the Virgin, is proved by the sudden revival of these motives, and of many others, which, in the sphere of Constantinople, had fallen into desuetude since the ninth century. Simultaneously with their arrival at the centres of Greek culture in the thirteenth century, the same iconographic features reappeared in Italy, where they also had existed in many Roman churches dating from the eighth and ninth centuries, presumably painted by members of the numerous Greek and Syrian colonies which flourished in the country at that time. And they reappeared, in the West, nowhere but in Italy. Here again is concrete evidence of the homogeneous flow of a popular humanising influence from the East, and of its simultaneous effect on both Greece and Italy. In Sicily and Calabria the Greek monastic influence was still strong; and it was doubtless by that agency that the new ideas and artistic motives were translated.

In Italy, where a native art was as yet unknown, the phenomenon is explicable enough. But that the art of Constantinople, a sophisticated, self-contained entity, supported by the Church, working on a principle of interpretational vision, and possessing a magnificence of colour and material which must have imbued its artists with a full measure of self-sufficiency; that this art should suddenly have admitted, or in some cases revived, a number of extraneous themes with which to complicate and derange its schematic evocation of the Christian mystery; is a fact which must cause surprise. The tendency to the dramatisation of religious observance, also arising from the East, has been described. But the capital itself was the seat of a native movement towards humanisation, whose effect was visible not only in the acceptance of the new themes, but in an alteration of the actual character of representation, in an added gentleness and sympathy, and in a new appreciation of earthly beauty. This development was in no sense the product of Cappadocia and the monastic tradition; the popular art was crude, almost savage, in its disregard of such ideals. The movement in question derived from the revival of Platonic and classical learning, which began as a reaction against the iconoclast atmosphere of theological controversy in the ninth century, and attained its particular efflorescence with Psellos in the eleventh.

IV. The Humanist Renascence in the Capital: Platonic Fashions

The movement against ecclesiasticism began at the court. The Cæsar Bardas, regent and uncle of Michael III. the Drunkard (842-867), was a man of singular morals, whose daughter-in-law was also his mistress. His attitude towards the Church is illustrated by his choice of Photius to be its head; for the most eminent Patriarch that Constantinople ever produced was a layman till within five days of his enthronement. It was the policy of the time to impress the best brains of the Empire into ecclesiastical service, and to reward them with its emoluments; in the previous reign of Theophilus, Leo the Mathematician had been appointed to the see of Salonica (840), despite a similar absence of qualifications. A temporary wave of scepticism, perhaps unique in Byzantine history, overtook the higher ranks of society. Michael III. and his companions made a practice of arraying themselves as prelates and aping the liturgy, the Emperor on one occasion satirising the prevailing dissensions in the Church by crying, "Theophilus (a courtier known to his intimates as 'the pig') is my Patriarch, Photius is the Patriarch of the Cæsar, and Ignatius is the Patriarch of the Christians." Such antics foreshadow the wholesale paganism of Renascence Italy six centuries later.

The character of the Cæsar Bardas evoked the admiration and curiosity of his friends; his efficiency as a ruler the tribute of his enemies. Like his brother-in-law Theophilus before him, he was the centre of a clique of remarkable and learned men, which included Photius, Leo of Salonica, and Constantine and

Methodius, apostles to the Slavs; and to his initiative was due the refoundation of a university in Constantinople, to replace that which Leo III. the Isaurian had closed. Rooms in the Palace of the Magnavra were assigned to teachers of geometry, astrology and philosophy; and though this revival of profane studies provoked the usual mediæval lampoons, thenceforth the classics remained a continual source of inspiration to Byzantine culture. Photius himself was accused of having denied Christ to a Jew for the sake of that same Greek wisdom which cost Faust so dear. Wisdom he certainly had; the collection of a library on every conceivable subject was his main interest; and he possessed several classics which have since perished. His house became the seat of a reading-club, one of whose members, having been called from Constantinople on a journey, requested, on his return, that he might be informed as to the works studied during his absence. To this circumstance posterity owes the Patriarch's analysis of 279 of his own books: " History was represented by authors from the earliest to the latest period. . . . Geographers, physiologists, writers on medicine and agriculture, grammarians, as well as orators and rhetoricians, furnished entertainment to this omnivorous society."[1] This bibliophil tradition was continued by Arethas, Archbishop of Cæsarea, for whom, in 895, the famous manuscript of Plato, now in the Bodleian, was copied.

The rediscovery of Plato marked the wane of the encyclopædic phase in Byzantine culture. That such a phase existed in the East, prior to the advent of the schoolmen in the West, is often forgotten. Its chief exponent was the Aristotelian defender of pictures, St. John Damascene, whose enormous compendiary of

[1] Bury's *History of the Eastern Roman Empire,* p. 447.

human knowledge, the Ἔκδοσις ἀκριβὴς τῆς ὀρθοδόξου πίστεως, was translated into Latin about 1150 under the title of *De fide orthodoxa.* On this work was based Peter Lombard's *Quattuor libri sententiarum,* a book whose importance was considered by Roger Bacon to surpass even that of the Bible. Both St. Thomas Aquinas and St. Bonaventure borrowed many of their opinions from St. John Damascene. Meanwhile, however, another tradition was gaining ground in the sphere of Constantinople.

The pursuit of Platonic studies in the East continued intermittently from the ninth century onward. But it was only during the eleventh that the Platonic spirit truly expanded, to exercise its effect on the whole character of Byzantine thought. The period between the virtual extinction of effective government at the death of Basil II. Bulgaroctonos in 1025 and the accession of Alexius I. Comnenus in 1081 was one of the most troubled and unsatisfactory in the history of the Byzantine state. The year 1071 witnessed the defeat of Manzikert at the hands of the Seljuk Turks, from which the Empire never properly recovered. Yet intellectually this age was the most significant that Constantinople ever produced; without its precedent, it is difficult to see how the Italian Renascence of the fifteenth century could have come about. The reign of Constantine IX. Monomach (1042-1054) had witnessed the inauguration of a new policy, which consigned the rule of the state to the intelligentsia. The result was instability at the centre, and disaster without. But in compensation for the first encroachment of the Turks in Asia Minor, Europe, in all probability, owes to the Byzantines its present knowledge of Plato.

The whole spirit of the age, the enthusiasm of new discovery and of the deliverance of the human intelligence from the limited boundaries of ecclesiastical approval, was concentrated in the purpose of Michael Psellos.   In yet another university, founded by Constantine IX. Monomach, he was called to the chair of philosophy.   After a short time, disturbed by the jealousy of the court, and obsessed with a desire for contemplative leisure, he retired to a monastery.   But asceticism, and the one-sided communing of religion, were little to his taste.   If he delighted in nature, his mind fed also upon the society of others.   After a year or two he returned to Constantinople, and became Prime Minister under Isaac I. Comnenus.   The latter abdicated in 1059. Thereafter Psellos gave himself to learning and speculation.

It was a brilliant age; and its thirst was not only for Plato, but for all knowledge.   Nor was its culture, as those who know the Byzantines by hearsay are prone to assume, of a wholly academic character.   Just as contemporary satire was turned against the ascetics and those who denied the world into which they were born, so Psellos railed against the pedants of his time.   The study of literature was expanded; commentaries on the ancient authors were written, new rules formulated for grammar and rhetoric. Scientific works, such as the medical formulary of Nicolas the Perfumer, which remained in use at the Paris school of medicine till the seventeenth century, were produced in abundance.   A soldier, Kekaumenos, could write a treatise on morals, parental obedience and domestic economy, for the guidance of his son. Mystics, such as Symeon the Young Theologian in the tenth century, and John Kyriotis in the eleventh, were already talking of the love that St. Teresa was to know.   Public life was invigorated by satire. To Psellos, the problem of first importance was the provision of educational facilities; and he himself taught arithmetic, geometry, music, astronomy, astrology, meteorology, divination, geography, and philosophy, in the new university. It was significant of the whole movement that all the teachers were laymen. Huge crowds attended Psellos' lessons. Even the Celts and the Arabs were become prisoners, he wrote to the Patriarch of the schism, Michael Cerularius. Egyptians, Persians and Abyssinians felt his effect; a stranger arrived from Babylon in quest of his wisdom. He wrote of demons, music, agriculture, and law. Foreshadowing the later middle ages in the West, he toyed with the mystery of numbers, conceived the soul in terms of geometry, and the health and maladies of the body in quantitative symbols. Classical precedent linked his mathematics with the musical harmonies.

So large a range of interests might seem, at first, to indicate no more than the typical Aristotelian, encyclopædic intellect. But Psellos was essentially a mystic; and his mysticism was of that objective nature, characteristic of his race and of the Byzantine civilisation, which consciously, rationally, subordinated the reason to a higher quest; just as Greco later subordinated his capacity for representation to a higher ideal of emotional expression. For Psellos, as for the painter, the beauty of the world and the knowledge of it were the means of insight into the deeper mystery. And it was to this end that he sought to revive the ancient Greek mode of thought. Like Plotinus, he studied Aristotle as a groundwork for Plato's metaphysics. But he reproaches Aristotle with having confounded the two worlds. Plato was the hero of his thoughts and taste. Yet again, Psellos was intent on a more defined God than Plato's.   Fundamentally, therefore, he was a Neoplatonist; and as such was his influence felt.   Henceforth, despite a temporary ecclesiastical reaction under Alexius I. Comnenus (1081-1118), during which a satire depicted Psellos ranged among the damned between Æsculapius and Hippocrates, Plato and the Alexandrine mystics remained the chosen reading of the Byzantines.   Throughout the twelfth and thirteenth centuries, scholars such as Michael Italicos and George Acropolites continued the expansion of this school of thought. In the fourteenth, Theodore Metochites, the Grand Logothete who erected the mosaics of the Kahrié, Nicephorus Gregoras, his pupil and apologist, Gregory Palamas the champion of the Hesychasts, and Demetrius Kydonis, were all preparing the ground for the Western Renascence of the fifteenth.   Then at last, came George Gemistos Plethon (see pages 128-9), a judge of Mistra, who attended the Council of Florence in 1438, and set that city agog with his exposition of Plato's teaching.   At Mistra, he was the centre of a secret and exclusive Neoplatonic society; and his last years were devoted to the elaboration of a new religion, which he confidently hoped would soon supplant both Christianity and Mahomedanism, and was not, admittedly, much different from paganism.   Later in the fifteenth century, the Greek Cardinal Bessarion obtained for Plato the official approval of the Roman Church, by invoking, as a precedent, the Neoplatonic doctrines of Psellos.[1]

[1] In view of its association with both the Byzantine and Italian Renascences, it is important to realise the essentially humanistic complexion of Neoplatonic mysticism.   The very fact of Alexandria's having been its birthplace is apt to invest the system of Plotinus with something of that dour and abstruse fanaticism which characterised Hypatia's murderers.   Plotinus was

Psellos and his contemporaries, both in scholarship and spirit, were the immediate precursors of the Italian Renascence. His, more than any other, approached the scientific, Florentine mind. But as such it lay outside the true development of his time. For the East was now at the brink of that great expansion of mysticism which, deriving from the revival of Neoplatonism, swept over the Greek lands in the twelfth century; and spreading ultimately to the West, was destined to extinguish an experiment in humanism, not dissimilar from that of Psellos, at the south Italian court of the Hohenstaufens. This movement, which culminated in St. Francis, far from being the precursor of the Renascence, retarded it for three centuries. When the Renascence came, it called again for Plato. But whereas, in the Italian Renascence, the effect of Plato was felt in the humanisation of knowledge and consequent exaltation of reason, in the Byzantine of four centuries earlier, it resulted in the humanisation of religion at the expense of reason. What the dramatic interludes in the church services, and the Cappadocian-monastic iconography had done for the people in revealing the human experience and human sympathy of Christ and his mother,

---

concerned primarily with the divinity in man, and how, by right conduct, man might become conscious of it. He was therefore concerned with the *beauty* of man. "Withdraw into yourself and look," he preached. "And if you do not find yourself beautiful yet, act as does the creator of a statue that is to be made beautiful: he cuts away here, he smooths there, he makes this line lighter, that purer, until a lovely face has grown upon his work." Only when a man is perfect shall the vision of God be vouchsafed him. "This is the only eye that sees the mighty Beauty. If the eye that ventures the vision be dimmed by vice, impure or weak, then it sees nothing. . . . Never can the soul have vision of the first Beauty unless itself be beautiful." Here is a mysticism closely akin to that mysticism which is art.

the Platonic revival of Psellos did for the more sophisticated intelligentsia of the capital. That the effect was immediately apparent in art, may be observed by comparing the almost contemporary cycles of mosaic at the monasteries of St. Luke of Stiris and of Daphni near Athens. Both are equally gorgeous in colouring and materials; both equally the product of the official and superbly competent art of Constantinople. Yet, while in the first there appears only the hieratic aloofness and majesty, demanding no more than the awe and homage of the beholder, which was characteristic of the post-iconoclast period, in the second this is combined with a new spirit, noticeable, particularly, in the figures at the foot of the cross. There is no accentuation of suffering or grief; this was to come; but a novel humanism is apparent, an insistence on the dignity and beauty of the human body, which is expressed with a sympathy and facility plainly deriving from the study of the Antique. This tendency survived, not, as in Italy, to become the instrument of reproduction and imitation, but to give reality to the predominant note of religious belief in the succeeding age, the human suffering of Christ and his mother.

Likewise, despite the extinction of the scientific spirit, the spirit of Plato survived. Throughout the fourteenth and fifteenth centuries the Greek emigrants to Italy carried with them the tenor of his doctrines, which their irrational intelligence, distorted by misfortune, could but imperfectly appreciate. Eventually the centre of Platonic learning shifted to Mistra, the capital of the Greek Despotat of the Morea. It is significant of Plethon that, instead of the glorification of logic, the chief outcome of his studies should have been the elaboration of a novel polytheism.

If the old faith was threadbare, the burden of his race remained: he must provide a new. If there is something ludicrous about this last misshapen bud of Greek philosophy, it is dispelled by contemplation of the flower at its side. The painters of Mistra held the same principle; theirs still were faith in the Reality of the universe and the interpretation of the visible world by that means, instead of the mere inquiry into it and reproduction of it. The long and jealously guarded wisdom was flown to more congenial shores. Colour and light remained with the East.

V. THE TRANSLATION OF THE NEW THEMES, SPIRIT, AND TECHNIQUE, TO ITALY, AND THE EMPHASIS ON THE DOUBLE PASSION

Thus two distinct forces converged for the final reformation of Byzantine art under the Palæologi: on the one hand, the popular demand for presentation, at once intelligible, sympathetic, and dramatic, of those events in the gospel which seemed to bring Christ and his mother into closest relation with unhappy man; on the other, the humanisation of taste in the central and learned society of the Empire, by means of classical, and, particularly, Platonic studies. But before proceeding to the examination of the chief monuments of later Byzantine painting preserved on Athos and at Mistra, a further problem, of profound importance in the cultural evolution of Europe, demands elucidation. This is the astonishing resemblance, both in spirit and iconography, displayed by the works of Duccio, Giotto, and the Italian precursors of the Renascence, to the frescoes still preserved on the Holy Mountain and in the now deserted capital of the Peloponnese. The resemblance, it is hoped, is made suffi-

7

ciently clear by the plates at the end of this book.   Nevertheless, it may not be irrelevant to summarise the most striking features common to both, and thus to provide concrete evidence of that psychological and cultural impulse which came to Italy from the East, and without which it may be that the lives and works neither of St. Francis, nor of Dante, nor of Duccio, nor of Giotto, nor of many subsequent Italian artists, would ever have assumed the form which has now placed them in the category of European achievement.

The flow of trade, emigrants, *objets d'art,* and ideas, from the Levant to Italy, may be traced, without interruption, from the fall of the Western Empire to the decline of Venetian sea-power in the seventeenth century.   Between 606 and 750 alone, there were thirteen Greek-speaking Popes, who were mainly of Syrian extraction.   Sicily and Calabria were the home of numerous oriental colonies; it has been calculated that during the iconoclast period of the eighth and ninth centuries, the Greek element was increased by the advent of fifty thousand refugees, of whom a large proportion were iconodule monks.   And in Rome, until the schism of 1054, various shrines were officially assigned to the care of the Greek order.   Thus, quite apart from the more familiar examples of Byzantine mosaic in Venice, Ravenna and Sicily, a whole series of monuments exist in Italy which prove the existence of a popular and inexpensive art deriving not from Constantinople, but from the Cappadocian-monastic school of illustration, with Rome as its centre.   Thus, for example, the theme of the infant Christ suckling his mother's breast, while unknown within the sphere of Constantinople, is found both in the early Coptic frescoes of Egypt, and in Italy, though not in the more northerly countries of Western

Europe. The tradition of the large heads, stumpy bodies, and white, staring eyes, inherited by the Cappadocian school from the Hellenistic style of portraiture,[1] is particularly noticeable in the frescoes of Santa Maria Antiqua at Rome (mainly eighth and ninth centuries), in those of S. Clemente (847-855), in the tenth century painting of the Virgin at S. Urbano alla Cafarella, in a mosaic of the same subject at St. Paul's outside the Walls, and in numerous miraculously painted icons such as those of Trevignano and Viterbo. In the thirteenth century this tradition found its most complete expression at the hands of Margaritone d'Arezzo, whose panels, of which a large example hangs in the vestibule of the National Gallery, might almost be mistaken for those distinctive icons which the Anatolian Greeks continued to produce up to the middle of the last century.

With the reconquest of southern Italy by the Macedonian and Comneni Emperors, the official and more sophisticated art of the Greek capital began to take root in that country, that it might ultimately displace altogether the wholly unmeritorious art of popular illustration introduced from Asia. In 1066, the abbot Desiderius of Monte Cassino summoned artists from Constantinople to embellish his monastery. There ensued, throughout

[1] The astounding geographical extent of this style's influence is apparent in the third century frescoes discovered by Sir Aurel Stein at Niran in Chinese Turkestan and brought by him to Delhi, where they are now in the Central Asian Museum. The latitude of Niran is that of Pekin; the longitude several degrees east of Calcutta. These frescoes preserve exactly the crude, staring method of Hellenistic portraiture under the Roman Empire and might be mistaken, by anyone ignorant of their home, for the forerunners of the later Cappadocian school. They show, when compared with the sensitive compositions around them, that the effect of Western art on Eastern was as odious then as it is now.

Italy, a revival of mosaic decoration, of which examples may still be studied in St. Paul's outside the Walls, Santa Maria Maggiore, and St. John Lateran at Rome, and in the Baptistery and in the church of San Miniato at Florence. If the Cappadocian types were not wholly eradicated, the compositions at least assumed a more grandiose and splendid complexion. The more, however, that the mosaics tended to develop a distinctively Italian form, as in St. Mark's at Venice, the more the brilliant inner light and colouring of the true Byzantine art tended to disappear. Of this cardinal virtue, the first genuinely Italian painters in the thirteenth century had scarcely an inkling. Only in the frescoes of the church of SS. Cosmas and Damian at Rome, supposed to date from the thirteenth century, is the Byzantine principle apparent: the faces of the holy women at the tomb are built, not modelled, in planes of light, and bear a strong resemblance to those of the same lamenting personages in the Peribleptos at Mistra (see Plate 57. ii). None the less, in Italy, as in Greece, the same process was at work: the fusion of the sympathetic monastic art with the more facile and impersonal tendencies of the official. Right up to the thirteenth century, there was no true native development. " About 1250," reads Vasari, "several painters were summoned to Florence from Greece, by those who ruled the city, in order to re-establish painting, which was lost rather than forgotten." About 1250 . . . only sixteen years before the birth of Giotto.

Giotto lived from 1266 to 1336, and Duccio di Buoninsegna from 1260 to 1318. That the themes and iconographic details of these founders of the Florentine and Sienese schools were largely Byzantine is so universally recognised that a tendency has lately arisen to attribute to Greek painters many early Italian panels which a Byzantinist can see at once to be foreign to the Byzantine method. Even Mr. Berenson, having started, like most critics, at the wrong end, has fallen into this trap, confused by similarities of iconography and linear lighting.[1] Giotto and Duccio, springing from a long succession of Byzantine artists, provincial or otherwise, utilised Byzantine themes, compositions, emotions, faces and even clothes; but it is important to realise that their conception of form, though approximating to the Greek Macedonian school (see below), was essentially non-Byzantine. They modelled; the Greeks built. In colour, though Duccio retained something of the Byzantine sequences in his succession of figures, their purpose was harmony and naturalistic shadow, instead of discord and emotional light. They were, in fact, the founders of a new and alien tradition, which, though it created the most beautiful works known to man, became no more than a prison—a prison whence it has taken West European art five centuries to escape. Only through the realisation of this can their significance be appreciated. And bound up with that significance is the fact that, despite their novelty, they were actually produced by a religious movement which had its seat among the mediæval Greeks, and which brought about a parallel development in the character of Greek representation also, though fortunately not in the Greek artistic technique.

[1] A case in point being his wrongful attribution of the Hamilton Madonna in New York. The infallible test of difference lies in the modelling round the eyes. In Italian painting, they are invariably half closed, and the flesh beneath them shades gently away into a flat cheek. In Byzantine, there is always a definitely outlined triangle of dark beneath the lower lid, and then a patch of light. This gives an impression of dignity and unhappy experience, which the vapid sanctity of the Italian conception lacks.

The difference in circumstances between Giotto and Duccio, who may be taken, for convenience, to represent their respective schools, needs some explanation.   Florence was the true home of the Renascence, that worldly spirit of enquiry, which invested every object from the altar to the fire-dogs with surpassing beauty, and for which subsequent generations have paid with a barren slavery to Antique imitation.   The temperament of the Florentine artists, even of Giotto, was not adapted to the illustration of religious incidents.   Realism, in terms of human emotions, had been displaced by heroics in terms of human body.   Siena was different, like its landscape.   In fifty miles the cultivated hummocks have given place to contours, sweeping and arid, which inspire the beholder, particularly in the summer heat, with a desolate awe.   St. Francis' slogan, mysticism for all, found its devotees in Florence and the Lombardy Plain, as elsewhere.   But it was typical of Giotto's essentially Western mind that he should immediately translate it into allegorical figures, Poverty, Chastity, Justice and Injustice.   In Sienese art, such material statements cannot be conceived.   For in Siena, the mystic impulse from the East, which unloosed St. Francis, found a more congenial home; there were no conversations with birds; the note of suffering was struck on a higher and more exclusive plane, and the result was St. Bernadino and St. Catherine.   Consequently Duccio adheres more closely than Giotto to the Byzantine principle of depicting the Christian drama, not for its own sake—as did Giotto—but for the sake of the mystery enshrined in it.   As Ghiberti (1378-1455) observed to Vasari, Duccio's Maesta, " though very mixed with modern," is done " almost in the Greek manner."   Plates 11. iii, 19. i, 37. ii, 39. ii, 42. i, 43. ii, 48. ii, 53. ii, 55. ii, 59. ii will show how largely Duccio derived from the Byzantines. In the works of Giotto, the resemblances are not so marked. Nevertheless, the resemblances are there (see Plates 12. iii, 25. ii, 35. ii, 52. i, 75. ii); and in both cases must be explained. For Giotto and Duccio, and the painters of Athos and Mistra, whose models they appear to have followed, could never have had the smallest acquaintance with one another's works. Iconographic details might be translated by means of portable icons. But for the similarities of emotional aim, facial appearance, and actual technique, explanation must be sought in a common psychological religious movement, based on a common literature.

The position is aptly summarised by Professor Mâle in the second edition of his *L'art religieux de la fin du moyen âge en France;* the problem being to discover why, while the French artists of the thirteenth century were still reproducing the severe, dogmatic iconography of the encyclopædic age, the Italians were already engaged in depicting the events of the gospel with a new and moving realism. "It was the orientals," he says, "who had transmitted to Italy, as early as the thirteenth century, many of the themes of this new iconography. The East had anticipated the West, and that by several centuries. Far earlier than the West, the East had understood the painful realities of the Passion of the Saviour. The doctors of the Greek Church early began to meditate on the wounds of Christ and on the sufferings of the Virgin at the foot of the cross. . . . It is strangely surprising to discover in the sermons of George of Nicomedia, written in the ninth century, a whole series of sentiments which do not appear in the West until five centuries later. The latter writes of the Virgin's anguish on the hill of Calvary with the force of our mystics at the end of the Middle Ages.   "*When men thought,*" he says, "*that Christ was dead; when the crowd was dispersed and the soldiers had retired to their meal; then the Virgin could draw near the Cross to kiss the feet of her son, and the scars of the nails. . . . 'O! that the nails might be thrust into my limbs,'* she cried; '*that I might suffer all his pains with my body.*'" The Taking Down from the Cross is no less moving.   "*Imagine,*" he says, "*the Mother erect and endeavouring to be of use, receiving the nails as they were withdrawn, kissing the unloosened limbs, striving to receive them in her bosom. . . .   When they had stretched the divine body on the ground, she flung herself upon it, to bathe it with scalding tears.*"

"The sermons of George of Nicomedia were no exception; a century later the same sentiments reappear with equal force in the works of Symeon Metaphrastes, who wrote a lamentation over the Virgin holding the body of her son on her knees.   "'*O head torn by the thorns that I feel in my heart,*'" she cries. . . .   "'*Behold you now my son, between these arms that once bore you with such joy.   Then it was your swaddling-clothes that I prepared; now it is your shroud.   Child, you have slept on my bosom; dead, you sleep there still.*'"

"Thus, as early as the ninth and tenth centuries the Greek writers had discovered those tones which the West was not to hear till long after, and had imagined those unhappy scenes to which the artists of the East gave reality almost at once.

"Italy, saturated with Byzantine influence, must have been early acquainted with these products of the East; but she did not really understand them till the day when St. Francis of Assisi opened her eyes; then she also was affected by the Passion of the Saviour. Sympathy made her feel what she had long copied without emotion. It was in the time of Cimabue, Giotto and Duccio that she annexed the fair works of the eastern artists; and it was then that she infected them with a new life."

Thus Professor Mâle shows how the exaltation of suffering, of the passions of Christ and the Virgin, which was the predominant religious and artistic motive of the Byzantines in the fourteenth and fifteenth centuries, was communicated from Greece to Italy.

In depicting scenes from the life of Christ, the Italians took their stand largely on the writings of St. Bonaventure and the Meditations of the pseudo-Bonaventure, both written towards the end of the thirteenth century. Much of these works' picturesqueness, whether by the agency of itinerant icons or texts, was borrowed from the Greeks. In the Meditations, for example, God appears in the background of the Annunciation, and is there placed by Giotto; precedent is forthcoming in many of the Greek homilies, such as those of James of Kokkinobaphos mentioned on page 84. The Meditations also describe the affixing of Christ to the Cross by the unusual means of three ladders; exactly such a scene is to be found in the Peribleptos at Mistra (see Plate 49. i) and also in the Macedonian iconography of Mount Athos (see Plate 49. ii). The actual St. Bonaventure, who composed a whole office in imitation of the Byzantines devoted to the sufferings of the Passion, says that Christ had wished to be received into the arms of his mother. This was a new departure; the usual recipient was St. Joseph of Arimathea. Duccio paints the incident; but it is also to be seen at Mistra in the Peribleptos. Again, it has usually been supposed that the pseudo-Bonaventure derived his contention that Christ reserved his first reappearance for his mother from his own imagination; the same idea, however, had already been put forward by the Byzantine hymn-writer Romanos the Melodious (either 491-518 or 713-716). Giotto and his school painted the Crucifixion with only the single and central cross visible. But Duccio and Lorenzetti depict all three; and three crosses are equally found in the Peribleptos, where they are no less a novelty in official Byzantine iconography. Similarly there appears both at Mistra and at Siena the scene of the Betrayal in the Garden, combined with the kiss of Judas and Peter's attack on Malchus; precedent for this can only be found in Cappadocia (see Plate 45. i).

How the elaboration of the Passion of the Virgin, hitherto supposed to have derived from the imagination of St. Bernard in the first half of the twelfth century, was developed in the East long before, has already been shown. The dramatic scene of the holy women mourning over the body of Christ, which the Italians were ultimately to transform into the *Pieta,* was transferred from Cappadocian iconography to Greece and Italy almost simultaneously. It is found both at Mistra and on Athos; Giotto, Duccio and Lorenzetti all paint it, carefully reproducing the spectacular detail of the female figure with arms upraised in grief (see Plates 55, 56, 57. i). This motive remained totally unknown in the further West. The scene of the Dormition of the Virgin was also a novelty in Byzantine iconography. Duccio paints it simultaneously with its appearance on Mount Athos and at Mistra (see Plates 65, 67, 68. i, 69). He depicts, also, her burial by the apostles; this scene, though comparatively rare in Byzantine art, is found in the church of the Brontocheion at Mistra. By the end of the fourteenth century, the Greeks were illustrating the whole life of the Virgin in the twenty-four stations of the Akathist hymn. Analogy was found in the West in the fifteen meditations on the same theme of the Mysteries of the Rosary.

Such are the outstanding literary and iconographic evidences of a common movement in later Byzantine and early Italian painting. The new impulse to accentuate every incident whose tender dramatic sympathy could evoke a corresponding emotion in the beholder had led the artists of both countries to have recourse, partly to the popular monastic iconography, and partly to the creation of entirely new themes, based on imaginative writings. The frescoes of the Macedonian school on Mount Athos were executed in the first quarter of the fourteenth century and were therefore exactly contemporary with Giotto and Duccio. But it is a curious fact, that the majority of the paintings at Mistra were not in being till half a century, or, in the case of the church of the Pantanassa, a whole century, later. This disparity in time has led casual observers to enunciate the theory that the Byzantine artists were influenced from Italy.

Apart from the fact that many of the points of resemblance mentioned above are to be found in the frescoes of the Macedonian school on Athos, the most prejudiced examination of the monuments of Mistra will reveal no trace of that softening influence which Italian painting later exercised on the Greek island schools in the seventeenth or eighteenth centuries. In the first place, the Byzantine compositions are considerably simpler than the Italian; it is the latter who are expanding, not the former; and the introduction of extraneous figures and picturesque backgrounds is invariably the mark of an artist who is adapting an already existent theme to a new temperament and audience. Where, on the other hand, the Byzantines exhibit a tendency to enlarge their scenes beyond already prescribed limits, as in the Raising of Lazarus or the Entry into Jerusalem in the Pantanassa at Mistra (see Plates 1, 34. i, 36. i), there is no sign of any borrowing from the Italians, either in colour, form, or picturesque detail. On the right of the Entry, in fact, the clothes of the group emerging from the city are of that fantastic cut and pattern which characterised later Byzantine fashions, sacred or otherwise. In this scene, both in the Pantanassa, and in the Peribleptos (see Plate 36. ii), one figure of this particular group is draped in a most distinctive mantle, patterned in brown and white herring-bone; while his feet are shod in peculiar white slippers which have the effect of tennis-shoes worn with dark socks. No analogy for this dress is forthcoming in Italian costume of the period; though in Italy, equally, it was becoming the custom to introduce modern dress into biblical scenes. Then again, there is evidence of actual distortion of scenes from their proper meaning on the part of the Italians. In the Greek version, the Lament of the Virgin over her son's body was conducted preparatory to embalmment, deriving, thinks Professor Millet, from native funeral rites. But Duccio and Giotto, unfamiliar with such a custom, have transformed the marble slab on which the body lies, into the mouth of a tomb. Final and most convincing proof, as far as Mistra is concerned of the indigenous character of Byzantine art in the fourteenth and fifteenth centuries, is the character and technique of the painting. The earlier Macedonian school, as exemplified on Athos, had shown a tendency to lose its light and soften its contours, after the manner of contemporary Italians. But at Mistra, there is a definite reversion to the old forms of mosaic and colour reaction. And it was this tendency, which the yet later Cretan school was to accentuate and imprison, and El Greco to carry to its climax.[1]

[1] How violent was the controversy originally aroused by the " Byzantine question " is revealed by E. Muntz writing in the *Revue de l'art chrétien* in 1893 : " If the discussion has become thus inflamed, it is because numerous Italian *savants,* prompted by a patriotism as narrow as it is despicable, have forced themselves to deny the part played in the development of their art by the artists from the East. It is impossible to reprehend too strongly a bias of this kind, whose aim is nothing less than the falsification of history. Italy has sufficient claim to glory in the works of Antiquity and the Renascence, without needing to grudge the Byzantines their assistance during less brilliant epochs." But those were tranquil days. The present Italian Government demands that not only criticism, but art itself, shall be national. Said the Fascist Minister of Education and Fine Arts in 1926 : " Artists must prepare themselves for the new imperialist function to be carried out by our art. Above everything, we must categorically impose a principle of *Italianita.* Whoever copies a foreigner is guilty of an insult to the nation, like a spy who admits an enemy by a secret doorway." Even in 1930, it is hard to conceive the mind able to evolve such nonsense.

CHAPTER 4

THE MONUMENTS

Note.—*Though this chapter is necessarily categorical in form, it is important to the general argument that the colour-analyses of the paintings at Vatopedi (pp. 116-119), at Xenophontos (pp. 151-153), and at St. Paul's (pp. 154-159), on Mount Athos, and particularly of those in the Peribleptos (pp. 135-138) and Pantanassa (pp. 138-145) at Mistra, should not be omitted by the reader.*

IT is not intended, either in this chapter, or in this book, to compile a full catalogue of the frescoes of Mistra and Mount Athos. Those described are chosen either for their artistic eminence, or else for their importance in illustrating the chief train of development in later Byzantine painting. Analysis of their method of composition and conception of form is reserved for the following chapter, where it may profit by comparison with those of Greco. For the moment it is hoped that the plates will give sufficient idea of the structure to which colour is applied; and that they will also make plain the diversities in style and ability which characterised the Greek artists from 1300 to 1600. Byzantine art has been called, by those unfamiliar with it, a static art. The enumeration of the chosen monuments in order of date will perhaps convince the reader of the active transformations witnessed by the last three centuries of the last specifically Greek culture.

I. THE MACEDONIAN SCHOOL ON MOUNT ATHOS

The series opens on Mount Athos. Upon that long and narrow mountain-range in the northern Ægæan, culminating in one massive pin-pointed peak, hermits had congregated since the beginning of Christianity; and there had been classical temples there before. A combination of circumstances,[1] originating in the tenth century, gave rise to the foundation, on the shores of the promontory, of numerous monasteries, magnificent in their buildings, and lavishly endowed with treasure and estate by the Orthodox potentates, prelates, and merchants, of Eastern Europe. The power of the hermits was absorbed in that of the monasteries; and there developed a federal republic, immune from all interference in its affairs, save by the actual head of the state. So strange and impracticable an institution must quickly have been absorbed at the close of the Middle Ages, had not the Turks, softened by the monks' timely surrender in 1430, recognised and preserved, until 1912, the administrative autonomy of the mountain. Even under the rule of the Palæologus dynasty (1261-1453), the Athonite community, with its large patronage of artists, its libraries and copyists, its atmosphere of contemplative retreat from a world of growing chaos and misery, its predominant Hellenism during a period of foreign encroachment from both East and West, and its incomparable natural beauty, must have occupied, with Mistra and Constantinople, the position of a cultural centre. And it is from this epoch, at the beginning of the fourteenth century, that the earliest surviving paintings date. But after the fall of Constantinople in 1453, the Mountain stood alone as the

[1] See *The Station,* by Robert Byron, ch. iv.

last fortress of the Byzantine tradition. Though the Œcumenical Patriarch remained in Constantinople, Athos, henceforth, was the true centre of Orthodoxy and the only one which, by reason of its remoteness of position, independence of constitution, and the number of its inhabitants,[1] could still exercise the patronage necessary to continue the artistic tradition of the Orthodox Church. For painters and craftsmen throughout the Greek lands it was a natural focus of talent. Thus there came into existence a second cycle of paintings, which date from the sixteenth century.

The first cycle, now contained in three churches and one chapel on the Mountain, is the work of a school generally known as the Macedonian, and was executed, by various artists, in the first quarter of the fourteenth century. The name Macedonian, originated by Professor Millet, implies a wide field of activity. And it appears that a single school of artists, mainly, if not wholly, Greek, was at work during this period throughout northern Greece and the Balkans. Fine paintings from the hand of the Greek Calliergis, in the year 1315, survive at Verria near Salonica; others, dating from later in the century, on the shores of Lake Ochrida. In Serbia, the Greek artist Eutychios painted the frescoes of Nagoritcha in 1317; further cycles, whose inscriptions are in Greek, may be seen at Studenitza (1314) and Gratchanitza (1321). In Rumania, the Macedonian school, though since Italianised in restoration, is represented in the fourteenth century church of St. Nicolas Domenesc at Curtea of Argesch. Bulgaria, curiously enough, contains earlier paintings than any, at Tirnovo, Sofia and Boiana; these date from the thirteenth century or

[1] The monastic population has always been about 5,000, as it still is.

earlier. But their artistic merit, judged from photographs, appears to be considerably less than that of the others.

It is reasonable to suppose that the Macedonian paintings on Mount Athos represent the flower of the school. The artists were working within the cultural sphere of Constantinople, where the exquisite mosaics of the Kahrié were at that time in process of erection. And the spacious Athonite churches gave their talent freer play than the cramped edifices of the Balkans. Their iconography is distinct from that of the Cretan school which succeeded them. Their facial types, while attaining a hitherto unprecedented gentleness in the females, seem to have perpetuated something of the old Cappadocian violence and crudity in the males. Particularly this emerges in their bearded apostles, where it is equally noticeable in the contemporary works of Duccio (see Plates 39. ii, 42. i, 48. ii). Their colour is subdued and harmonious; so that the pictures have lost that unique interior light which had hitherto distinguished the central school of Byzantine art, and was again to be revived at Mistra and on Athos by the later Cretan school. The Macedonian artists, plainly, had a new aim in view; they were intent on the dolourisation of their compositions, as the spirit of their age demanded. The ecstatic brilliance of the true Byzantine tradition was lost to them.

i. THE PROTATON (Plates 11. i, 15. ii, 24. i, 25. i, 39. i, 42. ii, 47, 84. i, 85. i, 85. ii).

This church, situated at Caryes, the capital of the monastic republic, dates from the period of the hermits. In 961, two years before the foundation of the first monastery, Leo Phocas, brother of the future Emperor Nicephorus II., assisted in its reconstruc-

8

tion. Its form, that of the basilica, is unique on the Mountain, and would appear to date from the sixth or seventh century. The existing frescoes were executed at the beginning of the fourteenth, and the freedom of the compositions shows that the artist profited by his escape from the universal Greek cross type of church (see Plate 6) to the broader surfaces here offered.

Though discreetly restored about 1540, and probably since, the paintings have preserved their original delicacy of colouring and singleness of tone. The prevailing tints are a dark and light wine-red shaded with meaningless black or indigo; a silvery green, which alone retains the proper Byzantine light; a rich flaming pink; a dull olive-tinted amber, having reddish shadows; and an unpleasant sea-blue relieved with white. The flesh-tints are naturalistic and tinged with pink. These colours are permuted indefinitely. In the scene of the Washing of Feet (see Plate 42. ii), Christ is robed in deep wine-red, Peter in amber with ruddy shadows, and the figure behind him in sea-blue. The seated Christ on Plate 11. i is clothed in greenish indigo, from which emerges a light slate-coloured sleeve. The halo, as always, is ochre. The Sleeping Christ on Plate 24. i has auburn hair, white blouse, Prussian blue braces, and a lower drapery of amber. The Supper (Plate 39. i) attains a greater variety and brilliance, the buildings in the background showing a pronounced buff yellow, with vermilion roofs. Christ is robed in reddish indigo; the table-cloth and apples are purple. The figure on Christ's right wears flaming pink; that on his left, white, shadowed in cold blue. Beneath the traditional scenes are ranged the usual saints, whose faces (see Plates 84. i, 85. i, ii) have escaped from the ordinary conventions and give an impres-

sion of vivid portraiture.   This is confirmed in a striking manner
by acquaintance with the ascetics of the present day.

ii. The Church of the Monastery of Chilandari (Plates 33. i,
    34. ii, 40. ii, 41. ii, 52. ii, 61. i).

The church of the Serbian monastery of Chilandari was erected
in its present form by the Kral Stephen Miloutin about the year 1300.
In 1302 painters were at work in another chapel in the monastery.
And it is certain that the frescoes of the main church were completed a few years later.   In 1744, Barskij, the Russian traveller,
was so moved by their beauty that he termed them superior to
any on Athos, comparing them to the mosaics of Chios, and
speaking of " this art always fresh, tender and natural."   But
in 1804 they were restored; and the process was carried out
with such completeness (fortunately rare on Athos) that, with
the exception of occasional portraits like that of the Kral Miloutin,
not one vestige of the original paint or colour survives.   The
entrant, having admired the weathered antiquity of the church's
exterior, is suddenly confronted by the blue-bell, geranium, and
apple-green, of a Victorian natural history book.   The paint is
dull and flat.   And the highlights, though neatly preserved,
exhibit no luminosity.

None the less, it is a remarkable fact, and a tribute to the
efficacy of strict iconography in the evocation of the Christian
mystery, that these compositions have retained much of their
ancient force and austerity.   The mind of the original artist seems
gradually to emerge from beneath the saccharine ineptitude of
his successor.   There is more vigour than at the Protaton, and
in such scenes as the Lament over the Body of Christ, an equal

sympathy.   The Ascension (see Plate 61. i), depicted on the
curving vault above the iconostasis, is still, despite its modern
over-coating, of great beauty.   On a very dark-blue ground, the
central figure is of gold, with burnished shadows.   While the
four supporting angels, whose flying wings are tipped in pink,
or, where reposed, in brown, are robed successively in light blue,
pink, dull scarlet, and greenish amber.

iii. The Church of the Monastery of Vatopedi (Plates 11. ii,
     37. i, 41. i, 43. i, 48. i, 50, 55. i, 58. i).

The church of Vatopedi, one of the biggest on the Mountain,
dates from the end of the tenth century, and presents a magnificent
example of a large Greek cross interior with all its old fittings,
including a seventeenth century gilt iconostasis, intact.   An inscription in the narthex reads : "This divine church was restored
during the reign of Andronicus (II.), the most Orthodox king,
Comnenus and Palæologus, by means of a subscription from the
priest-monk Arsenius in the year 1312.   The present narthex has
been renovated and repaired through the interest and care of the
most holy *proïstamenoi* of this most sacred monastery, and at
the expense of certain pious and Christ-loving Christians, by the
hand of the monk Benjamin and his brothers from Galatista, in
the year 1819."   The first sentence reproduces the old inscription;
and it is from the year 1312 that the paintings date.   Those of
the nave, which were restored in 1789, constitute a cycle distinct
from those of the narthex.   But the date of both is approximately
the same.

In the case of these frescoes the process of restoration has been
unusually judicious, and seems to have been carried out only

where absolutely necessary. Thus in the Transfiguration, while the top half of the scene, above a crack in the plaster, has been wholly renovated, the bottom retains the original dull harmonies for which the Macedonian school was distinguished. The frescoes are in no sense wholly repainted as at Chilandari, and in many of them the greater part of the original paint is still visible.

The cycle contained in the church proper constitutes, without doubt, the greatest extant memorial of the Macedonian school. In the Protaton (see above), the prevailing tone is a dim, dirty pink distilled from wine. Here the colour is colder; the severe blue of dulled ink, relieved by occasional touches of more brilliant blue, red, green, mauve, and ochre, suffuses the church. At first, indeed, the paintings are barely visible; the beholder, gazing up at the mysterious, arching walls, is conscious only of a dull haze, behind which the familiar actors in the familiar scenes are only shadows. Then, gradually, the detail emerges; a ray of sunlight shifts, or a staring window is veiled; and the figures appear, austere and touching in their sombre and restricted colouring. Only the faintest and most misleading impression can be obtained from the illustrations. For the scenes are depicted on a vast scale. It can scarcely be imagined, for example, from Plates 37. i and 50, that the Entry into Jerusalem and the Crucifixion are life-size. There is a grandeur about them which recalls the Byzantine interior of the middle period. Simultaneously they are infected with all the sympathy and insistence on the suffering of the Passion, which the religious feeling of the fourteenth century demanded.

In these two scenes, the Macedonian school reaches its climax. Comparatively speaking, they are unrestored. The Entry is a masterpiece of composition; the naturalism of the background is harnessed to express the emotion which the sober arrival in front must inspire.   Christ is seated sideways on the ass, whose prancing tread and pricked ears are implicit with triumph.   Robed in dark but brilliant blue, he turns his head to the remonstrances of the apostles.   Before him, the Jewish crowd is waiting, skirted in dull white and cloaked in red.   Palms are waving.   Behind rears the city, a cluster of red domes and roofs, into an indigo darkness scattered irregularly with stars.   And above Christ's head grows a tree, firmly and naturally rooted to a gentle eminence.   A palm it might be.   Whatever its kind, it is a living tree, all twisted and anxious with the solemnity of the moment, as though some Byzantine Van Gogh were finding his soul in the thought of it.   Look now across the church to the Crucifixion, no less gigantic, more than life-size.   Here the form of the composition has changed.   All the lines, from the weeping angels' handkerchiefs to the draperies of the miserable, straining mother, are straight, rigid.   Christ stands, rather than hangs, anatomically correct.   The tension is in those below.   The colour defies analysis.   It is all cold blue relieved by a dull dark mauve and touches of green.   Here there is no red.

Other, less important scenes in this cycle display a greater variety of tones.   In the Washing of Feet (Plate 41. i), Christ's robe is red, and those of the apostles are successively warm buff, sea-blue, grass-green, bright mauve and ochre.   The floor is green, the buildings buff, and the sky a distinguishable blue.   Unfortunately restoration has hardened the shadows.   In the Descent into Hell, Christ appears surrounded by an aura of fine rays, which are coloured in sea-blue, brick-red and green.   The rocks are ochre; and of the suppliant figures, the foremost is in white, the hinder in wine-red.

The other cycle of paintings, in the narthex, is remarkable for the fact that its skies are light, powdered with the silhouettes of stars. This characteristic, almost unique in Byzantine painting, accentuates the resemblance to the contemporary works of Duccio (see Plates 43. ii, 48. ii), compared with which the frescoes of the nave are immeasurably superior in their grandeur and emotional appeal. In prevailing colour, those of the narthex approach more nearly the paintings of the Protaton. A pinkish warmth pervades them. In the Betrayal in the Garden (Plate 48. i), Christ is robed in a dull purple, and the lower apostles in salmon pink, both of which harmonise with the ochreous buff earth. The other apostles are clothed in blueish white, olive and dull mauve. On Descending into Hell (Plate 58. i), Christ is draped in the colour of brown sugar, with the exception of a lilac sleeve, bound at the centre in black. The suppliant figures are again white and wine-red.

iv. The Chapel of the Prodrome, in the Cell of Denys of Fourna, at Caryes (Plates 8. i, 8. ii, 10. i, 10. ii, 12. i, 24. ii, 28. i, 28. ii, 29. i, 29. ii, 30. i, 30. ii, 67. i, 78. ii).

The series of frescoes contained in this diminutive building, about fifteen feet square, present problems of iconography and date which no attempt has yet been made to elucidate. Professor Millet, confused, it appears, by the assertion of the Greek writer Porphyrios that the inscription accompanying them was the work of the forger Simonides (see pages 154-5), whom he supposes to have antedated it by three centuries, ascribes them to the year 1701. Subtract 300, and the date becomes more probable. Save for the obviously later additions in the dome, there seems every reason to believe that these frescoes were originally completed before the fall of Constantinople.

A careful examination of them will immediately reveal, not only that all the compositions, with the possible exception of the Dormition of the Virgin (Plate 67. i), have been grossly and carelessly repainted, but that in some cases, such as the medallions of saints behind the iconostasis, the arrangement of the various themes has been deliberately altered by the interposition of floral borders, beneath which the old names are still perceptible. In places where the original paint has survived, such as the skirt of Salome in both the Dancing and Execution scenes (Plate 30. i, ii), in the figures addressed by the preaching Baptist (Plate 29. 1), and in much of the desert surrounding the infant John and the angel (Plate 28. ii), a very delicate brush appears to have been at work, and one which could scarcely have been produced in the Greek lands as late as the eighteenth century.

Iconographically, this cycle of scenes from the career of St. John the Baptist, though not unknown in Orthodox decoration, is distinctly unusual. In the illustrations of the same subject preserved in a few of the later churches and refectories on the Holy Mountain, the iconography is wholly different. The nearest parallel, on the other hand, is found in the mosaics of the Baptistery of St. Mark's at Venice, which were executed in the middle of the fourteenth century. It may also be noted that Salome, beneath her green dress, is wearing surprising scarlet shoes. These were the proper emblems of Byzantine royalty, and seem to point to the fact that the Emperors were still reigning in Constantinople. It is scarcely conceivable that such freedom of detail and choice of subject as are here visible should have invaded the very sanctuary of Orthodox iconography at the date mentioned by Professor Millet, a time of acute cultural depression. The comic touch of the man seated at the head of the banqueting with a fork in his mouth (see Plate 30. ii) belongs essentially to the fourteenth or fifteenth century. While the depiction of Jonah (Plate 10. ii), in a niche beside the altar, seems to be without precedent in later iconography. Against a sea of blue and green, the prophet appears in profile, dressed in pink sleeves and amber mantle, while his nether portions are caught up in the scaly maw of an ochre whale. In his hands he holds a scroll bearing the words: "I cried by reason of mine affliction unto the Lord, and he heard me." In the distance, facing the prophet, stands the city of Nineveh, turretted and embattled, upon a coast of emerald green and white, sustained by chocolate cliffs.

The antiquity of the paintings is also confirmed by further iconographic analogies. Immediately above the altar, thus symbolising the Trinity by juxtaposition with Christ's holy elements, are represented God in the guise of an old man (Plate 8. i) and the Holy Ghost in that of a dove (Plate 8. ii). These are related by two contiguous circles. Such a composition is unknown elsewhere on Athos. But it appears in the very earliest Byzantine art, and is also found in the Peribleptos at Mistra, which was decorated at the end of the fourteenth century. The purity of design displayed by the circle of the Holy Ghost, and the three smaller circles attached recalls the finest examples of Byzantine pattern, and finds no analogy in post Constantinopolitan art. Another somewhat uncommon feature of the chapel

is the Sleeping Christ over the door (see Plate 24. ii). This
is found in the Protaton (early fourteenth century), and in the
Peribleptos at Mistra (late fourteenth century). It is also reproduced at Xenophontos on the Mountain. The paintings of this
monastery, it is true, were not executed until 1544. But in many
other ways, they give the impression of being the work of a
Cretan artist following the Macedonian iconography of the
fourteenth century, to which the Sleeping Christ undoubtedly
belongs. Thence also derives the figure of Noah (Plate 10. i),
holding a miniature ark, which is again found in the Protaton.

The colouring of the whole chapel seems to oscillate between
the dull harmonies of the Macedonian school and the cold brilliance of the Cretan; thus indicating the same fusion as displayed
by the churches of Mistra. In the Dormition of the Virgin
(Plate 67. i), a rosy light pervades even the white and amber
tints; the foreground is dead grey; the faces are soft; and many
of the draperies white shaded in beryl green. Of the single figures,
that of Noah (Plate 10. i), though considerably retouched, presents a rich, subdued scheme of tones: the mantle is of deep wall-
flower red, beneath which hangs an underskirt of blueish black;
the background is divided into three zones of dead black, white
and grey. Those of St. Athanasius and St. Ephraim the Syrian,
equally restored, are robed in wine-red, burnt red, grey and
amber.

The single scenes of the Baptist's life and death, still preserve,
between their coarse overpainting, touches of great delicacy. The
wilderness into which the angel leads the youthful John (Plate
28. ii) discloses two rocky eminences, the first grey shadowed
with ochre, the second a dark, meaty red. Beneath these grow

olive-trees and flowers, the former bearing their natural foliage of greenish, evanescent grey. The angel is draped in a voluminous vermilion cloak, beneath which hangs a tunic of beryl green and a wine-red skirt. The child, already in fur, appears to have preferred the fox to the camel.

He next appears, as a grown man, preaching baptism to the multitude (Plate 29. i) against a background of black sky and tall grey-green trees, coarsely restored in white. The ground is chocolate-red, starred with green plants. The saint, though retaining his fur, has now assumed an over-drapery of orange-brown lined with red. His hearers are clothed in the most singular manner. To his right stand a lady and a white-bearded man, the first in sky-blue skirt, rose-coloured tunic of the same pattern as the angel's, and vermilion top-hat; the second in brown buskins, vermilion tights, slate kilt, beryl green tunic with a white lining, and wine-red fez. The woman squatting at the saint's feet, and holding a baby, disports a geranium skirt and cold green tunic. Finally, the mock-heroic figures on the saint's left are dressed respectively in green tights, and vermilion tights sprigged with green; while their helmets are of grey, red, and brown.

The scene of the Meeting with Christ (Plate 29. ii) is yet more grossly disfigured with new whitening. The Master wears a dull blue cloak, lit and shadowed with different tones of the same colour. The ground is green. In the group on the Baptist's left appear the head and shoulders of a Falstaffian penitent, wholly draped in scarlet.

The final tragedy is depicted in three scenes on one wall (see Plate 28. i), in all of which the backgrounds and floors have been painted over in the crudest manner by one to whom the precepts even of Byzantine drawing were unknown. In the first scene the saint stands before Herod. The Tetrach is seated on his throne, which is placed on a double marble dais, whose technique is strongly reminiscent of architectural backgrounds in the Pantanassa at Mistra (early fifteenth century), but which has been half obliterated by restoration. Above Herod's head hangs an elaborate baldochino, with a green dome, gold cornice and tassels, and dull scarlet curtains patterned with sprigs. Herodias stands menacingly to one side. In the opposite corner of the wall, the actual Execution (Plate 30. i) is portrayed; the executioner, wearing a white tunic and sprigged shorts, hands the head to Salome, who displays an airy beryl green skirt, scarlet shoes, rose-geranium bodice, and white veil outlined in scarlet. The central panel is occupied with Herod's banquet (Plate 30. ii), in which the same canopy, and Salome in the same dress, reappear. The table-cloth is outlined in green, and displays a sprigged border. This sprigged pattern is also reproduced round the wainscoting of the chapel as an architectural ornament. The effect, at first sight, is curiously modern. But precisely the same decoration is found in Santa Maria Antiqua at Rome, a church whose paintings date from the seventh and eighth centuries.

The artist of the chapel, like Botticelli, had a strange predilection for sprigged stuffs. Beside those already mentioned, the Sleeping Christ (Plate 24. ii) is clothed in them; and also the God, the "Father without Beginning" (Plate 8. i) over the altar, whose mantle and tunic are white, the first shaded in green, the second in pink. The face is natural; the hair blueish. The whole background is a deep, dirty pillar-box red, the two sets

of circles and rays being grey, outlined in white. The white
Holy Ghost (Plate 8. ii) has a yellow halo, and is set on an inner
circle of yellowish red.

More space, perhaps, than is proportionate to their present
artistic merit has been devoted to the description of the Prodrome
frescoes, and must be excused by their unique iconography,
evident antiquity, and original fineness of workmanship. One
very curious feature is apparent in them: a marked resemblance
between such postures as that of the executioner on Plate 30. i,
or of the cup-bearer at the Banquet on Plate 30. ii, and the figures
of the Florentine schools of the fifteenth century, particularly
those of Botticelli. In later centuries, Italian influence certainly
filtered through, as may be observed in the frescoes of the Grecised
Venetian Zorzi at the monastery of Dionysiou (see below, pages
153-4 and Plates 32. iii, 45. ii, 63). But such influence was
essentially Venetian and baroque. In the chapel of the Prodrome,
whether this resemblance is to be explained by Italian influence,
or by a simultaneous native development on the part of the Greeks,
it is of an altogether earlier type. It is much to be hoped that
one day, when the monks have become aware of the value of
their artistic heritage to the whole history of European art, these
frescoes in the chapel of the Prodrome at Caryes may be properly
cleaned and restored.

II. THE CYCLES OF MISTRA

Professor Millet, and others, have sought to extend the classi-
fication of the Macedonian and Cretan schools to Mistra. So
individual, however, are the paintings contained in the churches
of that city, that they seem, more probably, to represent a native

efflorescence, which took place in the last half of the fourteenth century and the first half of the fifteenth. This individuality may derive, in part, from the fact that, unlike those of Mount Athos, such of the Mistra frescoes as have survived have done so completely unrestored. But though they display affinities, both with the warm flat harmonies of the earlier Macedonian school, and with the frigid brilliance of the true Byzantine tradition as exemplified in the works of the later Cretan artists, they form a separate, if transitional, cultural entity. Their influence, or the influence which produced them, was widespread. In Serbia, parallel works are to be seen at Ravenitza (1381), Ljoubostinja (1389-1405), and Manassia (1407), all of which were probably executed by Greek artists. And in Russia, at this date, arose a whole new school, led by the Greek Theophanes, who was responsible for the frescoes of the church of the Transfiguration at Novgorod between 1395 and 1405, and whose pupil was Andrew Roublev,[1] the native founder of the Novgorod school. This school continued predominant during the first half of the fifteenth century, and was only swamped by the Slav tendency to folk-decoration during the reign of Ivan III. (1462-1505).

The town of Mistra, climbing a precipitous spur detached from the main bulk of Taygetus, and overlooking the rich valley of the Eurotas, remained inhabited up till the War of Independence at the beginning of the last century; and, with the possible exception of Constantinople, is the only site which still preserves the character of Byzantine civil life. Regained from the Villehardouins by Michael VIII. Palæologus, it became, in 1339, the

---

[1] Icons by Roublev, dating from 1410, are still preserved in the Troitzkaya Lavra Museum near Moscow.

capital of a Despotat, whose status in relation to the imperial government on the Bosporus was that of a British dominion. In an atmosphere of the past, as yet unbroken by the archæologist, the visitor may wander up the tiny, twisting streets, and in and out the broken houses, each one terraced forward on its concrete cistern; he may find the skeletons still lying in their graves; he may picture the magnificence that once adorned the spacious hall of the Palace of the Despots; he may penetrate the impregnable battlements of Villehardouin's castle, situate on the very point of the pinnacle, and discover yet another cistern; he may descend to the Metropolitan church at the bottom of the town, and observe the eagle set in the pavement to commemorate the coronation of Constantine IX. Dragases, last Emperor of the Greeks, who fell on the walls of Constantinople in 1453. Inscriptions abound, to assign these vague memorials their places in Byzantine history. The monogram of Manuel Cantacuzene, the first Despot, who reigned from 1349 to 1380, appears on walls and over gateways, as it does on the cup presented by that ruler to the monastery of Vatopedi on Mount Athos. In the church of the Brontocheion, the four walls of a small chamber are wholly covered with the texts of four imperial chrysobuls, whose sealed parchments are unrolled by four hands depending from four rays, which radiate from the centre of the cupola. These, dispensed by the " King and Emperor of the Romans," date from 1314-1315, 1319, 1320, and 1322, the second being that of Michael IX. Palæologus, and the others those of his father, Andronicus II. In another chapel appears the epitaph of the Despot Theodore II. Palæologus (1407-1443), who is depicted, on one side, in the high jewelled headdress of his secular office, on the other, in his latter habit of a monk.

Anna Lascaris, of the family that once ruled in Nicæa, is also buried in the church.   At the Pantanassa may be read a reference to the last of the East Roman Emperors in the epitaph of Manuel Lascaris Chatzikes, "the servant of our Despot Constantine Palæologus," who died in 1445.   He also is depicted, wearing a long robe with full sleeves, and the high, pointed hat with up-turned peaks before and behind which may be seen in the Pisanello medal of the Byzantine Emperor John VIII.

The place has an air of reality, even though the reality is only of ghosts.   The visitor pictures the rulers and officers of the provincial capital, as their mules climbed the streets in single file, and twisted through the gateways and round the corners of houses, till they reached the platform overlooked by the many windows of the palace.   Even after the surrender to the Turks, building activity continued: the encircling walls of the Peribleptos were raised in 1514; the church of St. Nicolas, high up towards the castle of Villehardouin, was not founded till the beginning of the seventeenth century. During the history of the Despotat, Frankish principalities and Turkish incursions interrupted the landward journey to Constantinople; the sea was thick with hostile ships; yet though the political condition held little hope, learning and art flourished with an independent life in this remote outpost of Hellenism.

The outstanding figure of the fifteenth century was the Platonist George Gemistos Plethon, already mentioned as the occupant of a judgeship at Mistra, where he died, aged nearly a hundred, in 1450.   Though known to be opposed to the proposed union of the Churches, and already eighty years old, his reputation demanded his inclusion in the mission which the Emperor

John VIII. led to the Council of Florence in 1438. And such was the effect of his revelation of Plato on the Italians that his bones were later disinterred, and translated from the place of his death to Rimini at the instance of its Malatesta ruler. The secret society for the study of Plato, of which he was the centre and the intelligentsia of Mistra the initiates, has already been noticed, as also his great philosophical adumbration of a new religion. The latter work was afterwards destroyed by the Patriarch Gennadios, to whom it had been given by the Despot Demetrius Palæologus, following the latter's surrender to Mahomet II. and return to Constantinople.

Gemistos Plethon, like all Greeks, was keenly alive to current affairs. And in a series of seven addresses to the Emperor Manuel II. Palæologus, and his son the Despot Theodore II., he has left a picture of the misery prevailing in the Peloponnese during the last days of Byzantine independence: the open brigandage of the aristocracy; the unpopularity of conscription; the corruption and demoralisation of the people; the futility of monasticism; such were the evils which he condemned. His remedies were full of hope. He advocated a novel scheme of taxation, which should separate military and financial liability; a system of peasant proprietorship; and a policy of protection, saying, with regard to the latter measure, that the country produced all the necessaries of life save the iron needed for arms, and that the latter could be got in exchange for cotton. His words fell on deaf ears; the central government was helpless; and the division of the province on the accession of John VIII. (1427) between his brothers Theodore, Constantine and Thomas, put an end to all hope of reform, since their time was occupied in making war on

9

one another.   But his career, and his opinions, illustrate the measure of culture and enlightenment which the capital still preserved.

The paintings of Mistra, surviving in all the brilliance and delicacy of their original colouring, give an impression of freshness and humanism which is not to be found in the ascetic environment of the Holy Mountain, and which is generally associated with the term Renascence. Their people are real people, no longer merely the stereotyped adjuncts of the Liturgy.   The angry contorted faces of the Macedonian and Sienese schools have disappeared.   In the Pantanassa, the scenes are filled with picturesque details, introduced with the delicious irresponsibility of a Pinturicchio.   But the virtue and beauty of the paintings lies primarily in their colouring, in which province they far excel even the exquisite mosaics of the Kahrié in Constantinople.   Each component part of each scene, drapery, face, and rocky background, radiates an individual luminosity, which is achieved not only by highlights, but by carefully considered contrasts of colour.   That such an art should have blossomed during the last days of the Byzantine Empire, and under the conditions described in the writings of Plethon, is a tribute to the marvellous intellectual vitality of the Greek race; and shows how a full-flowered Byzantine Renascence, such as it foreshadows, might have surpassed all that Italy ever produced.   In fact, only one posthumous flower ever worked its head through the débris of the future.   This was El Greco.   And it is in Mistra, particularly, that the origins of his art are revealed.

i. THE METROPOLITAN CHURCH OF ST. DEMETRIUS (Plates 13. i,
    76. i).

The earliest cycles of paintings at Mistra are contained in this
church, which lies at the foot of the hill on which the town
stands, and is still used as a place of regular worship by the
inhabitants of the lower village.   The fact that services continue
to be held there, and a priest to be attached, has not prevented
the frescoes from falling into a miserable state of decay.   The
church is of basilica form, and may therefore be presumed to be
of considerable age.   In the year 1310 it was refounded by " the
humble Nicephorus, president of Crete . . . while Andronicus
(II.) Palæologus holds the sceptre of Empire with his son
Michael (IX.)."   This was the Metropolitan Nicephorus Mos-
chopoulos, and it is from the second decade of the fourteenth
century that the earlier cycle of paintings, representing the life of
Christ, the martyrdom of St. Demetrius, and a triple rank of
saints, must date.   The style of these frescoes indicates the tradition of an earlier epoch of the popular monastic art that flourished
side by side with the gorgeous age of mosaic in the sphere of Constantinople; Mistra was not yet a capital; and their place, though
not their date, is outside the Byzantine Renascence.   A certain
facility of design is apparent in the well-preserved Hetimasia
reproduced on Plate 76. i.   The Virgin in the apse (Plate 13. i),
austere and dignified, with her rose-coloured mantle hanging in
heavy folds above a grey skirt, is reminiscent of the Torcello type.
The infant Christ is clothed in tawny brown, shaded in slate.
And the background is indigo, save for a broad field of ochre
running round the vault, which stretches from the calves to the

hips of the central figure.   The remaining scenes in this first cycle, though not lacking occasional figures of graceful movement, seem cramped, and their actors ill-proportioned.   Their colours, in their present condition, are barely distinguishable.   But they can never have exhibited any particular luminosity.

The second series, which is engaged, in the nave, with the miracles of Christ, and in the narthex, with the numerous episodes of beatitude and damnation comprising the Last Judgement, must have been painted soon after the first, possibly at the restoration undertaken by the Metropolitan Matthew, of unknown date. The artist employed an impressionist manner, depicting his lights in coarse splashes.   But there is little virtue in the colouring. And again, for the most part, the figures are uncomfortably cramped.

ii. THE BRONTOCHEION (Plates 16. i, 76. ii).

This church was founded by the Protosyncellos Pachomius before the year 1311.   Its paintings appear to belong to a later date, probably in the second half of the century.   They show no traces of the uncouth art of the Metropolitan church; and their colouring displays none of that harmonious warmth which characterised the productions of the Macedonian school in the first quarter.   In general, yellowish green, amber, grey, and white, seem to combine with shadows of wine-red and slate.   The painting is smooth and precise; each colour-field is defined.   The artist seems to have had a peculiar talent for pattern and formal decoration.   One remarkable feature, illustrative of his insensibility to naturalism, is the brilliant emerald green ox in the scene of the Nativity.

The finest and, with the exception of those in the chamber of the chrysobuls, only reproducible piece of fresco surviving, is the head of Zacharias on Plate 16. i.   Placed within a circular design of rolled green leaves, the face of the High Priest looks down from its diminutive cupola with an expression of inhuman intensity. The whole composition is executed with that mastery of formalism in which the Byzantines excelled.   The face is of smoothest ivory, heavily shaded in ochre and green; the hair and beard are of a light opaque yellow, tinged with pink; the drapery is burnt rose; and the left hand holds a green scroll.

The Byzantine genius for design and composition is further revealed (by the aid of a lamp) in the square chamber containing the chrysobuls, already mentioned on page 127.   This unlighted accretion to the main church is surmounted by a small cupola, in the centre of which was originally Christ in his glory.   Now, only the outline of the glory is visible; and this is upheld by four magnificently drawn angels (see Plate 76. ii), whose outstretched wings overlap immediately above the centre of each of the four walls.   At the point of intersection, a ray, emanating from the glory, descends to the top of the wall, where a single sleeved hand grasps the rolled parchment, and lets it fall to exhibit the whole charter.   Between the hand and the wings, and encircling the whole cupola, runs an elaborate design of tied foliage.

The present condition of the Brontocheion is a dishonour which not only the Greek government, but Europe, and even America, must be called upon to remedy.   The church was originally half demolished by the deliberate work of the peasants, whose laudable intention was to repair the older and more historic fane of St. Demetrius with the borrowed stones.   And thus, half

demolished, it remains.   The head of Zacharias lies open to the
air, the rain, and the snow; only its position in the vault of a
cupola, which hangs in mid-air without visible means of support
and must assuredly collapse in the immediate future, has hitherto
preserved it.   The chamber of the chrysobuls, together with the
funerary paintings and inscriptions mentioned on page 127, are
among the most precious historical memorials of the later Byzantine Empire.   They, too, though sheltered from actual rain, lie
exposed to the air and its corroding moisture.   That their plaster
should already have adhered to the stones of the outer wall for so
long is miraculous.   That it will continue to do so is not possible.   Thus, while every country of civilised pretensions main-
tains institutions and men of learning in Athens for the purpose of
researching into the potsherds and cooking utensils of Antiquity,
while Americans are expending a million pounds sterling to
demolish the few remaining houses of Independence Athens in
order to explore the remote possibility of finding yet further products of a debased and unemotional art, the frescoes of Mistra,
unique in their importance as the one great historical link between
the art of painting in Western Europe and its original home in
Eastern, the proud epilogue of a culture which endured for a
thousand years, are left by an enlightened world to lie in the
open.   Within view of Mistra, some three miles off in the
Eurotas valley, lie the modern town and ancient site of Sparta.
Nearby, the contours of the ground indicated the presence of an
ancient theatre.   For three years in succession, the British School
of Athens, poorest of all the foreign academies in that town, has
issued piteous appeals for funds with which to continue its excavation of this miserable amphitheatre, where there is admittedly no

chance of discovering any so-called works of art, and which, once excavated, must remain untended in its olive-grove till the weeds have again concealed it. Excavation is a costly process. With the money already subscribed to this contemptible project, the neighbouring churches of Mistra might all have been rendered air- and water-proof, and heating might have been installed in them, thus preserving what is left, and preparing the way for a proper course of restoration. As it is, the paint continues to be corroded, the plaster to crack, and the stones to fall. Once the frescoes are finally destroyed, the pedants who control the funds of European culture will doubtless discover the value of Byzantine art and express a touching regret.

iii. THE PERIBLEPTOS (Plates 9. ii, 32. ii, 36. ii, 49. i, 57. ii, 59. i, 68. i, 79).

Definite evidence as to the date either of this church or its paintings is not forthcoming. But the style of the latter places them at the end of the fourteenth century or the beginning of the fifteenth. Their colour, though brilliantly lighted, is subdued, thus linking them with the Macedonian school, of which the scenes of the Putting Up to, and Taking Down from, the Cross, and the face of Christ in the Descent into Hell, are also reminiscent. On the other hand, much of their iconography, such as the groups watching the Ascension, and the Entry into Jerusalem (Plate 36. ii) with its extraordinary figure in the herring-bone mantle, is intimately connected with that of the Pantanassa, which was only founded in 1428.

Professor Millet has discovered the work of two or more painters in this church, who, though members of the same school, and doubtless working simultaneously, betray their individuality, the one by an exquisitely smooth finish of technique, the other by a more impressionist manner.

The masterpiece of the first is the procession of angels in the composition known as the Divine Liturgy (Plate 77. i). At the centre of a long frieze stands Christ, robed in the elaborately patterned vestments of a Byzantine Patriarch; before him is an altar; above his head the customary ciborium, supported on four pillars. Toward him, and then from him, defile with long and reverent strides a rank of angels, sexless yet human, and invested with a deep and beautiful religious feeling. The inscription formerly in the church of the Lavra on Mount Athos may again be quoted: "Seeing the tribune of the altar of the Lord, stand trembling, O man, and cast down thine eyes, for within is the Christ daily sacrificed, and all the ranks of the holy angels prostrate themselves before him in fear and ritual." In the present scene each angel carries some necessary adjunct to the celebration of the Eucharist, and is robed in a long white surplice, square-cut at the neck, reaching to the ankles, and having very full sleeves. The background is a deep sapphire blue; the angels' hair, bound with white ribbon, is russet; their wings are green, with blue insides. But the marvel of the whole is the miraculous painting of the surplices. The stuff, beneath which every movement of the limbs is visible, is in no sense transparent; it possesses, on the contrary, the liquid opacity of a pearl: in the lights, a white pearl; in the shadows, a pink; and this is achieved by a delicate opalescent finish, which accentuates, rather than diminishes, the textural value. The artist responsible seems to have excelled in the painting of white draperies. No less beautiful are those of the transfigured Christ (Plate 32. ii), again on a blue ground, in which the shadows, instead of pink, are orange. Another example of this highly finished brushwork may be seen in the head and vestments of St. John Chrysostom on Plate 79.

The other and more impressionist painter appears to have been chiefly engaged on scenes from the life of Christ. Those of the Passion, particularly that of the Lament over the body of Christ, are filled with a great sympathy; the colouring is subdued; but the form is nevertheless luminous. This quality is most noticeable in the three female heads at the Burial of Christ (Plate 57. ii). The faces are of deep apple-red, gently shaded to olive, the central one being wrapped in a claret-coloured veil to which light has been applied in impressionist splashes. This light, together with that on the cheeks, chins, noses, and foreheads, proves, on close inspection, to be painted in a brilliant sky-blue, calculated to achieve the very extreme of contrast with its ground. The use of this colour in the depiction of flesh finds analogy in the mosaic panels of Saints George and Demetrius (eleventh or twelfth century; see description on page 32), preserved at the monastery of Xenophontos on Mount Athos, where small cubes of it are introduced into the more or less naturally coloured cheeks for textural, rather than luminous, purposes. Of the importance of this precedent in relation to El Greco, more will be found in the following chapter. Another example of subdued tones combined with luminous brilliance is found in the scene of the Incredulity of Thomas. Christ himself is robed in indigo, and his draperies are heavy and unlit. But the apostles to his left seem as though clothed in an essence of pearls, pink, white, black, and yellow pearls, in order of their recession from the central figure. This pearliness is not that of the angels' surplices, but is more brilliant and translucent.

The condition of the frescoes in the Peribleptos calls for comment not less emphatic than that of those in the Brontocheion. The church, though whole, is disused. Being partially hollowed from the living rock, it is naturally damp. Its windows are unglazed; its doors a travesty. Here the reproach, if anything, is greater. The paintings survive, many of the scenes entire; and they are deliberately being allowed to rot away. In a hundred years' time they will be gone altogether. The theatre at Sparta will then hold its dominion over the tourist unchallenged.

iv. THE PANTANASSA (Plates 1, 14. ii, 17, 19. ii, 20, 22, 34. i, 36. i, 60. i, 60. ii, 77. i, 77. ii, 78. i, 83. i).

This church, terraced high up on the opposite side of the town to that of the Palace of the Despots, is attached to a convent whose seven or eight nuns are the sole remaining inhabitants of the deserted capital. Their situation, overlooking the valley from their white-pillared cloister and strange egg-topped campanile, is one of extraordinary beauty. And to their efforts, and to those of their predecessors, posterity owes the preservation, not only of their own most beautiful paintings, but of many of those already mentioned.

The church, whose foundation is probably contemporary with that of the whole convent, "was consecrated and sanctified," according to a now lost inscription, "by the most reverent Metropolitan Nilos of the most sacred Metropolis of Sparta, on the authorisation of the most holy Œcumenical Patriarch Denys in the reign of our most pious King (Despot) Theodore Palæologus

the Porphyrogenitus, in the month of September, 1428." The
founder, referred to as the κτήτωρ, was a minister of war, who
thus explains himself in an inscription surrounding the Mother
of God reproduced on Plate 14. ii: "Having enjoyed, O
Virgin, many of thy benefits, I, John Phrangopoulos, Protos-
trator, bring to thee a small gift, this church. . . ." Now the
word κτήτωρ invariably refers to the initial founder; and since the
second inscription is painted, the frescoes may be presumed to
have been executed immediately after the completion of the building in 1428.

These frescoes are the very flower of later Byzantine art. In
their colours, which have remained as fresh and brilliant as when
the artist left them, the interpretational method of colour reaction
attains a climax of success. The principle has been observed in
practice at the Peribleptos. But there, a certain blurring of the
divisions, a gentle transition from one tone to another, was perceptible. Here, each colour-field is rigidly defined, so that the
maximum of contrast with its neighbour is achieved. There is
no attempt at naturalism; that aim, towards which the Macedonian artists were moving, has receded. Nevertheless, an unprecedented humanism is apparent, a vivid joy in the artist's
power to evoke, not only religious emotion, but the concrete
beauty of the world. In the opinion of the West, humanism
was conditional on naturalism. The Byzantines knew better.

Outstanding in the whole cycle is the scene of the Raising of
Lazarus, a composition about ten feet high by twelve broad,
depicted on a curving plaster vault overlooking the nave (see
Plates 1 and 34. i).

The general background of the scene presents the colour and

tone, and has the same translucency, as bottled honey, slightly tinged with olive. The escarpment on the left, above the group containing Christ, is a definite green. The valley in the middle is deeply shadowed in olive. Such of the sky as has survived the cracking of the plaster is a rich navy blue, a colour quite distinct from the toneless indigo which forms the background to most of the Athonite frescoes. Thus far, the colouring is strikingly reminiscent of Greco's Agony in the Garden in the National Gallery in London. The buildings at the back, however, seek the most exaggerated contrast with the landscape, in a tint of crushed strawberry, which, in the doorways and shadows, gives the impression of having been burnt. Bearing in mind the surpassing brilliance of all the colours mentioned, it is not difficult to imagine that, if the artist is to bring his figures into the foreground against such a scene, and thus rescue his composition from the level of mere pattern, he must have recourse to measures unknown in Western art until the present day.

The group on the left (Plate 34. i) is depicted mainly in Prussian and sky blues, the only exception being the brilliantly lit apostle immediately behind Christ, who is clothed in a kind of pink-tinted brown, which discloses the top of a Prussian blue tunic. Of the group at the back below the buildings, the foremost figure is robed in a dark wine colour without highlights, the second in glowing amber, and the third again in sky-blue—that being the colour most completely divorced from the background. These separate compositions are intended to act as foil to the actual upraising of Lazarus on the right (Plate 1).

A most beautiful, moving humanism pervades these six persons, which culminates in the weeping figure on the left, and is accentuated by a little white flower with chocolate leaves that grows beneath the feet of the lid-bearers. The anatomy is no longer hieratic, no longer the anatomy of physically abnormal ascetics. The weeping figure is perfectly proportioned; the mummy expresses a tragic resignation; while the man unwinding is fired with a frantic vigour. His legs tread the ground with the classic assurance of Signorelli's frescoes at Orvieto. All the heads, legs, arms, and hands, of the picture are achieved by the use of a yellow vermilion, almost the colour of a dark crocus, lit with fine white lines, and shadowed, through olive, to dark wine-red. The tunic of the weeping figure is a brilliant grass-green, which is painted over in a masterly way with transparent sky-blue in order to emphasise the lights. This garment is edged with amber, lighted like a topaz and again shaded in wine-red. Both the garters and neckerchief are of the same sky-blue with the same claret shadows.

Lazarus himself is wrapped in a shroud of pearly opalescent yellow, to which the pinkish chocolate interior of the tomb acts as foil. The unwinding figure is dressed in an upper garment of dark wine-red, lit with white, beneath which flows a drapery of the same pearly yellow as the shroud, followed by sky-blue shorts, which, from a distance, appear to be white. The right-hand figure at the top wears a cloak of deep sky-blue, shadowed in claret and having a claret lining, beneath which hangs a robe of yellowish green, lit with sky-blue and white. The lid is marbled in crushed strawberry and buff; the right-hand bearer wears a purple and white kilt with sky-blue draperies; the left is clothed in the same pearly yellow. If the reader will now recall the honey colour and crushed strawberry of the background, and the dark blue and brown group on the left, he will perhaps retain some impression of the brilliance of the whole scene.

No less dazzling and translucent are the Angel of the Annunciation and its setting, reproduced on Plate 17. Behind this messenger, who is still propelled, though his feet have touched the ground, by a rust-coloured wing with grey-blue tips, flutters a cloak in the yellows and greens of a hard-boiled egg. With the exception of a grey-blue sleeve bound with a rusty ribbon, the other draperies are painted in a glacial beryl green, having white highlights, and washed over with transparent yellow for the shadows, till, on the bent knee, this becomes an opaque mossy colour. The bare feet, of crocus yellow and wine-red, tread a marbled floor of burnt pink, which colour is continued on the buildings in the background. The two slender marble pillars are the tone of purple grapes. Beneath the feet, a charming little quail, with a grey back and a breast striped in yellow, chocolate, and white, drinks from a pool, into which the basin of the usual pineapple-shaped Byzantine fountain is overflowing.

The insistence on the decorative values of marble, so prominent in this composition, and on the lid of Lazarus' tomb in the previous, again finds play in the scene of the Presentation of Christ in the Temple (Plate 22). The background is composed of an elaborate architectural setting, in which the excellent perspective of the curtained balcony on the beholder's left is a remarkable feature, and again, like the quail, recalls the joyous frivolity of Carpaccio or Pinturicchio. The building from which the balcony depends is lettuce green; its porch, a light opaque rose colour. The canopy of the ciborium, with its inevitable cone such as once sheltered the altar of St. Sophia, is of burnt pink; beneath it runs a circular balustrade of dark leaf-green marble. Symeon, standing on a throne of dark and light burnt pink, is robed in transparent blueish mauve. The Virgin wears a dark chocolate dress, with striking cold blue lights. The figure behind her is draped in a pale pink mantle, beneath which hangs a sky-blue skirt.

The scene of the Entry into Jerusalem (Plate 36. i), occupying a similar area to that of the Raising of Lazarus, is of a most extraordinary character, the felicity of the composition being marred by the overcrowding of figures and incident. The impression given by the whole is one of opalescent yellowish green, including the walls of the city, whose roofs are covered with slate, alternating with occasional vermilion tiles. On the beholder's left, however, the buildings change to a tint of crushed strawberry, shadowed with mauve, above which the rocks are a warm amber. Beneath the feet of the ass appears a peculiar little edifice, surrounded by trees, and displaying two gabled roofs of light red. The ass is white; its hindquarters have the air of a Pinturicchio charger. Coming forward to meet Christ is an astonishing group in white tennis slippers, which latter, at the back, give place to rust-coloured boots. In the foreground of this group stands a figure wrapped in a white cloak heavily patterned in tawny zigzags and circular dots. This singular garment, whose significance has been discussed on page 108, is also included in the same scene in the Peribleptos. Beneath appear a wealth of small actors facetiously removing their clothes to lay beneath the feet of the ass.

The groups watching the Ascension (Plate 60. i, ii) present a similar humanistic consciousness of the diversities of landscape.

Against a rocky background of translucent yellowish green, above which the sky is dark blue, stands a row of trees with olive-coloured trunks and varying foliages of silvery grey. In the group which includes the Virgin, the figures, counting from the beholder's left, are robed successively in pale wine-red, golden yellow, greenish white shadowed with olive and slate (the angel), rich cobalt lit with rusty lines (the Virgin), wine-red, leaf-green, and brilliant lettuce green. The opposite group presents the same colours differently arranged.

In the scene of the Nativity, the arriving Magi and their horses (Plate 20) present a surprising combination of colours. The foremost animal, grey-white, carries a rider in slate tights, dark green kilt, and a pale fawn-coloured cloak. The middle figure, of whose horse only the legs are visible, disports a dark green cloak which flies out behind him. The last is borne by a superbly modelled Arab, of a pinkish terra-cotta colour, shadowed in dark purple and lit with white, the edges of the latter being tinged with blue so as to obtain the extreme of contrast and relief. Beneath the horses' feet, a shepherd in a broad-brimmed hat blows a horn. Below the Virgin, another, more youthful, is conversing with his goats (Plate 19. ii).

A further example of anti-naturalistic colour is exhibited in the head of a saint reproduced on Plate 83. i, a magnificent exposition of the Byzantine method of giving form to a dark mass by the application of light. This is painted entirely in leaf-green, ochreous white, and dark chocolate purple.

Once again, the unfortunate state of many of these frescoes must be remarked. The plaster has been mended, but in many cases so coarsely that the subject is barely distinguishable (see Plate 19. ii for example). Both here, and in the Peribleptos, supposing that the frescoes continue to survive, a discreet but competent artist is required to fill in the cracks and restore the compositions to unity and coherence. The peculiar significance of the paintings of Mistra, both for their intrinsic beauty, and for their value to the history of European art, is perhaps apparent; their relation to El Greco, and therefore to the present, will be discussed in the following chapter. Meanwhile, the fact that they are slowly disappearing cannot be sufficiently reiterated. In the whole of Europe and America, among all the lovers of art and art-loving societies, can no money be found to save them?

III. THE CRETAN SCHOOL ON MOUNT ATHOS

The Macedonian school and its tendencies represented, in the provinces of colour and light, a departure from the true Byzantine tradition. In compensation, it achieved, as the religious feeling of its time demanded, a measure of humanisation hitherto unknown. To this humanism, by a further widespread development in East European painting of which Mistra has survived as the centre, was assimilated the ancient heritage of brilliant, shining colour. But while, in the Macedonian school, the feeling, human though it be, is dolorous and concerned mainly with suffering, the paintings of Mistra, particularly of the Pantanassa, are filled with the joy and beauty of life. Then, within three decades, Constantinople, and Mistra herself, had fallen to the Turk. The spirit of an East European Renascence, such as Gemistos Plethon and his followers might have brought about, was stifled. And, for subsequent artists, reft of a cultural centre, only strict adherence to tradition could preserve their work from that dead-level of peasant incompetence which forthwith over-

10

took the Slav offshoots of Byzantine civilisation. Colour, however, the colour and light of the Peribleptos and the Pantanassa,
remained to them. And in the first half of the sixteenth century,
there arose the renowned school of Cretan painters, who were
ultimately found at work throughout the whole Levant, from
Venice to Mount Sinai. Their art is not humanistic; it is barely
sympathetic. Their aim, once more, is to evoke the awe of the
beholder by their unearthly combinations of colour, by the accentuation of every shadow and every light, not for the purposes of a
dramatic chiaroscuro, but in order to invest each form with the
maximum of identity and energy. In the section entitled "How
the Cretans work," from the Guide to Painting by Denys, monk
of Fourna of Agrapha, it is clearly explained that, for the painting
of faces, feet and hands, the form must first be sketched in "very
deep black," and the flesh colour then added sparingly. "Be
careful," writes the monk, "not to cover the whole face (with
flesh-colour), but only the illuminated parts, and to diminish it at
the edges." Such a precept illustrates how the true Byzantine
conception of form was carried to its conclusion, and how the
Cretan artists, to a greater extent than those of Mistra, relied on
the pattern of their lights to weld their compositions to a unity.
Thus, just as the impulse which prompted the Macedonian style
produced the early Sienese and Florentine schools, so, in yet closer
relationship, that behind the Cretans gave birth to El Greco; and
the very extremes of European painting are directly joined to the
same Byzantine root. But it is the misfortune of posterity that,
with the exception of small painted panels, always a secondary
province of Byzantine art and bearing no true relation to the
fresco-like conceptions and palette of Greco, really fine mural

paintings of the Cretan school have survived, with their original colouring intact, only in one place: the chapel of St. George in the monastery of St. Paul's on Mount Athos. Elsewhere the works of the Cretan artists are either wholly restored or else the products of an insufficient cultural tradition. None the less it is possible to determine from the existing monuments the essential character of the art of the Cretan school, and its importance.

The actual history of the Cretan school is obscure. But the name, unlike the "Macedonian," is a native one, traditionally handed down to modern usage. It has been widely maintained by such authorities as Professor Sotiriou of the Byzantine Museum in Athens that the Cretan painters owed their fame and name to icons alone. Such a theory is immediately discounted by the extract from the Guide to Painting quoted above, which explicitly refers, in its instructions concerning pigments, to mural decoration. Nor are actual instances of fresco-painters lacking. Both Theophanes and Zorzi, who decorated the monastery churches of the Lavra and Dionysiou on Mount Athos in 1535 and 1547 respectively, were actual natives of Crete.

Theophanes was traditionally called a pupil of Manuel Panselinos, whose talent, though authenticated specimens of it are unknown, is still revered by the monks of the Holy Mountain. Their names are found bracketed together in a Russian Guide to Painting dated 1738. Panselinos is described by Denys of Fourna as "of Thessalonica." Thus, if the style of the master in any way resembled that of the pupil, it is plain that the Cretan style had finally displaced the Macedonian of two centuries earlier in the latter's very stronghold.

It is a fact that, during the sixteenth and seventeenth centuries, the trade in icons was an important factor in the advertisement of the island painters. Panels by them are to be found in the monastery of St. Catherine on Mount Sinai, in the Patriarchal church of Alexandria, in nearly all the monasteries of Mount Athos, in the church of San Georgio dei Greci at Venice, and, of course, in Crete, where a notable series from the brush of Michael Damascenos is preserved in the cathedral of Herakleion. The artists signed themselves κρής like a trademark; panels by Angelos Kres, Neophytos Kres, and Jeremias Kres, dating from the first quarter of the sixteenth century, may all be seen in the Greek Orthodox churches of Cairo. This habit Greco continued.

It may well be asked why Crete, that complex of gigantic, barren mountains jutting from the southern Ægæan, should have been the seat of so widespread an art. The circumstances were favourable. While the Greek lands, save for a few diminutive islands, had succumbed, or were succumbing, to the Turks, Crete remained Venetian; and there alone Greek culture continued to develop. It might be supposed that this development, of which an account will be found in the following chapter, bore a Venetian stamp; in fact, it did not. But while Cretan painting remained more or less free of Italian influence, it cannot be denied that the surviving frescoes of the island exhibit, but for a certain delicacy of colour, nothing more than the crude technique of the popular monastic art. This absence of notable works of art is probably due to the habit of all Cretan artists of talent to seek their fortunes outside their native island, and to the incessant insurrections of the Turkish period, which have destroyed or mutilated all but the remotest churches. Certainly the natural environment is such as to inspire any painter with exactly that pronounced conception of form and light which distinguished the Cretan school. As the sun rises and sets over mountains whose eternal peaks dominate every coast of the island, their arid slopes, cleft by incessant gorges and escarpments, assume precisely that glassy pattern of light and shade which gives form to the artists' figures, draperies, and rocky backgrounds. The island exhales an atmosphere of grimness and austerity. It could produce nothing, the visitor feels, which is not unique. Its native artists could no more have painted in the Macedonian style than the Italians have built in the Gothic.

i. THE REFECTORY OF THE MONASTERY OF THE LAVRA (Plates 7, 72, 74. i, 74. ii, 87. ii).

This building in its original form was probably contemporary with the foundation of the monastery and completion of its church, about the year 1000 A.D. In 1512 its ancient cupolas were replaced by the coved wooden roof which now covers it; and its walls were repainted. These restorations were due to the initiative of "the most all-holy and honoured Metropolitan of Serres, Gennadios"; thus he is described in the verandah, where he appears in the grasp of a military saint, holding a model of the refectory.

As illustrative of colour and technique, none of the paintings in the Athonite refectories is of any value. Either they are blackened with the perpetual smoke of candles and lamps; or else they have been carefully, but uncompromisingly, restored. Even when, as in the present case, the refectories have fallen into comparative disuse owing to the idiorhythmic rule of life, which allows the maintenance of private kitchens, the renovations appear to have been conscientiously carried out. That of the Lavra, of which a general view will be found on Plate 7, exhibits, none the less, one composition of great dignity and beauty, "the Dormition of our holy Father Athanasius" (Plate 87. ii). This was St. Athanasius of Athos, who founded the Lavra, the earliest monastery on the Mountain, in 963, and was killed by the fall of the main dome of the church about the year 1000.[1]

In the centre of a landscape of hermits, very similar to that surrounding the Dormition of St. Ephraim the Syrian on Plate 86, the saint lies encompassed by the walls and inhabitants of the monastery; above him appear the domes of the church which caused his death, together with the now demolished cell and library above the narthex, where he lived. The scene is full of sympathy and feeling, and is very large, measuring roughly sixteen feet by seven. Another remarkable composition is the elaborate Last Judgement (see Plates 72, 74. i, ii), which occupies the three walls of the south transept. The features common to this and Greco's Dream of Philip II. are remarked on page 191.

ii. The Church of the Monastery of the Lavra (Plates 12. ii, 33. ii, 38. i, 49. ii, 52. i, 53. i, 69. i, 69. ii, 82. i, 83. ii, 85. iii).

A dedicatory panel, inserted into the scene of the Dormition of the Virgin over the doorway into the nave, reads as follows: "The church of the mother, virgin, maiden, is decorated from floor and foundations by means of the subscription, care, and peregrinations, of Neophytos, President of the illustrious Verria, and hailing from the city of Athens, during the Patriarchate of Jeremias and the abbotship of Cyprian, in the year 1535, by the hand of the monk Theophanes." This Theophanes, who has

[1] See *The Station*, by Robert Byron, pp. 53 and 54.

already been mentioned as the pupil of Panselinos, worked also
at the Meteora monasteries, where, in the year 1527, he described
himself as "monk of Strelitza in Crete." At the monastery of
Stavronikita on Athos, where he was employed in 1546, he was
assisted by his son Symeon.

The frescoes of the Lavra church, like those of the refectory,
appear to have undergone the most thorough restoration. Though
the light and delicacy of their paint has thus been wholly lost, the
work of renovation must have been entrusted to an artist of some
talent; and the felicity of the original modelling of the faces and
draperies is still apparent in such scenes as the Exaltation of the
Cross (Plate 85. iii) or the Dormition of the Virgin (Plate 69. i, ii).
In the scene of the Transfiguration (Plate 33. ii), the rocks are a
dull ochre, and the draperies invested with a mauve tint; the aura
of the central figure is grey and white. These tones seem to pre-
dominate throughout the church. One remarkable head, sensitive, unconventional, and evidently taken from life, is that of the
servant in the Supper at Emmaus (see Plate 83. ii), whose shock
of tousled hair is red.

The authors regret that they were unable to visit the Meteora
monasteries, where it may be possible to examine the work of
Theophanes in its original state, and thus to judge how far his
real talent is displayed or concealed in the present church.

iii. THE OLD CHURCH OF THE MONASTERY OF XENOPHONTOS
(Plates 6, 13. ii, 21. i, 23. i, 24. iii, 27. ii, 27. iii, 38. ii, 44,
51. i, 51. ii, 54. ii, 56, 62. i, 62. ii, 65, 67. ii).

This church, a fine example of the small Greek cross type, is
now disused; and the absence of the elaborate furniture prescribed

by the Orthodox ritual makes it possible to obtain a true idea of the decorative value of the paintings which cover every available wall-space (see Plate 6). Two artists worked here: one, Antony, decorated the nave in 1544; the other, Theophanes, who is not to be confused with the artist of the Lavra, was employed, in 1563, to duplicate certain scenes and to decorate the narthex. From his hand are the latter's Ascension, reproduced on Plate 62. i, and probably the Crucifixion with three crosses on Plate 51. ii. The paintings were restored in 1902-3.

Certain features in the work of Antony, such as the Sleeping Christ over the doorway (Plate 24. iii), and the sun and moon, with their peculiar veilings, on either side of the crucified Christ (see Plate 51. i), recall the iconography of the Macedonian school. His colouring is completely distinct from any on the Mountain or at Mistra. The skies make no pretence of being blue or indigo; they are flat, charcoal black, and thus accentuate the extreme luminosity of the burnt siena, faint burnt pink, amber, olive, and wine-red, with which his scenes are depicted. In that of the Entry into Jerusalem (Plate 38. ii), the ass is painted in blue-grey and yellow-grey, against a rocky background of dead burnt siena. The seated Christ wears a mantle of dark grey and a skirt of chocolate. On the beholder's right, the walls and buildings of the city show a dirty, rank yellow. And the foliage of the tree is olive. The masterpiece of the cycle is the Crucifixion (Plate 51. i). Here, against the prevailing flat, black sky, a body of translucent olive green, having touches of pink in its lights, is nailed to a burnt siena cross; the robes of the woman beneath are of that colour and grey; the buildings ochre; the moon is grey and white; and the sun a tawny chocolate. In the Dormition of the Virgin (Plate 65), the same tints are interspersed with wine-red. The significance of these frescoes, with their austere palette and violent lights, does not derive, save when taken altogether as a decorative cycle, from artistic merit. Their inept drawing and obvious difficulties of composition show how the Byzantine cultural tradition was already on the wane. But, beneath these crudities, an extraordinary emotional realism is apparent. The Crucifixion (Plate 51. i.), with its livid body, and disturbed planets, is ghastly; the agony of the Lamenting Women (Plate 56) is intensified by the cadaverous human shell beneath them. In the Dormition of the Virgin (Plate 65), a real beauty of composition is attained, which depends mainly on the rhythm and pattern of the lighted draperies. In this respect, these frescoes, more than any other, approach the individual genius of Greco. Even the method of painting is the same. The highlights have doubtless been subsequently intensified; but the frescoes bear no sign of having been wholly repainted; and the bold, coarse impressionism of their technique certainly derives from the original Antony. Such brushwork, modified by the limitations of canvas, was Greco's most potent instrument in the achievement of his unearthly luminosity.

iv. THE CHURCH AND REFECTORY OF THE MONASTERY OF DIONYSIOU (Plates 32. iii, 45. ii, 54. i, 63, 70, 71. i, 71. ii, 75. i).

Almost the entire monastery of Dionysiou having been burnt in the year 1534, the church, according to an inscription, was refounded and decorated at the expense of "John Peter, Voivode of all Moldo-Wallachia, during the abbotship of Matthew the priestmonk, in the year 1547." The painter employed, records a *typikon* of the monastery, was a native of Crete, and bore the Venetian name of Zorzi; "an admirable artist" he is termed. This sentiment posterity can scarcely echo. Though he was responsible for the only instance of accurate architectural perspective on the Holy Mountain, that in the background of the Pentecost scene (see Plate 63), he could not escape the Italianate influence implicit in his name. His colour is a mere sequence of Preraphaelite reds and blues, the former pervading even the aura of the transfigured Christ on Plate 32. iii. His draperies are too windy; and his attempts at graceful posture unfortunate, when combined with the rigid iconography of the Orthodox Church.

Happier and more original, though presumably not his work, are the apocalyptic paintings which decorate the refectory cloister, and probably date from the same year (Plates 70, 71. i, ii). That of the Four Horsemen is more than quaint, exhibiting a mobility almost Persian in its sense of equestrian action. The interior of the refectory, again of the same date, contains a Last Judgement (Plate 75. i), whose composition bears a remarkable iconographic resemblance to that which Giotto executed some 250 years before in the chapel of the Arena at Padua. A heavenly Ladder in a corner of the refectory dates from the year 1603, and was erected in memory of Father Demetrius of Pesikos.

v. The Chapel of St. George at the Monastery of St. Paul (Plates 14. i, 15. i, 18, 23. ii, 31. i, 31. ii, 35. i, 38. iii, 61. ii, 64. ii).

The date of this tiny barrel-vaulted chapel, perched up on the back-wall of the monastery, where its slender square tower rises to assist the peak of Athos in its passage to the sky, is concealed by what is possibly the most obscure Greek epigraph in existence. Persistent scholars, familiar possibly with the official signatures of Patriarchs, have deciphered the following sentence: "This lovely temple of the great martyr George was decorated, in the year 1423, by a subscription of Mitrophanes, the treasure-keeper of the great church of Christ (that of the monastery), by the hand of Andronicus Byzagios, and consecrated to St. George on the day of the inauguration of this church, the feast-day of the saint, instead of on the day of the Entry (that of the Virgin into the Temple: November 21st), the Metropolitan of Salonica officiating, in the abbotship of Ananias, 1425." It has been observed, however, that, immediately beneath this inscription, there are visible the remains of older Slav hieroglyphics, among which Professor Millet, by the aid of a special light, has discerned the date 1555. The explanation of this contradiction is that, about the year 1844, when he founded the new church now occupying the courtyard beneath, the abbot Sophronius Calligas entrusted the restoration of this inscription to the forger Simonides; the reason doubtless being the then revival of Greek patriotism, and the wish to obliterate, somewhat ungratefully, all traces of Slav benefaction. Professor Millet therefore dates the paintings from the year 1555. If he is right, there can be wanting no greater testimony to the continued vitality of Byzantine art in the century following the fall of Constantinople. The paintings appear to have escaped restoration entirely; and though their transparent delicacy is in many ways reminiscent of Mistra, the prominence of their lights, and absence of any marked sympathy or humanism, are essentially characteristic of the later Cretan school. Of this school, they are the only cycle on the Holy Mountain that has escaped restoration, and in which the true virtue of Byzantine colouring, as observed at Mistra, is still apparent.

In the scene of the Raising of Lazarus, reproduced on Plate 35. i, the castle in the middle background glitters white against a mouldy indigo sky; while on either side rise rocky eminences: the first translucent as dark honey, lit with white and shadowed in olive; the second of a darker tone, amber, with tawny shadows and honey lights. In the foreground, the snowy white of the castle is continued in the swathings of the mummy; the lid of the tomb is marbled in beryl green; and of those carrying it, the foremost is dressed in transparent burnt pink, the hinder in blueish mauve. The group beneath the castle are mainly white, touched in with the same mauve or pink. Christ, erect, with auburn hair, displays a rich wine-red sleeve and skirt, over which is draped a mantle of white, shaded in sharp blue and black. The figure behind him is amber, and the one behind that, slate, shaded in cold blue. The colour of the faces is natural, but has a slight tan, which appears black in the photographs, and thus distorts the reproductions.

In the scene of the Transfiguration (Plate 31. i, ii), of which, owing to a beam, the camera was unable to obtain a straight view, there are three distinct sets of rocks: the first, counting from the beholder's left, are depicted in a peculiar burnt mauve, very light, with chocolate shadows; the second, in amber, with olive shadows; and the third in beryl green; the prominences of all three being discreetly touched with white. Atop the mauve rocks, on Christ's right, stands Moses, a figure of ethereal beauty, tightly draped in a kind of honey-coloured silken tulle, with olive shadows, and light touches of reddish gamboge. The draperies of the central figure are white, with honey shadows; the circle and the diamond of the aura successively dark grey, light grey and white, with black rays; but the curving square, between the circle and the diamond, is of two shades of amber, edged with white. On Christ's left stands Elias, draped in slate colour, with a cold blue sleeve. The collapsed apostles display more numerous colours, as becomes a foreground. That beneath Moses is draped also in honey-colour; but this has both olive and deep red shadows, and is lit with very pale blue and yellow. The central figure is clothed in slate and cold blue. And the last has a drapery of beryl green, heavily shaded in wine-red. In the intermediate groups, Christ appears in the same dress as in the Raising of Lazarus.

The scene of the Presentation in the Temple (Plate 23. ii), exhibits an architectural setting of great beauty. The building on the left, which, in the photograph, is partially obscured by the wooden cross of the iconostasis, displays a white front, shaded in olive green and honey yellow, and an amber pediment, above which appears the hint of a tiled roof outlined in scarlet. The ciborium in the centre is marbled in pale plum-colour and burnt siena, and is supported on pillars of rusty chocolate. Symeon's throne is also marbled, beryl green. The floor is ochre. Symeon is draped in slate, mauve, and white. The Virgin wears a mantle of rich burnt chocolate, beneath which hangs a cold grey-blue skirt. The figure behind her disports an aquamarine mantle, and a white skirt shadowed in amber and red. Joseph wears the same colours as Symeon. The bible on the altar attracts the eye with the brilliant pink edges of its pages.

In the Nativity, reproduced on Plate 18, the rocky background is honey-coloured, shaded to a foreground of amber and olive, and plentifully lit with white.   Above the peak appears a star of grey and white.   Of the angels on the beholder's left, the hindmost displays beryl green draperies; the middle a rusty red tunic with mauve lights and claret shadows, over which hangs a honey-coloured mantle; the third, a mantle of mauve and white and a cold blue tunic; all the wings are burnt siena, with the feathers outlined in white. The angel on the beholder's right, or the Virgin's left, is clothed in a mantle of mauve and slate and a tunic of burnt pink shaded in wine-red, and converses with a shepherd in a beryl-green mantle shadowed in pink, beneath which deeply tanned legs find rest in buskins coloured like autumn leaves. The three horses on the Virgin's right are successively greyish white, dull reddish pink, and olive grey.   The Virgin herself, lying on a cushion of burnt pink, wears a mantle of deep wine-red with rusty lights; her skirt is of pale Prussian blue.   The manger, baby, ass and sheep are grey and white; the ox amber. In the row at the bottom stands an olive-tree with silvery grey foliage.   Beneath it sits a grey and white dog.

It will be seen from the photograph that a large crack cuts across the middle of this scene.   In Professor Millet's reproduction, published in 1926, this blemish, though apparent, does not show an actual parting of the plaster.   Already, half the whole cycle has completely disappeared; and the sad condition of many of the remaining scenes is illustrated by the mutilated, though still beautiful Entry into Jerusalem reproduced on Plate 38. iii. The process of disintegration is continuing, as the monks themselves admit.   The chapel lies in an unfortunate position, immediately beneath the peak of Athos, which rises 6,000 feet above it in a series of huge precipices. Even in summer, this mountain acts as focus to every vagrant cloud in the Ægæan sky. During winter terrific storms sweep round it; and the monks, though efforts at reconstruction have been made, and though the chapel is not disused, are impotent against the elements. Must these frescoes also, the gem of post-Constantinopolitan art in Eastern Europe, be allowed to perish? The original bloom on the painting, which alone on the Mountain has escaped restoration, cries at least for a fixative. Under present conditions it can be wiped off with a feather brush.

vi. The Chapel of St. Nicolas Adjoining the Church of the Monastery of the Lavra (Plate 64. i).

" This divine and holy chapel of our divine and holy monastery, which is honoured in the name of Nicolas, greatest among prelates and worker of miracles, was decorated by the subscription and peregrination of Cyprian, worthiest even among monks, during the abbotship of our most sainted father Ignatius, priest-monk, in 1560, by the hand of the most hapless Frangos Catellanos of Thebes in Bœotia." This artist also worked at the Meteora monastery of Barlaam in the year 1565. His frescoes at the Lavra, of which a Pentecost is reproduced on Plate 64. i, exhibit a charming delicacy and sense of design. Their colouring is over-sweet, a rose-pink prevailing.

vii. The Church of the Monastery of Docheiariou (Plates 21. ii, 23. iii, 32. i, 58. ii, 86).

This building is the largest church on Athos, and was erected in 1568, the paintings being executed on completion. In 1855 the latter were wholly and ruthlessly restored. Thus, as at Chilandari, their remaining virtue lies in their decorative ensemble, which is enhanced by the size of the church, and in the force of the stereotyped compositions beneath the hard modern colouring. Two paintings at least, however, appear to have escaped renovation. One is a seated Virgin, in which her chocolate mantle is lighted with lines of dull gold in the manner of an icon; by her side stands a charming vase of red and white flowers. The other is the large landscape scene, about fifteen feet high, showing the Dormition of St. Ephraim the Syrian (Plate 86). As in that of St. Athanasius of Athos at the Lavra, a great sympathy pervades the lower group. Around are depicted the usual hermit scenes. The importance of this composition, and of Byzantine landscape generally in relation to Greco, is discussed in the following chapter.

viii. THE REFECTORY OF THE MONASTERY OF DOCHEIARIOU (Plate 9. i).

This building, whose date, and that of its decoration, are uncertain, contains a remarkable series of apocalyptic paintings. That of God, illustrated on Plate 9. i, displays a figure robed in a grey mantle and a rosy skirt, in whose hands is a golden book, and at whose lap stands a snow-white ram with olive green horns. "And I saw," wrote St. John in the fifth chapter of the Revelations, "in the right hand of him that sat on the throne a book written within and on the backside, sealed with seven seals. . . . And, lo, in the midst of the throne . . . stood a Lamb as it had been slain, having seven horns and seven eyes, which are the seven Spirits of God sent forth into all the earth."

ix. THE REFECTORY OF THE MONASTERY OF CHILANDARI (Plate 40. i).

The frescoes in this building, unlike those of the monastery's church, have escaped restoration, and were painted in 1621. They depict both the Akathist Hymn and the story of St. Sabbas, the founder of the monastery. In the apse, above the chief seat, is a fine composition of the Last Supper, which is reproduced on Plate 40. i.

x. THE CHURCH OF ST. NICOLAS AT MISTRA (Plate 16. ii).

This building was erected at the beginning of the seventeenth century, and though largely roofless, still preserves the figure of the Announcing Angel reproduced on Plate 16. ii. On to a pavement of marble, tesselated in green, blue, wine-red, and amber, the celestial creature flutters down, the feathers of the wings being outlined in gold, and the body draped in a mantle of deep wine-red brilliantly lit with scarlet, beneath which hangs a skirt of the typical Mistra sky-blue. This figure, both in colour and strength of line, is very attractive.

It is hoped that the above outline will have impressed the reader with the salient characteristics of later Byzantine painting. If he can preserve the impression, the following chapter will perhaps explain how this last product of East European culture was ultimately expanded and carried westward.

CHAPTER 5

THE CLIMAX OF INTERPRETATION

THE first, most distinct, and ultimately most enduring impression received by the beholder of Greco's greater pictures is that he is in the presence of a mind; a mind concerned not exclusively with beauty or drama, melancholy or joy, as those of other artists, but busy with all the lessons and all the knowledge of the world; a mind, not versatile like those of the Renascence, which diffused their power in engineering, speculation, and debauch, but concentrated wholly in the purpose of expression through a single medium.   Such minds have generally chosen words.   Greco's chose paint.   It may be supposed that his intellect was neither subtle nor consistent; that, in fact, he was one who saw the truth and grasped it, rather than pursued it by tortuous processes.   This, when that truth is truth, is the definition of genius.   But, though Greco's pictures, like the sculptures of Chartres, may well take their place in histories of philosophy, their author was primarily, and above all his thoughts, an artist and technician.   Few great men can show such a balance of accomplishment.

Yet, other artists have had thoughts also.   Blake strove to express them, and failed for lack of exactly those technical qualities which Greco possessed.   Giovanni Bellini invested grotesque allegories with the frigid, calculated beauty of the early Renascence. Botticelli carried the static humanism of the later Middle Ages to

a climax of loveliness.   Michael Angelo at times burst away
from his slavery to the Antique.   Some melody seems to be
emerging from the concatenation of realism and symbols which
still deafens the twentieth century.   But where others have moved
timidly, or without sufficient capacity, Greco rushes in and con-
quers.   His language is the language of enormous perception.
He did not peep at the world through science, Christ, or Antique
heroics; he looked it in the eyes as a hunter his lion; arriving in
the West from without, he saw it as it lay, maudlin and baroque,
clay for Greek detachment to mould into a permanent memorial
to the verities of human character and human aspiration.   The
conventional religious clichés, the whirling clouds, the anæmic,
semi-bearded Spanish faces, the ill-formed bodies, the idiosyncrasies of friends, the occasional allegory, the local view—all were
material to hand.   The Byzantines, by depicting the mystery of
the Gospel, had sought to express the mystery of the faith; Greco,
by depicting Spain, sought now to express the mystery of the
world.   The method of both was the same: intelligible incident
and form were used to envisage man's inner quest.   In the process, following the iconoclast controversy, the Byzantines had succeeded in discarding symbolism; Greco now discarded formalism
as well.   Mentally, their method remained the same.

I. Greco's Character: Cretan Culture and Society
after the Fall of Constantinople

The outposts of Greek independence, Constantinople, Mistra,
Trebizond, had fallen in the middle of the fifteenth century.
Already, since 1204, poverty and foreign encroachments had been

eating into the vitality of Greek life; now the Turks had annexed the crumbling structure for their own damnation.   Byzantine culture, as we have seen, was not immediately extinguished; but being robbed of its central channels, a drought set in.   There was only the past. The artists sank to copyists. By the opening of the seventeenth century, the Cretan school had lost its pre-eminence and the process was complete.   And though Greek painting never descended to the folk-level of the neighbouring Slavs; though it always retained, till destroyed completely by the oleograph of the nineteenth century, something of the brilliance of colour and technical delicacy which the Byzantines had perfected; it relied, during the seventeenth and eighteenth centuries, on ecclesiastical formula alone for its inspiration; and the value of its then works, judged by universal standards, is decorative and no more.

Domenicos Theotocopoulos, known to history as El Greco, was born at Candia in Crete in 1541.   Of the Cretan landscape, of the peculiar atmospheric environment exhaled by that grim and luminous island, something has been said (see page 148).   But environment does not suffice. There have been great sons of the soil, forceful and enduring soldiers and statesmen hailing from barbarism and illiteracy, or incalculable publicists like St. Francis, whose very attraction has lain in their native simplicity. Such qualities are precisely those which Greco had not. His greatness was a poise, which had sifted the intellectual fashions of post-Renascence Europe; a sophisticated equilibrium between the cold enquiry and amorous mysticism which characterised his time. He was witty; he was extravagant in living and violent of opinion; the learned men of Spain rejoiced in his company.   His theory of art as a science, to be practised scientifically like other sciences, defied Aristotle; he wrote about architecture; he had a zest for legal battle, and conducting his own cases in a foreign country and tongue was usually successful.   He was a man in whose acquaintance we should have delighted.   Such endowments, though their potentiality is innate, are not the products of the soil.   They are developed only by education and society.   The first step, therefore, in the estimation of Greco's achievement, is to examine the conditions of his early life; conditions far different from those of his less fortunate compatriots on the mainland.

At the partition of the Greek Empire in 1204, Crete fell to Boniface of Montferrat, who promptly sold it to the Venetians. And for 465 years, till the famous twenty-one-year siege of Candia that ended in 1669, the Venetians ruled in the island.   They ruled it to good purpose; first as a trading-station; last as a military bulwark against the Turk.   Its importance was such that scarcely an account of travels in the East during this period survives without reference to it as a port of call.   In so long a time, and under such conditions of activity, a homogeneous society formed.   But it is a curious fact that, despite the steady influx of Venetian colonists, and the unceasing passage of Greeks to Venice, that society bore not an Italian, but a Greek, stamp.   It was the Venetians who joined the Orthodox Church, and founded Orthodox monasteries, which still exhibit their charters blazoned with the Lion of St. Mark.   It was the Venetians who borrowed the Greek tongue, and finding it their speech, wrote it in Latin script; of the converse no manuscript has survived; whereas in Asia Minor, up till 1923, the Turkish vernacular written in Greek was a common phenomenon.   Nor, astonishing though it seem, did the native art of painting show itself susceptible to the gorgeous and facile taste of the ruling republic. Writes Gerola, an Italian, and as such avowedly unsympathetic to all manifestations of Byzantine culture: "It seems inexplicable that, at the most splendid and brilliant period of Venetian painting, when the works of that divine art were spreading as far as Crete, when the Cretans themselves were hastening to the lagoons to perfect themselves in an art so renowned—that, even then, the painting of the island did not surrender to the attractions of new and genial inspiration. On the contrary, not only in the Greek churches, but also in the Latin, frescoes were still executed exclusively in the Greek manner; and in the Venetian temples themselves, the Byzantine hagiography reigned supreme."[1]

More striking evidence, however, of a progressive native culture is provided by the numerous and unique literary productions of the island. The earliest of these, dating from the middle of the fifteenth century, bears a distinctly national character: lamenting the vanished glories of Constantinople and the lustre of such monarchs as Constantine the Great and Justinian, it hails Crete henceforth as the centre of Hellenism; Constantine Dragases, the last Emperor, is made to request decapitation with his dying breath, that his head may be despatched to his beloved Cretans. Another poem, written by Sachlikis about a hundred years later, presents a vivid picture of the life of the island, and of the harmonious relations then prevailing between Greeks and Italians. Sachlikis belonged to the local aristocracy, the ἀρχοντορωμαῖοι, whose prestige the Venetian authorities were at

---

[1] Exceptions, of course, are to be found in the panels of painters like Michael Damascenos, Greco's contemporary, who were actually trained in Venice.

pains to reinforce with titles of their own.   At the age of fourteen he forsook his books and sought prostitutes instead.   His
days were devoted to hunting and the breeding of hounds.   At
length he was ruined; his friend the governor found him employment as a lawyer; but unable to retrieve his fortune by honest
means, he reverted to his old life, and eventually expiated his
extravagance in prison, where he committed his experiences to
verse.   Later, he wrote a poem of admonition for the son of a
friend: there were three things, he said, that a young man should
avoid: street-walking at night, harlots, and dice.   Such, if he
chose to taste its pleasures, was the society into which Domenicos
Theotocopoulos was born.   Him, too, we may imagine, in view
of his future disregard of the marriage-tie, casting a greedy four-
teen-year-old eye on the ladies of Candia.

The best known of the Cretan poems was written about a century after Greco was born by a Cretan of Italian descent named
Vincenzo Cornaro, who hailed from Sitia in the east of the island.
Entitled *The Erotokritos,* its ten thousand lines did not prevent
its dissemination throughout the Greek lands; and until the War,
wherever Greeks were there it was found also, from New York
to the Crimea.   In the great cities of the Levant, despite occasional crudely printed editions, it descended by oral tradition till
the beginning of the last century.   Its hero and heroine became
proverbial among the Greek people, as Hamlet or King Arthur
are to the English; and though its epic form was borrowed from
revived Western classicism, and its plot may even have derived
from that which gave Shakespeare the tale of Romeo and Juliet,
its idiom, allusion, and sentiment, show it to be the product of an
essentially Greek society.   Another Cretan poem is *The Fair*

Shepherdess, a comparatively short pastoral of five hundred lines, whose inspiration, apart from the contemporary fashion for pastorals, appears to be entirely native, and which describes the natural beauties of the island with the sensitive appreciation typical of the Greek of to-day.   This work was edited and published in 1627 by the Cretan, Nicolas Drymitinos.   As he states that there were already several texts to choose from, it was presumably composed in the latter half of the sixteenth century.

In addition to poems, there were plays, whose tenor, construction, and measure of artistic originality, have lately been revealed to English readers by the three translations of Professor F. H. Marshall, supplemented by a critical introduction from Mr. John Mavrogordato (see bibliography).   The first play contained in their joint volume is entitled *Abraham's Sacrifice,*[1] and is based on Luigi Groto's *Lo Isach,* which was published at Venice in 1586.   A careful comparison of the two reveals a Shakespearian parallel.   For it is the Greek author, who, like Shakespeare, is expanding and humanising the Italian plot, thus producing a curious effect of transition from the mediæval mystery play to the modern family drama : Isaac promises to bring his mother back some apples and scented foliage, at the same time leaving a message for his teacher, in case the latter complains that he is late; Sarah replies with a gift of pears, which she has saved for her "darling child" from the day before.   The second play, a typical "Elizabethan tragedy of love and blood," was written by the Cretan, George Hortatzis, and was published in 1637.   The dedication, to John Mourmouris, reveals the same pride in Cretan

[1] A Dutch translation was performed with success in Holland in 1920.

culture as the signatures of Theotocopoulos and his less distinguished fellow-artists:

"So out of thousand persons dowered with an abundant grace,
    By virtue famed or letters' art or else by wealth or place,
    Who shine as do the stars of heaven in Crete from end to end,
    And shed on her their lustre bright and old-time brilliance lend,
    E'en as in those far distant times when Minos held his sway,
    And Crete him as her overlord deemed honour to obey,
    Thee have I singled out from all, most noble Mourmouris,
    Thou orator. . . ."

The third play is the Gyparis, "a pastoral tragi-comedy," in which the author, who was probably a native of Rethymno, "transferred the scene from Arcadia to Mount Ida, and gave the theme of a hopeless love redeemed at the last moment by divine intervention to real Cretan shepherds and shepherdesses."

These plays are only the best known examples of a numerous collection, of which other examples are still preserved in the library of St. Mark's and await an editor.   The whole series, says Professor Hesseling in his *Histoire de la littérature grecque moderne,* exhibit a skill, "from which one may conclude that there is no question of isolated attempts, but of the remains of an abundant output."   And they were written, in his opinion, "for a public of cultivated and sophisticated townsmen." "Those which have been published," says Mr. Mavrogordato, "are not masterpieces; but they are outstanding achievements in the body of modern Greek literature, which tends to be rather overweighted with folk-songs and other forms of popular art.   The language in which they are written, after allowance has been made for the numerous Cretan formations, provides a normal and lively idiom. . . .   It is a relief to find the perfectly natural spoken language applied to a thoroughly sophisticated theme; and the natural beauties of the untaught mind, the lament, the love-song, and the proverb, adapted and refined by the conscious art of an educated poet."   Thus, as the author remarks, "there was in Crete a Greek community sufficiently cultured to demand the perform-ance of plays of the same general type as those which were being enjoyed all over Western Europe."   And he asks whether, given peace and stability, a "modern Greek culture of permanent value to Europe might not have developed."   To which all that can be said is that Europe received from that society Greco instead; and has at length, by continuing his example, begun to forget Pheidias.

Greco's fearless and direct habit of speech and mind were typical of the remarkable islanders amongst whom he was born.   It was the Cretans whom, at the last siege of Constantinople, the whole Turkish army was unable to dislodge, and who were eventually allowed to depart honourably and unscathed.   Cyril Lukaris, the great Patriarch of the seventeenth century, who corresponded with the Archbishop of Canterbury in the reign of James I., and ulti-mately threatened such a revival of Orthodoxy that the Jesuits persuaded the Turks to drown him, was a Cretan.   Eleftherios Venizelos, whose personality led the victors of the Great War into the deepest follies of the Peace, is a Cretan to-day; and likewise the Patriarch Meletios, now of Alexandria, whose personal strength alone saved him from the murderous intentions of a paid mob at Constantinople in 1921.   The mountains give the race its character; but their barren escarpments imprison its activities. Like the Irish, the Cretans have sought their fame in other lands. In Venice, particularly, they formed the nucleus of a Greek colony, which numbered 5,000 in 1470 and by 1606 had risen to

14,000.   One of their number, George Palæocappa, became rector
of the university of Padua in the sixteenth century; the calligraphy
of another, Angelos Vergitzes, was employed to design the famous
type known as *Grec du Roi,* which was set up at Paris under
Francis I.   Mark Musurus, another, helped found the Aldine
press,[1] was a friend of Erasmus, and talked to Pope Leo X. of the
glories of Constantinople that would come when the Greeks regained their capital.   And the Cretan Demetrius Ducas super-
vised the printing of Cardinal Ximenes' famous polyglot bible at
Alcala in Spain.   Nor was he Greco's only predecessor in that
country.   On his arrival at Toledo, his compatriot, Antony
Calosynas, already enjoyed a reputation in that city for his skill
both as a doctor and a poet.

These Greek exiles were proud of their race; but they were
prouder still of the fact that they were Cretans.   Another of their
number, Zacharias Calliergi, set up a press of his own in Venice,
and in 1499 published the *Etymologicum Magnum.*   This book,
undertaken at the expense of a rich Cretan, Nicolas Vlastos, and
under the patronage of Anne, daughter of the unfortunate High
Admiral Notaras, who was executed by Mahomet II., contains a
prefatory poem by Mark Musurus, extolling the part played by his
fellow islanders in its production.   " As the soaring eagle," it runs,
"impelled from heights incognisable, routs the birds of prey; as the
sun, mounting his chariot, outshines his sister's light; and as she has
made of the stars but a vanity; so has the ancient form of these
characters, born of file and reed, been eliminated.   I marvel how,

[1] In 1604, there was living in Toledo, aged seventy-five, Manusso Theotocopoulos, presumably Greco's elder brother.   The name Manusso suggests
some connection with the famous family of printers.

with chisel and scalpel, this range of intricate types has been cut and chased, and how the impalpable accents have been firmly fixed between the straight-set lines and impended on the vowels. But why do I marvel at the Cretans' talent, since it was Minerva's self, at her father's behest, who taught them the beauties of art? A Cretan has cut them. A Cretan has fashioned the bits of copper. A Cretan has fastened them each to each. A Cretan was the lead-founder. A Cretan, namesake of victory (Nicolas), has borne the cost. A Cretan (Musurus) celebrates these events. It is the Cretan Jove who smiles on the Cretans. Therefore let us turn suppliants, and hope that the father of the benefactor, having thus named his son, may not see the name belie its prophecy. May Nicolas vanquish all competitors. Jove has assented. For the types of divine Hellas are the pride of the sons of the Greeks."

It is clear from this poem that the Cretan scholars and workmen in Italy at the end of the fourteenth century already formed a kind of patriotic brotherhood, conscious and arrogant of success. And when at length the boy Domenicos Theotocopoulos, not unfamiliar with the dissolute society of towns and fairly grounded in the education of his time, had acquired the spirit, colour, and technical processes of his native art, and grown conscious of the power within him, every precedent called him from his island. He was a subject of Venice; numbers of his countrymen were already there established. Thither, therefore he sailed. And he remained in Italy some fifteen years.

II. Greco's Character : Venice and Rome

It is in no sense the object of this chapter to present a complete survey either of Greco's life or of his painting.   These have been undertaken in more authoritative books.   And students of art are already familiar with, and weary of, the repeated estimates of Greco's debt to his Italian contemporaries.   Those estimates the present writer is concerned neither to deny nor to sustain.   It has simply been his intention to reveal, through a cursory examination of the psychological circumstances that produced later Byzantine painting and of its surviving monuments, that the basic elements of Greco's character, taste, thought, and æsthetic conception, were essentially Greek, and essentially a product, however belated, of the Byzantine civilisation.   The logic of the case is embodied in the St. Maurice.   This picture was painted between 1580 and 1584.   The artist must have begun it within three or four years of his arrival in Spain.   He had spent a decade and a half in Italy.   And the St. Maurice derives from past or contemporary Italian painting as nearly as Cézanne's *Bourgade dans les arbres* from a Japanese miniature of Fuji Yama.   Nor can any previous Spanish painting help in the least degree to explain its origin. These facts have not hitherto been explained, because the later manifestations of mediæval Greek culture have not hitherto been regarded as an interesting or accessible province of history. Titian, Tintoretto, and Michael Angelo, nourished the seed, like the sun, the rain, and the wind.   But the seed was there.   Once it has been shown that it was there, Titian, Tintoretto, and Michael Angelo, become relatively unimportant.   The stages of Greco's

Italian sojourn may therefore be summarised in as few words as possible.

The young Greek became a pupil of Titian. And his early pictures certainly show that at first he was much influenced by Tintoretto. The very distinction between these two Venetian masters is important. For whereas the first was the very incarnation of the High Renascence, radiating its warm colours through the length and breadth of Europe, the austere feeling of the second tended to resist that worldly movement. Both in the form of his figures, and in the dependence of his compositions on their pattern, he recalls the mosaics of St. Mark's and of the surrounding islands. Further, it may almost be said that the distinction between the whole of Venetian colouring and that of the Umbrians derived from the former's affinity with the Byzantine; for Venice and her chiefest and earliest monuments were Byzantine. But of the principle of colour relation possessed by the painters of Mistra and by Greco, the Venetians, even Tintoretto, beyond a certain obvious tendency to shot stuffs, had no inkling.

The art with which Greco found himself in contact, cannot, therefore, have been unsympathetic; it were not as though he had fallen into the clutches of Perugino and Raphael. For its scenic grandeur, delicious insight into human pleasure, textural use of paint, and sheer capacity for representation, he doubtless paid it homage. But except for a temporary interlude, exemplified by his portrait of the Maltese knight Vincentio Anastagi, he did not succumb to a mere imitation of it, like his compatriots in the town. The various versions of his Christ in the Temple, painted during his Venetian period, exhibit unmistakable traces of his native tradition: the brilliant touch of cold honey yellow in the foreground is a colour that no Venetian ever employed; and the rhythm of the bodies is the one feature which Tintoretto borrowed most markedly from the Byzantine monuments around him, and which he never used with half such success as Greco. Nevertheless, in this protracted tutelary stage of his life, Greco learned much: a supreme dexterity in the application of actual paint, and in the achievement of textural contrast by the sudden transition from large to very small brushes; and, most important, an ability, not only to draw, but to place his figures in such circumstances and positions that none but he could have drawn them. It was this ability which enabled him to accomplish the final liberation of that seed which had been implanted in European art by the iconoclast controversy of the eighth century, and which, in fear of Hellenistic naturalism, had retired its chastity, during the intervening centuries, within an armour of formalism. Singlehanded he tore aside his own cumbrous garments, the garments of a millennium. The body was his own; Venice the scissors. He accomplished another Renascence; for us, the more profound.

The process was complete, though the fruit of it was yet to be seen. And the time came when Greco moved to Rome. There was despatched, in his interest, a letter of recommendation "to the Cardinal Farnese-Viterbo, November 16th, 1570.

"There is come to Rome a young Candiot, a pupil of Titian, who in my opinion is a painter of singular talent; among other things he has done a portrait of himself, which astounds all the artists of Rome. I should deem it a favour, were he under the patronage of your most Illustrious and Reverend Lordship, without other contribution towards his upkeep than a room in the Palazzo Farnese for some little time, until he can find better accommodation. Therefore I beg and beseech that it may please you to write to Count Lodovico, your majordomo, to provide him with an upper room in the palace; your Illustrious Lordship will be doing a virtuous action worthy of you, and I shall feel highly grateful. With reverence I kiss your Lordship's hands, and remain,

"Your most Illustrious and Reverend Lordship's most humble servant,

"JULIO CLOVIO."

Clovio, whose real name was Glovichisch, was a Croatian miniaturist of repute, of whom an excellent portrait by Greco is preserved in the Museum at Naples.

"A portrait of himself which astounds all the artists of Rome"; this was no poor achievement for a young artist of twenty-nine. Nor were other tributes lacking. An account of Greco, written about the year 1620 by G. Mancini, the doctor of Pope Urban VIII., reveals the following estimation: "During the Pontificate of Pius V., there came to Rome a man who was universally known as the Greek (*il Greco*). Having studied in Venice, principally the style of Titian, he and his method of painting acquired the high regard of the profession. Having departed thence for Rome, at a time when few men were there of so decided or so apparently fresh a manner, he attained great merit, all the more because he gave great satisfaction in certain private commissions, of which one can be seen to this day in the house of the lawyer Lancilotti; it is considered by some to be the work of Titian."

Nevertheless, it was the generation preceding Guido Reni and Domenichino. Already the cultivated taste of the period was looking forward to that invertebrate sweetness which was to rot the art of Catholic Europe during the next three centuries. Throughout his life Greco was the focus simultaneously of admiration and disapproval. The latter sentiment now found vent in a poem from the pen of Marino (1569-1625), published in his volume, *La Galleria*: "The idiot painter painted two pictures: in the one, Deucalion; in the other, Phaeton. So fair a task completed, he inquired what price would be commensurate with, and worthy of, his lovely design. And the oracle jokingly replied that the one should be drowned and the other burnt."[1]

Violent words, such as greatness always evokes from the mediocre. It is possible that Greco, had he read them, would have enjoyed them. For such were his own tactics. He was of an age and power to see clearly the forces which opposed him, the hollow beauty of the Italianised and decaying classicism; forces which he might not destroy, but of which he should at least be independent. Mancini records another incident: "Opportunity having offered to cover certain figures in Michael Angelo's Judgement, which Pius had considered indecent, he (Greco) then exploded with the statement that were the whole work cast to the ground, he would have executed it with sincerity and decency, and in no way inferior to the standards of fine art. This becom-

[1] This poem, and Mancini's manuscript in the British Museum, were brought to the author's notice by Dr. Tancred Borenius. Deucalion was the Noah of Greek mythology.

12

ing known to all artists and amateurs of this profession, he was obliged to depart to Spain." Such was the prelude to that conversation of forty years later, with which this book opens: "A good man Michael Angelo; but he could not paint."

III. Greco's Character: the Environment of Toledo and Evidence of Spanish Contemporaries; his Library

Mancini's account, of which there seems no reason to doubt the accuracy, provides one link of great importance in Greco's life, which has hitherto been missing. This is the reason why he went to Spain. Philip II.'s demand for artists to decorate the then building Escurial was doubtless the primary attraction, and offered the natural refuge to an artist driven from Italy by ridicule. For, in the opinion of contemporaries, Michael Angelo's Last Judgement, scarcely thirty years old, was the greatest *tour de force* that a European painter had yet achieved. By 1577, Greco was in Toledo, had been there some time, since the paintings commissioned for Santo Domingo el Antiguo were in process of completion, and he was already sufficiently well known to receive an order from the chapter of the Cathedral to paint the Divestment of Christ (Plate 46), which hangs to this day in the sacristy for which it was designed. Here, once more, the influence of Titian and Venice is apparent in the glowing, unrelieved crimson of Christ's robe. But there is much, now, that is foreign to Italy: the splash of honey yellow again in the foreground; and the cold light, accentuated by a dark and colourless sky, which dominates the scene. The golden summer of Venice is evaporating in a winter moonlight; white, blue, violet and a steely grey have come out.   The picture was finished in 1579.   Thereafter, in his heart, Greco was Byzantine again.

Even to-day, with tourists arriving from Madrid, and a power-house adjacent to the Alcantara, it is difficult to believe that the world can show a more beautiful city than Toledo.   It was a curious coincidence that took Greco to this town.   Susceptible to landscape, as his paintings of it show, he might never, had he remained in Italy, have escaped altogether the seductive and har-monious trammels of the Italian countryside.   In Spain there is something of the Greek lands, of that barren southern fire burn-ing in rock and dust which the Byzantines borrowed for their art.   And to watch the sun rise and set on the hills surrounding Toledo is to see reflected the ripple of light and shadow on the Cretan White Mountains.   In front, the silver Tagus; above its gorge, diminutive on a table of rock, the impalpable city, spires, towers, domes, and battlements, lengthening to the time of day; and all around, the sweeping Spanish contours, dappled in the oblique light, and composing to a picture as masterly and rhythmic as any paint, wherever the eye rests; such a scene, such an environment, must immediately have called to the surface all the latent and inherited instincts which the siren charms of Italy had obscured.   All of Greco's palette, for which his native land can show no precedent, derives from here: particularly the grey and violet, those positive, steely colours with which he carried the luminosity of his ancestors to such astounding conclusion.   Simi-larly, just as the Byzantines in their angular, tightly wrapped folds, reproduced the angular faces, rust-coloured and claret-coloured, of their own mountains, so Greco responded to a more expansive natural formation.   The coarse and impetuous sweeps of his paint, relieved by patches of intimate and flawless delicacy, seem perforce to derive from a country which makes anyone who has ever held a paintbrush wish that he were holding it again. The Spanish mountains and the Greek mountains are united in their opposition to the overpowering formlessness of the Alps or the frivolous tittups of Italy.   Each has colour and each has form. Greco took of both.   And Spaniards themselves rhapsodise over his feeling for their national characteristics.   Above all, he was a Toledano; he loved the town; glimpses of it fill the corners of his pictures; a whole vista appears in the Laocoon.   And in the Burial of Count Orgaz, the contemporary notables stand in a row, each a portrait, memorial to the society which gave the artist his home.   Toledo and Spain were the Greek's material.   Their spirit he could understand, and, like his forbears their material, he interpreted it.

The modern visitor sees in Toledo a typical southern hill-town, an impracticable place with streets so narrow that two vehicles are unable to go abreast.   On Greco's advent, it was not yet twenty years since Philip II. had removed the court and government from this rock to the sandy nucleus of Madrid.   The old capital remained the seat of the Primate, the focus of the Castilian aristocracy, and the home of art and letters.   Cervantes himself resided there during Greco's sojourn.   And the artist, reserved and extravagant as his character seemed to contemporaries, moved in a circle of poets, littérateurs, and scholars, who had the good sense to admire both his work and his wit, and in whose company he plainly took pleasure.   The blight of the Spanish state, precipitated by the minute incompetence and moribund Catholicism of the king, had already begun; Greco himself witnessed its turning-point, the expulsion of the Moriscoes.   Such accidents passed by the Toledan intelligentsia.   We see Greco in its midst, earning a lavish income, surrounded by his family, looking from his windows over the Tagus gorge or walking the hills for his views, and absorbed, wholly, in his art.

Giuseppe Martinez, in his *Discursos practicables . . . della Pintura,* written between 1650 and 1664, says that Greco arrived in Toledo "with a reputation so great that he let it be clearly understood that nothing could surpass his art."   Law-suits in support of this contention were his joy from the beginning; fight and independence were in his blood; and who should say that he, a Greek, and a genius too, deserved less of Spain than Spaniards? The first was in 1579.   Into his composition of the Divestment of Christ (Plate 46), he had inserted, despite the evangelist's assertion that they were "looking on afar off," the two Marys. The chapter of the Cathedral, on account of this iconographic inexactitude, withheld payment.   Eventually a compromise was reached by independent mediation, which granted the artist a certain sum, but not that originally stipulated.   Thereupon he appealed to the governor of the town, who was obliged to threaten him with prison, before he would accept the smaller award.   His temper in the matter is illustrated by his blank refusal to make any statement as to why he had come to the place.   Similar complications arose over the Burial of Count Orgaz, for which Greco received a first contract in the year 1584, and another in 1586, the latter stipulating that the painting should be finished by the end of that year.   At the artist's request, the council of the archiepiscopal see appointed assessors to determine its value.   This they fixed at 1,200 ducats, about £573 in gold value, and by modern standards worth from five to ten times as much.　Such a handsome price shows the estimation in which Greco's art was held; and the size of the income which resulted is confirmed by Martinez' assertion that he "earned numbers and numbers of ducats."　In this particular case, the parish authorities, who viewed the picture as a memorial tablet, considered the price too high.　They had cause to regret their parsimony; for other assessors, newly appointed, fixed the worth of the picture, not lower, but higher by a third, at 1,600 ducats.　Upon further delay, Greco lost patience and hurried into litigation, the judgement in the suit being that the 1,200 ducats should be paid him within three days.　At this he was angrier than before, and determining to receive the extra four hundred ducats, registered an appeal with the Pope himself.　But a few days later, doubtless fearing the costs of such a proceeding, he cancelled it, and on June 20th, 1588, accepted the 1,200 only.　His, however, was the last word: "As surely as the rate of payment is inferior to the value of my sublime work, so will my name go down to posterity . . . as one of the greatest geniuses of Spanish painting." Nor was it only in his own interests that this haughty temper was exhibited. On one occasion, his pupil Tristan, who had executed a Last Supper for the monastery of Sisla, found himself at odds over the price, which he had fixed at two hundred ducats.　The monks, having appealed to Greco to revise it, were alarmed to see him fly into a rage and threaten his pupil with a stick; at which they begged him to be calm, since Tristan was still very young. "It's clear to me that he's nothing but a child," was the reply; "he has the face to ask two hundred ducats for a picture which is well worth five hundred.　I shall keep it myself, if you don't give as much." To which the monks acquiesced, swearing regretfully that they would not be caught again.

His final triumph in the courts was his successful resistance, conducted in person about the year 1603, against the decision of the fiscal authority of Illescas to tax a painting which he had executed for the hospital of that town. Thereby he created a precedent for the whole of Spain, often referred to by later jurists, that works of art should be exempt from all impost. Yet when no question of his personal rights was at stake, he used to say that no money was adequate recompense for paintings such as his, and preferred to lend them only, to persons "who would not have refused him the price he wanted." At Seville, finding his art disapproved, he is recorded by Manuel de Melo to have remarked that he would rather be poor than make a fool of himself.

Contemporary, and almost contemporary, writers have left accounts of Greco's other idiosyncrasies. "He was a great philosopher," wrote Pacheco, who knew him, "very witty, and he wrote about painting, sculpture and architecture;" elsewhere: "he was original in all things, as in painting." Martinez also bears testimony to his eloquence, and speaks sarcastically of his "absurd ostentation": "he earned a great deal of money; but the unique fortune that he left behind him was two hundred unfinished pictures." That a painter should have hired musicians to have played to him at meals appeared the summit of wastefulness; that music might have helped him in his art and thoughts, or rescued him from them, does not occur to the writer. He lived in a suite of twenty-four rooms, with kitchen and garden. At his death in 1614, an inventory was made of his possessions by his son George Manuel, which, though it discloses a strange paucity of clothes and furniture, preserves the details of a library containing 130 books. These details are further supplemented by an inventory of George Manuel's own possessions, which was taken seven years later, on the occasion of his marriage to Doña Gregoria de Guzman.

The books reveal the wide range of Greco's interests and culture, and seem in a sense, to complete the fragmentary portrait of his character. In his native language, besides a lexicon, there were twenty-six, a large number at that date. These included Demosthenes; Xenophon; Isocrates; Homer; two copies of Aristotle's *Politics* and one of his *Physics;* Plutarch's *Moral Philosophy*; Æsop's *Fables*; Euripides; the commentaries on Aristotle's *De Anima* of Philoponus, the Alexandrine philospher of the fifth century A.D.; Lucian in two volumes; and Hippocrates. In Alexander, the undying hero of Hellenism, Greco appears to have taken particular interest. Written in Greek, he possessed Plutarch's *Lives* and the account of Alexander's campaigns by Arrian, historian of the second century A.D.; in Latin, the *Deeds of Alexander,* by Quintus Curtius, compiled in the first. In Latin, also, was a work or works of Boethius, the minister of Theodoric and the founder of scholastic philosophy.

Interest in the Church and the early Christian writers was equally represented, the books being entirely in Greek, and comprising the Old and New Testaments in five volumes, Josephus, Justin Martyr, two works by St. Denys the Areopagite, including one on the *Celestial Hierarchy,* the Constitutions of the Holy Apostles, the *Orations* of St. John Chrysostom, and the *Ethics* of St. Basil. It is also stated that an account of the Council of

Trent was in Greek.   But it seems more probable that this was in Latin.

In Italian, Greco still possessed the book from which his early lessons must have been taken, the *Vocabolario, Grammatica et Orthographia de la Lingua Volgare* of Alberto Acharisio, published in 1543.   His subsequent proficiency in the language is confirmed by the presence of works by Petrarch, Ariosto, and the poet, Francesco Milanese.   He owned also the *Amadigi* of Bernado Tasso, father of the great Tasso, together with a Description and a History of Italy.   The scope of his interests appears in treatises on the Art of Painting, Military Discipline, and the Conservation of the Health.   Geography was represented by the *Relationi Universali* of Giovanni Botero.   Another author mentioned is Camillo Agrippa, who wrote on Navigation and the Science of Arms in the middle of the sixteenth century.   Two books stand out above the others as relating to Greco's peculiar turn of mind. The first is that of Artemidorus on the *Interpretation of Dreams;* the second, the *Ten Dialogues on the Reading and Writing of History* by the mystic Francesco Patrizzi, of whom more will be said on page 205.   Lastly, the inventory of 1614 includes the *Justificazion del Capitano Francesco Piniero,* together with fifty unspecified works in Latin or Italian, seventeen in Romance Spanish, and nineteen on architecture.

It is the last two groups which George Manuel's second inventory illumines.   The Spanish books, which have decreased from seventeen to ten, include translations of Cornelius Tacitus and of that earliest love-fiction, Heliodorus' *Æthiopica;* treatises on Medicine by Bairo da Turino, on Arithmetic by Perez de Moya, and on Navigation by Martin Cortes; a *Miscellany of Various Readings* by Pero Maxia; *Flos Sanctorum* by Alonso de Villegas; *Papal and Catholic History* by Gonzalo de Illescas; *Republics of the World* by Jeronimo Roman; and *Prodigious and Marvellous Tales of Divers Events* taken from the French. The architectural works, which, being of greater use to George Manuel, have increased from nineteen to twenty-one, form a very complete collection, comprising Vitruvius in Latin and Italian; a book by Palladio (probably *Quattro Libri dell' Architettura*) and an *Antiquities of Rome* possibly also by him; the drawings of Juan de Herrera for the church of the Escurial; Vignola's *Five Orders of Architecture;* Besson's illustrated work on cranes and levers; a book probably to be identified with Braun's *Civitates Orbis Tarrarum;* Vignola, Sirigatti, and Barbaro on Perspective; and various works by Labecco, Serlio, Rusconi, and Alberti. Finally, there were six manuscripts on architecture, one illustrated, which, in view of Pacheco's remark on page 183, are not unlikely to have been by Greco himself.

Thus we can picture Greco not only as an artist and a " character," but as a man of unceasing intellectual activity, speaking or reading ancient and modern Greek, Latin, Italian, and Spanish, and seeking mental stimulus in every subject from religious philosophy to modern warfare.

The above details are far from giving a complete survey of Greco's life. They illustrate, simply, what kind of man he was, and what circumstances most contributed to his achievement. The sophisticated society of Candia, enjoying its own Greek poems and its own Greek drama; the environment of Venice in the heyday of power and wealth, and the technical secrets of Titian and Tintoretto; the gradual recognition of the young

painter's accomplishment, and, simultaneously, the gradual disapproval; the interlude in Rome; and, finally, the expansive,
sympathetic influence of the Spanish landscape and the society
of the late capital; such were the accidents which carried the
last exponent of mediæval Greek culture to success.   One other
thing there was: his own, the Cretan, character.   We see a
youth, who, at the age of twenty-nine or thirty, would have
destroyed Michael Angelo's Last Judgement, because he despised
it, and because he could have done it as well; an aggressive pros-
perous angry stranger in a further land; and an old man of wide
reading and incessant activity, who was noted for his wit,
philosophy, extravagance, conceit, and also for his painting.   The
vanished empire, the invaded city, could have asked no more
robust embodiment of their vagrant spirit for an epilogue.   On
April 7th, 1614, Domenicos Theotocopoulos died, in the seventy-
third year of his age.   And on the morning of the following day
he was attended to his grave by the aristocracy and intelligentsia
of Toledo, among whom he had spent nearly forty years of his
life.   Thus ended the Byzantine civilisation.   The epilogue was
also a triumph.

IV. Greco's Derivation from Byzantine Art: Iconography and Landscape

It has been assumed, throughout this book, that the reader is
familiar with the essential features of Greco's painting.   A
categorical comparison, therefore, between the pictures of the
artist, and those of his tradition, is all that remains to complete
the revelation of his origins.   The general resemblances, most of

which have already been noticed, are plain to anyone who has visited both Athos and Mistra, and Toledo and Madrid.   And a study of detail confirms them.   They fall under three headings: Iconography and Landscape; Colour; and Form and Light.

ICONOGRAPHY

Of the three great pictures painted by Greco during the first decade of his stay in Spain, two derive their compositions mainly from prescribed scenes in Byzantine Orthodox decoration; while a mysterious and puzzling feature of the third can be explained by the same precedent.

In the Divestment of Christ (Plate 46), which hangs in the sacristy of Toledo Cathedral, the frontal position of the central figure, the spears in the background, and the rhythmic agitation of the crowd, are all identical with that Betrayal in the Garden which is found in the tenth century churches of Cappadocia (see Plate 45. i), which occurs at Mistra in the Metropolitan church of St. Demetrius, and which was painted by both the Macedonian and the Cretan schools on Mount Athos (Plates 47, 48. i, 45. ii). Owing to the change of incident, the Marys have replaced Peter's attack on Malchus.   But a more convincing proof of the relationship between the picture and the frescoes than even the general scheme of composition is the two peaky, semi-demented faces on either side of the Saviour, which appear without variation in the dozen or more versions which Greco painted of the Divestment. These are found, with their same leer, though without their Spanish beards, in the Byzantine Betrayals from the tenth to the sixteenth century (see Plates 45. ii, 47, 48. i).

In the case of the Burial of Count Orgaz, much discussion has been evoked as to the significance of the heavenly scene in the top half of the picture.   Christ is in the centre; on his right the Virgin; on his left a naked and elongated figure, which some have assumed to be the Count Orgaz arriving in heaven, and others St. John the Baptist.   The latter ascription makes possible the theory that this composition represents a baroque version of the Byzantine Deisis (see Plate 2. ii), in which the Christ enthroned is attended by his mother and precursor on his right and left respectively.   This derivation on Greco's part, if derivation there was, cannot have been an artistic one; there is no pictorial resemblance between the two compositions.   With the lower half of the Count Orgaz (Plate 66), this is not the case.   Here, the composition is achieved by means of distinct and symmetrical lines : at the back, the vertical figures of the cortège; in front, the curving figures of the two bearers; and then, the horizontal implication of the sagging corpse, uniting the whole.   It is a composition which, in its very simplicity, stands apart from any in contemporary art.   And precisely that simplicity, and precisely those three classes of lines, are exhibited in the various examples of the Dormition of the Virgin reproduced on Plates 65, 67. i, ii, 68. i. In these, again, the horizontal corpse is united to the rigid central Christ, with his head slightly inclined in grief like those of the Toledan notables, by the curving backs of the sympathisers at either end.

As regards the St. Maurice at the Escurial (Plate 81), the chief links with Byzantine painting fall under the subsequent headings of Colour and Form and Light.   Iconographically, however, there is one question which has puzzled observers ever since the picture was painted.   This is the peculiar costume of the three foremost figures, who are arrayed in skin-tight jerkins, with cloaks or neckerchiefs tied at the throat, and short kilts ornamented with a number of thicker strips depending from the waist. "Mock-Roman" these dresses are usually called; and are presumed to derive from the classical heroics of the age; just as, in eighteenth century French architecture, a hollow effigy of Roman armour is frequently made the centrepiece of a group of trophies placed in a pediment.   It seems far more probable that Greco, casting about for a costume which would allow him play in the depiction of human anatomy, while permitting him, at the same time, to forego the enormous expanses of flesh tints necessitated by the entirely naked, bethought himself of the traditional Orthodox uniform of the military saint; for such was St. Maurice.   These saints were always clothed in much the manner that Greco adopted and simplified, as will be seen from the picture of SS. Theodore Stratilates and Theodore Tiron, reproduced from the church of the Lavra on Mount Athos on Plate 82. i.   Here the same sword, the same kilts and the same cloaks are apparent, though in place of the leather jerkins, the saints are wearing a kind of armoured corselet.   It must be remembered, however, that these military saints, of which one or two are to be found in nearly all the cycles of later Byzantine painting, are dressed not as mock-Romans, but in the ordinary uniforms of the Byzantine armies, for which minute regulations were laid down, varying with each regiment.   In 1439, the Emperor John VIII. Palæologus and his suite entered Florence.   And soon after, Piero della Francesca, who was in that city at the time, was commissioned to paint the still existent frescoes at Arezzo, which depict the victory of Heraclius over the Persians and his recovery of the

Cross.   In these frescoes, the Byzantine armies and officials are clothed in the uniforms with which the Emperor John was surrounded.   And, in the centre of the battle scene, there appears a warrior riding a white horse, who wears exactly such a leather jerkin as adorns the three figures of the St. Maurice (see Plate 82. ii).   This figure, and many of those around him, also wear the flat, chased helmets, some of them crested like the dorsal fin of a perch, which frequently appear on the heads of military saints in Byzantine churches.   Nor do these frescoes provide the only precedent for Byzantine military uniform in Italian painting.   In the Procession to Calvary, executed by Ugolino da Siena in the first half of the fourteenth century, and now in the National Gallery (Plate 82. iii), soldiers in the same kilts, cloaks, and helmets, are convoying Christ to his fate.   There seems no doubt that the representation of actual Byzantine uniforms was a regular tradition in the iconography of later Byzantine and early Italian painting, and that Greco consciously followed this tradition.

Near the St. Maurice in the Escurial hangs that strange composition, the Dream of Philip II. (Plate 73), in which it is plain that Greco has derived many features from a mediæval, and therefore a Greek, Last Judgement.   The mouth of the monster of hell, though here affronted by Greco's superior talent instead of presenting the usual profile, is a familiar cliché in the Athonite monasteries, and may be observed in the refectories of the Lavra (see Plates 72, 74. ii) and of Dionysiou.   Equally recognisable are the forward hands and the unnaturally obtuse angle of the kneeling knees of Philip II.; this difficult position was always that of the groups of righteous suppliants, surrounded by cloudy frillings, in the Byzantine compositions, and is found on Plate 74. i in the section depicting "the choir of pious kings."

The single portrait of Christ is a subject which may be said to have been almost unknown to the painters of Western Europe in the sixteenth and seventeenth centuries.   In Byzantine and post-Byzantine art, on the other hand, the lowering Christ Pantocrator was the recognised occupant of the dominating central cupola in any church or chapel (see Plate 12. i, ii).   Greco also per-petuated it (Plate 12. iv).   In the three-quarter length picture in the museum at Toledo, all the usual features are apparent, with the exception of the book in the left hand.   So strong was the tradition, that the artist adopted the formal halo, an adornment unknown in his other pictures, and evidently re-pugnant to his sense of realism.   It is true that he shaped it as a diamond instead of as a circle; similarly he ruffled the drapery; but in that as well, the traditional arrangement is visible, the heavy fold of the mantle over the left shoulder, covering the left arm and carried across to the right side, and the inner tunic, with its low neck cut in facets, which do not appear in Greco's depic-tions of Christ in other scenes.   The hands, too, like all Greco's hands, are of a tapering Byzantine character; two fingers of the right are raised, as they always were ; the thin, bony thumb goes up to meet them; the other two are crooked down.   A similar likeness appears in the construction of the full-staring face, with its undeviating gaze: the symmetrical shadows encroach on the cheeks to give it the forbidding hatchet-shape; and the nose is heavily darkened at the sides according to the Orthodox pre-scription.

The Baptism in the Prado (Plate 26), though superficially

bearing small relation to a Byzantine composition, offers another
example of Greco's fidelity to the iconography of his forbears.
As in the Protaton (Plate 25. i), and in the churches of the Lavra
and Xenophontos (Plate 27. ii), on Mount Athos, Christ stands
on a lower level than St. John.   In the traditional manner, the
latter's right hand is held above Christ's head; one of his legs is
stretched forward and bent.   In the centre descends a vertical and
symmetric dove, which is encircled by a flood of light, geometric
in the case of the Byzantines, diffuse and shimmering in that of
Greco, but exactly the same in place and character.   Below it, a
winged angel, feathers dark at the tips, and, on Athos, outlined
in white, ministers.   Above, in Greco's picture, sits God in white.
In the Byzantine compositions his presence is indicated only by a
large geometric aura, to which, in the Protaton, is added a protruding hand.   But God is not unknown in Byzantine painting.
Both in the chapel of the Prodome at Caryes (Plate 8. i), and
in the Peribleptos at Mistra (Plate 9. ii), he is found, also in
white; in the first, three-quarter length; in the second, seated, as
in Greco's picture; and in each case, as in the latter, in conjunction with the dove beneath, and also, either by an actual representation, or by the implication of an altar, with Christ.   Thus,
Greco has combined two of the traditional iconographic motives
of the Orthodox Church in a single composition.

In the general province of physical characteristics, the most
obvious debt of Greco to his forbears was his tendency to elonga-
tion.   In the case of his hands, this has already been noticed; but
its most marked effect was in his bodies.   It was evidently inten-
tional; for the proportions of the St. Maurice figures must satisfy
the most academic taste.   In the depiction of single saints, such

13

as the St. Bernadino (Plate 80), he reverted to the traditional exaggeration of Orthodox decoration. "Learn, O my pupil," wrote the monk Denys of Fourna in his Guide to Painting based on immemorial practice, "that the body of a man is nine heads in height." Actually, it should be seven. Much in Greco, for which the ignorant have sought astigmatism as the cause, is explained by this injunction. Facially he was generally Spanish. But in certain cases, as in the Christ already mentioned, and in the depiction of ascetic types, he recalled the forbidding galleries of Orthodox saints. The portraits of St. Jerome by Greco and of St. Euthymius at the Protaton on the Holy Mountain, reproduced side by side on Plate 84. i, ii, seem almost to have been drawn by the same hand. St. Jerome, it may be noted, is dressed as a cardinal; and in the Burial of Count Orgaz, St. Augustine is robed as a bishop, such as he was, and St. Stephen as a deacon. This again is in accordance with the Byzantine habit of investing the heroes of the Church with the vestments to which their rank would have entitled them if still alive.

LANDSCAPE

There is one last province of Greco's painting into which it might confidently be expected that no trace of his Byzantine antecedents could possibly have intruded. This is that of his landscapes, in which, more nearly than anywhere else, he approaches the impressionist founders of modern art. The reader thinks instantly of the stormy glimpse of Toledo in the Metropolitan Museum at New York, and its astonishing affinity with the painting of Cézanne. And he thinks again of the long panorama of Toledo (Plate 94), with the hospital of St. John on a cloud in the foreground, and its astonishing dissimilarity from any picture on earth.   In these, surely, Greco has discarded the last vestiges of the hieratic Orthodox tradition.   Yet there exists from his hand another landscape, and one painted in a manner no less impressionist.   This represents Mount Sinai, with the ancient Greek monastery of St. Catherine, the seat of a diminutive autocephalous church, crouching at its foot (Plates 90, 93. i, ii).   It was presumably painted while Greco was in Italy, since it is known to have hung in the collection of Fulvio Orsini,[1] who died in the year 1600.

This picture, nineteen inches long and sixteen and a half high, is one of the greatest evolutionary curiosities in European culture, the very duck-billed platypus of Western painting.   At once it is the first modern landscape and the last mediæval one.   For, as the prints on Plates 91 and 92 show, it is directly based on one of the fantastic Orthodox formulæ which have circulated from time immemorial over Russia and the Levant, to represent, for those who are unable to be pilgrims, the holy places of the Church. Critics have had occasion, now and then, to quote Giorgione as Greco's precursor in landscape.   A more striking example of one who was not Greco's precursor, of the very phase of landscape-painting that he never traversed, could scarcely be chosen.   Giorgione carried the Italian classical landscape to its apotheosis.   Greco avoided it altogether.   The picture of Mount Sinai shows how nearly related are realism and formalism, and how one may develop directly from the other, without any mediation on the part of the laborious picturesque.   It also provides the final and

[1] This fact, and the authority of Dr. A. L. Mayer, vouch for its anthenticity.

irrevocable proof of Greco's habit of borrowing from the iconographic formulæ of his native land.

It is interesting to note that this little picture was not the only
imaginary landscape that Greco painted with the aid of a print
or drawing from some other source. In the Instituto de Valencia
de Don Juan at Madrid, there hangs an extraordinary canvas,
four feet high by three broad, which is entitled Allegoria de la
Vida de los Camaldulenses (Plate 88). Above the figures of
St. Benedict and St. Romuald appears a circular panorama of the
hermit community which the latter founded at Camaldoli, near
Arezzo, in A.D. 1012.[1] It is highly improbable that Greco ever
visited this little frequented fastness of solitaries. And it seems
certain that he derived his impression of it from some contemporary print such as that in the British Museum, of which a
section is reproduced on Plate 89.[2] Comparison between this
and the painting reveals how Greco, faced with a disordered
and insupportably romantic composition, reduced it to exactly
such a formula as might have been used by his native Church
under similar circumstances. Many of the details are identical;
but they have become symmetrical, and have been arranged in
precisely that manner which is still employed in the depiction
of such holy places as Athos and Jesusalem. The two scenes
representing the Dormitions of St. Athanasius of Athos (Plate
87. ii) and of St. Ephraim the Syrian (Plate 86), at the monasteries of the Lavra and Docheiariou on Mount Athos, illustrate
how this principle of formalisation was applied to what may con-

[1] It still persists unchanged.
[2] The print is undated; but it exhibits the style, though not the ability, of
Callot. Whether the temple in the middle ever existed is obscure.

veniently be called "lifescapes"; many of their subsidiary figures
bear a strong resemblance to those of Greco's Mount Sinai.   How
accurately such formulæ could travel is shown by the icon of the
Dormition of St. Ephraim (Plate 87. i), which was painted by
Emmanuel Tsanphournari, a member of the Greek colony at
Venice, in the sixteenth century.

The picture of Mount Sinai, painted in youth, shows Greco
advancing from formalism to realism; that of the Camaldulensian
community, dating from his middle period in Spain, receding to
formalism again.   In his last years, he painted the famous
panorama of Toledo (Plate 94).   In tone, this is a lighter picture than photographs allow: the sky is grey, pierced by rents
of cold blue, and projecting tufts of white cloud.   Into this the
town, like a sad European mirage, lifts its reticulated contour
from a long hill of golden green, and stretches out into the distance.   In one corner of the canvas reclines a strange allegory,
holding a cornucopia, and sculptured in some such colour as gold
leaf on a foundation of brown paper, only slightly green, and
black in the shadows.   In the other, but a little nearer the centre,
is a boy, dressed in the same green as the grass, who holds a map
of the town, so careful and accurate that it might be the work of
an expert cartographer.   Near it, perched on a cloud, hovers a
building with a dome.   Above all, in the sky, a little heavenly
group dominates the whole scene, deftly impressed in a scattering
of greenish yellow, cold blue, wine-pink, and, at the very top,
one touch of orange vermilion, which gathers to itself the transparent red over-painting of the grey clouds, and forms the pivot
of the whole picture.   Such an odd medley seems, once more,
to recall the Byzantine landscape, and its subordination of natural

features to hieratic convenience; save that here, in place of ecclesiasticism, there is frivolity, conscious and delicious, such as our age particularly loves. But, for the benefit of a more meticulous generation, there is written, near the map, an ironic apology: "It has been necessary to put the hospital of Don Juan Tavera in the form of a model (that on the cloud), because it not only so happened as to conceal the Visagra gate, but thrust up its dome or cupola in such a manner that it overtopped the town; once put thus as a model, and removed from its place, I thought it would show the façade before any other part of it; how the rest of it is related to the town will be seen on the map.

"Also, in the story of Our Lady who brings the chasuble to St. Ildefonso for his embellishment, so as to enlarge the figures, I have availed myself, to a certain extent, of their being heavenly bodies, in the same way as lights, seen from afar, appear large, however small they be."

The beholder would laugh, were it not for the tears in sky and city, and the artist's old age. Once, however, Greco discarded these tricks, and painted the view pure and simple which is now in New York. And this is as close to our serious moods as Mount Sinai to the Byzantine.

V. Greco's Derivation from Byzantine Art: Colour

Greco achieved the principle of colour relation, in which lies the fundamental virtue of all his art, by two means: in relation to the whole composition, by a sequence of unconnected colour-fields; and in relation to individual form and light, by means of small inharmonious planes of varying tones. It is clear that, even in relation to his compositions, he thought wholly in colour. Dürer, to take the extreme opposite, drew his pictures, and then tinted them like a cartoon. From Greco's hand, scarcely an authenticated drawing has survived; even in the exhaustive list compiled by George Manuel of the works of art in his studio at his death, there is only one. On the other hand, a small Annunciation in the Prado, about nine inches by seven, illustrates clearly enough his method of hurriedly setting down the main colour-fields of a composition in an impressionist manner, before proceeding to a larger work. The regular, almost mathematical, sequences of colour employed over large areas by the painters of Athos and Mistra have been described in the last chapter. Exactly the same principle, and mainly the same colours, though more varied in their application, are repeated in Greco's paintings.

In relation to individual form, an analogy with the Byzantine method is found in Pacheco's description of Greco's technique, Pacheco having probably seen him at work. According to this passage, it was Greco's habit to touch and retouch his paintings over and over again, "in order to leave the colours distinct and apart (*desunidos*), and to produce those cruel splashes (*crueles borrones*) with the object of affecting bravado (!)." The Byzantine method, though exceptions, which in themselves provide a precedent for Greco's vigorous brushwork, are forthcoming in the Peribleptos at Mistra and the church of Xenophontos on Mount Athos, was almost geometric in the exactitude with which it defined the colours of a drapery or a rock, to represent light, shade, and norm. For Greco, such geometrising was precluded by his realism. But he retained, most markedly, the principle of the hard outline. This may conveniently be observed in the particularly luminous example of his work in the National Gallery: the Agony in the Garden. How, the beholder asks, till he wonders if the paint is not phosphorescent, is the extraordinary effect of Christ's robe obtained by a simple juxtaposition of white and wine-red? The answer lies partly, of course, in the absolute contrasts of the surrounding indigo and moss-yellow. But, in actual detail, the effect is achieved simply by the sharp division of the white from the red, the first accentuating its brilliance, the second its depth, as they meet. This device recalls the interposition of light blue on the horses' necks in the Nativity of the Pantanassa at Mistra (see page 144). And it is in this particular aptitude that lies one of Greco's chief distinctions from the Venetians. Tintoretto was given to obtaining his lights by charging a wine-red drapery with yellow—a favourite combination both of Greco and the Byzantines. But, in his case, the colours are not left "distinct and apart"; they merge into one another; and the effect, though it serve the general pattern, is one of shot silk, instead of inner light. Hence, in this sphere, his comparative failure and Greco's success.

A few obvious examples of resemblance will illustrate the tradition to which Greco was bound.

As indicating Greco's habitual treatment of flesh, the following passage from Meier-Græfe, relating to a portrait, may be quoted: "If one stops to consider the anatomy of the face, one receives the impression of a fantastic structure. The right eye is far lower than the left; the mouth, but for the beard, would be a shapeless piece of flesh; the right ear, almost separated from the head, would seem monstrous. The joke is that one can separate nothing, that the coloured flow of dark pink and yellow binds the separate points more organically than any draughtsmanship could do." That yellow, as a rule, was a primrose colour. And its combination with wine-red, usually considered peculiar to Greco, is exactly reproduced, though in a larger sphere, in the mummy and tomb of the Lazarus of the Pantanassa at Mistra (see page 141 and Plate 1), in which the pearly, opalescent yellow of the shroud stands out against a pinkish chocolate. But replace this primrose by crocus, and the same combination may be found in the flesh of the same scene. There, heads, legs, arms, and hands, are all achieved by the use of a yellow having vermilion depths, lit with fine white lines, and shadowed, as always in Greco's pictures, with dark wine-red. Facially, also, another analogy is forthcoming. In the head of the Virgin by Greco in the Prado, the skin of the face contains not only wine-red and yellow, but touches of definite blue. In the heads of the lamenting women at the Peribleptos (see page 137 and Plate 57. ii), the same characteristic is noticeable: a brilliant blue is used to indicate the usual white highlights; while, in both cases, this colour is invisible from a distance. It may reasonably be argued, however, that the artist of the Peribleptos was using his blue simply to obtain an effect of form and light, while Greco was aiming merely at accentuating the textural depths of the skin. For this latter process, precedent is immediately found in the superb mosaic panels at the monastery of Xenophontos on Mount Athos, whose description has already been given on page 32. In the faces of these, small cubes of brilliant cærulean are introduced with precisely the same object as Greco had in mind; the lights are depicted by other and lighter tones altogether. It was this cold, immaterial blue which

Velasquez diluted, and which places the Rokeby Venus on a pinnacle among paintings of the human body.

The detailed use of this sky-blue, in other than large fields relating to the whole composition, while unusual on Athos, is frequent at Mistra. In the same scene of the Raising of Lazarus (Plate 1), the tunic of the weeping figure is of a bright grass-green—another favourite colour of Greco's—which is over-painted blue with masterly transparency in order to emphasise the highlights. A remarkable parallel to this scheme is found in the picture of St. Thomas at Toledo, where Greco has compressed all the contrasts of a whole landscape or story on to a single figure. The mantle of the apostle is a cold slate-colour, whose highlights of buff yellow are separated from the background by dark strokes of wine-red. The shadows, on the other hand, as though to obtain the very extreme of contrast, are depicted in grass-green and cobalt, exactly the colours of the weeping figure's tunic, though here there is no over-painting. In the latter process, however, Greco was by no means deficient, as is shown by the long panorama of Toledo (Plate 94), in which the grey and stormy clouds present, on close inspection, a thin coating of scarlet —invisible from the distance of a few yards, but giving exactly that curving prominence to the sky which is needed.

In addition to the green and cobalt, the tunic of the weeping figure in the Pantanassa displays an amber hem, which, in its turn, is edged with claret. But for the blue over-painting, the total combination of colours lavished on this garment is apparent in Greco's picture of St. John the Evangelist in the Prado, where a mantle of wine-red, lit with faint olive yellow planes, discloses a tunic of brilliant grass-green charged with planes of amber.

This green and amber is also to be found in the kneeling figure on the beholder's left of Greco's Pentecost in the Prado.   At times the artist seems almost to have been actuated by malice in his ruthless application of concatenating lights.   On the cold azure of the Virgin's robe in San Vincente at Toledo, great splashes of burnt pink produce an effect which is scarcely coherent.   The same combination may be observed, though in a more sombre and formalised context, in the Virgin of the Pantanassa Ascension (Plate 60. i), where her robe is of dark cobalt, relieved by heavy lines of rusty grape colour.

Reference has already been made to the vivid grey which Greco occasionally employed to accentuate the brilliance of its more active neighbours.   Such a grey must have derived, largely, from the Toledo landscape.   But it is found, notwithstanding, in the Byzantine paintings: a definite grey, playing its part in the whole colour composition, and not employed merely for shadows on white drapery, or to depict, naturalistically, the ass on which Christ entered Jerusalem.   The rusty wing of the Announcing Angel in the Pantanassa (Plate 17) is tipped, each feather, with this colour; amid the spring-like riot of mossy yellow and lettuce green which envelops the ethereal figure, and the burnt rose marble of the background, this matter of fact touch produces a surprising, static effect, arresting the eye at an unexpected point. The same colour, and the same reaction, are also imparted by the regal and erect figure of the Virgin which dominates the apse of the Metropolitan Church of St. Demetrius at Mistra (Plate 13. i).   Here it is applied in a solid field to the under-skirt; the mantle above is a dark rose-colour with white folds; and the background of indigo and ochre.   On the part of the Athonite painters, the most frequent use of grey was in the depiction of celestial lights, in exactly that context where an Italian would have exhausted the resources of his palette in an attempt to imitate the rainbow.   The Transfigured Christ in the chapel of St. George at St. Paul's (Plate 31. i, ii) is surrounded by an aura of geometric compartments in greyish black, Greco grey, and white, with only an ochre square in the middle to throw the white robe of the figure into relief.   The same grey is employed with peculiar effect in the sombre frescoes of Xenophontos (Plate 21. i, 27. ii, iii), where the divine presence, denoted by an effulgent grey and white circle, protrudes, on one side the star of the Nativity, on the other, the dove of the Baptism, each at the end of a ray in the same tones.

This grey was particularly the inheritance of Velasquez, and was transformed by his facile brush into a more elusive silver. The blind esteem in which that artist was held by a previous generation is perhaps explained by the fact that Whistler also used grey.   None the less, Velasquez, if not a great man, was a great painter.   And from as early as Palomino (1653-1726), Spaniards have been quick to recognise his debt to Greco. Velasquez, this writer reports, proclaimed himself a disciple of Tristan; and Tristan was Greco's only pupil who afterwards reproduced any of his manner.   It is impossible to explain Velasquez without the Greek antecedent.   All over Europe, the robust warmth of Rubens and the Venetians was paramount. At the court of Spain, the tones were cold and measured.   Señor Cossio, writing at the apogee of Whistler and Corot, admits that, "to the glory of both, Greco was the only master of Velasquez, and Velasquez the only pupil of Greco."   Señor Beruete, who was no admirer of Greco, was forced to the same conclusion. In some cases the resemblances are obvious. The portrait of Innocent X. in the Doria Palace in Rome plainly derives from Greco's Cardinal Niño de Guevara. The Las Lanzas in the Prado has borrowed its composition and landscape colour from the St. Maurice. But great as Velasquez was, greatly he lost. The light is gone; "the blue and pink vibrate so little that they become relatively dirty" (Meier-Græfe). Once again, all is harmonious and representational; there are only solid, exquisitely depicted facts. Thus genius may be implanted in a great man, or in a little one. Generally the world prefers it in the latter.

VI. Greco's Derivation from Byzantine Art: Form and Light

Francesco Patrizzi, whose Dialogues on history were found in Greco's library, enunciated a theory in his *Nova de Universis Philosophia* that the fundamental condition of being, of all development, of the validity of sensory perception, and of all knowledge, was light. Whether Greco, as he might easily have done, ever came under the influence of the author in person, or of the work in question, is unknown. But the coincidence may at least serve as a text. For, among all Greco's unique and strange qualities, the cold and entirely self-contained luminosity of his pictures is the one which distinguishes him most completely from any other artist ever known to Western Europe, and which links him most strongly with his Byzantine precursors. Such stress has already been laid on this quality, and on this link, that repetition of it must seem superfluous. Nor can words well assist the proof.   The identity of the colours and colour-principle obtained by Greco and the Greeks, together with the part played by the pattern of light in their compositions, have been examined in some detail.   But the effect, as opposed to the means, is one which scarcely admits of analysis.   It is only possible to repeat: the light is there; it is a cold impersonal light; and in both cases, it is an internal light, emanating independently from within the object, and interpreting it.

Certain facts, however, may be noted, to reinforce a statement which the eye, observing both Greco's paintings and those of the later Byzantines, can immediately take for granted.

It is impossible to emphasise too strongly the distinction between the reserved, intrinsic lucidity of Greco and the Byzantines, and that warm radiance, usually known as chiaroscuro, which found apotheosis in Rembrandt and absurdity in Caravaggio.   The term chiaroscuro implies an external source, and a corresponding welter of shadow and mystery.   To the Byzantines, being formalists, shadow and mystery were entirely foreign.   But even Greco, with all his realism, never employed them.   His conjuring ability, when he wished to conjure, disdained such a trick.   Instead, he turned people upside down, or made clouds of glass, as in the *gloria* of the Count Orgaz. Equally unknown to both was the conception of warmth as an artistic virtue.   Harmony is implied in the very word; and it was precisely that which both sought to avoid; their compositions were conceived more organically; each plane and field of colour stood to express an individual, aristocratic significance, besides playing its part in the economy of the whole.   Cold, the opposite of warmth, does not make for harmony.   On the contrary, it

accentuates differences.   It may be said, in fact, that the idea of
a warm light, with which Italy must have rendered him only too
familiar, was actually repugnant to Greco; that the glacial, moon-
lit effulgence of the St. Maurice remained his ideal no matter
what the scene.   Reproductions of his picture containing a boy
blowing on a lighted coal, with a monkey in the background,[1]
seem to suggest chiaroscuro in its most pronounced form.   But
the reality reveals that the light of the coal is white, snow-white;
and that all the colours retain their separate coherence.   Such
also is the case with the Burial of Count Orgaz (Plate 66),
whose prevailing tone, despite the richness of the vestments, is
that of November.   There are torches in the background; but
they are white, snow-white.   And the surplice of the priest on
the right is made of white Bristol glass, not milky, for milk has
colour, but the white of uncut diamonds.   Parallel for such
translucency in crumpled stuff can only be found in Byzantine
mosaic or painting, of which latter may be instanced the olive
and honey-coloured figure on the right of the Transfigured Christ
in the chapel of St. George at St. Paul's on Mount Athos (see
Plate 31. ii).

The extent to which Greco depended on the pattern of light
for the unification of his compositions is obvious in the worst
reproductions; and the strength of the tradition from which he
derived this reliance may be judged by the frescoes of Xenophontos
on Mount Athos (Plates 38. ii, 44, 51. i, 56, 65), painted in 1544,
three years after the artist's birth.   It was doubtless the importance
of maintaining this unity, this tempestuous rhythm of light and
dark, which led the Byzantines, when gold was no longer avail-

[1] Of which one version is now at Chesterfield House.

able, to adopt the constant indigo or black of which their skies, though occasionally relieved by stars or celestial portents, invariably consist. This was another rule which Greco inherited, and which, despite occasional clouds and rays to accentuate his pattern still further, he never infringed with colour.

Such an idea of the functions and emanence of light naturally exercised a corresponding effect on the Byzantine conception of form. It has been suggested that the habit of inverted perspective, which the Greeks perpetuated in Duccio and Giotto, derived from the artist's imagining himself within the object portrayed, so that, as it progressed in the direction of the beholder, it necessarily diminished. Such indeed was the Byzantine vision of form as expressed in terms of light and dark. The head, the arm, was conceived primarily as a dark mass, instead of as a given space to be invested with form by the application of shadow. This principle is explicitly stated in Denys of Fourna's Guide to Painting, in relation to flesh-depiction; and the interest of this instruction lies in the fact that it exhibits the *exact converse* of the rules for the same process prescribed in mediæval Western manuals, such as that of Cennino Cennini. For the preparation of the proplasm, or groundwork, according to the usage of the celebrated Panselinos, "take white lead, ochre, green and black," writes the monk. "Grind all this together on marble, and collect the mixture in a pot; then ground the places where you will paint the flesh." Ochre, green and black: the darkest possible combination. Next he gives a recipe for the glycasm, or half-tone: "Take two parts of flesh-colour, and one part or a little less of proplasm; unite these in a shell, and you will have a glycasm which will enable you to depict such flesh as you wish."

Then: "When you have applied the proplasm (the dark first), and drawn in a face or another part, you will do the flesh with the glycasm (the half-tone next) . . . You will add flesh-colour on the outstanding parts (the third and natural tone in patches only). . . . Last you will use white with reserve (the fourth and final gradation) in order to give the light, mixing the touches of white, and those of flesh-colour, first gently, then more forcibly. This is how flesh is done, according to Panselinos."

The single head of a saint on Plate 83. i, reproduced from the Pantanassa at Mistra, illustrates a favourite, though by no means universal, technique of applying the luminary white in a series of lines, as an academic western draughtsman might apply his shadow. The continuance of such formalism was not to be expected of Greco. But Greco may none the less be said to have adhered to the basic principle involved. Primarily, all his forms, with the exception of his portrait heads, are dark shapes given meaning by boldly applied light. This is true painting; there is nothing sculptural in it. Turn, for example, from the legs of the unwinding figure in the Raising of Lazarus at the Pantanassa (Plate 1), to those of the man with his back turned in the foreground of the St. Maurice (Plate 81), or of the youth constructing the cross at the bottom of the Toledo Divestment (Plate 46). In all three figures, despite the greater formalism of the Byzantine, the muscles and movements of the limbs are apparent not in a plastic, modelled sense, but in the running junction of the light and dark. When, in addition to this, an active contrast of colour is involved, the realism is doubly enhanced.

Thus, the sources of colour and of light having been investigated, the climax of Greco's art, and of all Greek painting, is

14

come to: the St. Maurice. Hidden away in the Escurial lies an æsthetic experience which the world can offer but once to any man. Enthusiasm is inept; generalisation odious; posterity disdains the one, revises the other. But let posterity recall, that for our generation, in the nineteen-twenties and thirties, this picture marked an advance in representational art, which no surviving monument, before or since, had surpassed; and furthermore that it expressed, in the highest degree, that impersonal, inward beauty of the glorious earth which others had sought through religion, and we still were seeking, we knew not how. Through this, at least, amid the deserts of print, of histories, of controversies and licentious memoirs, posterity, if it wishes, may know us.

Greco received the commission in his prime.[1] It was 1580; he was thirty-nine. The impression of Spain was still fresh upon him; the revived tradition of his race was in its first flower. And it was his opportunity, the opportunity which, in all probability, he had come to Spain to seek. The Escurial was in its newness, an impressive monument to all the hopeless folly and materialism of its time. Royal favour meant fame, employment, setting magnificent, field inexhaustible. The artist was on his mettle; he made reservations with a view to complete success. "It has come to my intelligence," wrote Philip II., while the Armada was already building, "that for lack of fine colours, and payment for labour on the work, he (Greco) will

[1] That he, as yet almost unknown in Spain, should have been thus chosen to decorate the very core of Philip's gigantic and much-beloved project may possibly have been due to the good offices of his compatriot, the Cretan Nicolas de Torre or Turrianus, who was at that time the official copyist of the royal library.

not undertake it.   And since it suits me . . . that it should be completed as soon as may be, I instruct you (the Prior) to supply him with some of those (colours) which he demands, especially ultramarine.   And as regards money, you may supply him with some on account."

The picture was painted to measure, for the high altar : nine feet ten inches in breadth, fourteen feet nine inches in height.   It was not finished, despite the royal interest and assistance, till August 17th, 1584.

Then the king, forswearing his last chance of reputation, withheld his approval.[1]   Greco, one feels, must in his heart of hearts have expected this result.   He had put his whole soul and being into the picture; and he must have known, by this time, that this was not the sort of thing that kings, any more than Cathedral chapters, demanded.   "That it did not please his Majesty," wrote Siguenza in 1605, "is not surprising; for he pleases few people; although they say it has a lot of art in it, and that the artist knows a lot. . . ."

To describe the picture is useless.   Conceived with the restricted palette of a fresco, but in such colouring, submarine blue from the rim of the Ægean, and yellow distilled from lemons and spring flowers, that it holds the moon prisoner for its assistance, it simply exhibits the superlative of all the principles which comprise the one principle of interpretational art, and whose

---

[1] Mancini throws a new light on this incident. He says: ". . . but when there appeared on the scene Pelegrin of Bologna, Frederico Zuccaro, and certain Flemings, who artfully and with smooth cunning came forward against him, he (Greco) decided to leave the court and retire." Actually Zuccaro did not arrive till eight years later; but other painters were there.

origins and progress it has been the purpose of this book to elucidate.

VII. Greco's Hellenism

Italy and Spain had left their impress on Greco. As parts of the world, sheltering components of the human race, he had imbibed their worth and assimilated it in his art. But fundamentally, in his directness of vision during an age twisted with obscure subservience to Catholicism and absolutism, and in his own opinion, he remained a Greek.

From the St. Maurice, rebuffed, he proceeded to the sober composition of the Burial of Count Orgaz. That nobleman had died in 1323. Eleven years before, certain monks of the order of St. Augustine had been obliged to forsake their convent on the banks of the Tagus on account of its unhealthiness; and the count had rendered them a signal service by procuring from the queen Mary of Molina another site, on which he desired that their new building, like the old, should be dedicated to St. Stephen. On his death, he was borne to the parish church of Santo Tomé in Toledo, which he had previously enlarged; and such had been the excellence of his life, that the saints Augustine and Stephen, who, as has been seen, had most benefited from it, honoured his funeral in person; and taking the corpse from its bearers, placed it in the grave themselves. In commemoration of the event, a chapel was built. But in 1564, some 250 years later, the village of Orgaz, jealous for the memory of its illustrious *seigneur*, brought an action against the parish priest of Santo Tomé for having failed to comply with the count's instructions that an inscription should be erected in his memory. The inscription was then executed.   And the priest saw fit to commission a picture which should portray the miracle that had attended the original interment.

The choice of Greco as the artist reveals a strange coincidence, and one which perhaps explains the enormous care and technical ability which he lavished on this picture and which afterwards caused the assessors to rate its value so high (see page 181). For this Count Orgaz was also, in part, a Greek, and one whose antecedents must have inspired any compatriot with reverence. Contemporary chroniclers, writing of the picture, describe him as "Don Gonzalo Ruyz of Toledo, descended from the clear lineage of Don Esteban Illan, who was a descendant of Don Pedro Palæologo, third son of the Emperor of Constantinople (from whom are descended the Dukes of Alba and the Counts of Oropesa and Orgaz). . . ."   Such an assertion might be dismissed as a mediæval fiction, were it not corroborated elsewhere. The Spanish traveller, Pero Tafur, while visiting Constantinople in the year 1438, observed with regret that the royal arms were not those which he had expected.   For he also was a descendant of this prince.   "I enquired of the Emperor (John VIII.)," he writes,[1] "why he did not carry those arms which it was formerly the custom for the Emperors to wear, that is the arms of my family. . . ."   To which John VIII. replied that his ancestor, who had retaken Constantinople from the Latins, "could never be prevailed upon to relinquish the arms which he formerly bore, which were and are two links joined. . . ."[2]

[1] *Travels of Pero Tafur,* Broadway Travellers Series.
[2] This is obviously a reference to the four "B's" of the Palæologus shield (see *The Byzantine Achievement,* by Robert Byron, pp. 241-243).   Tafur's

That Greco should have been aware of the ancestry of Count Orgaz is not unlikely, in view of the monument to the family's founder in Toledo Cathedral (see note).   But whether he was or no, there is abundant evidence of his inspired affection for his race.   In the decades that followed the battle of Lepanto (1571),

---

narrative continues: "Nevertheless the old arms, which are checky, can still be seen on the towers and buildings and the churches of the city, and when people put up their own buildings they still place the old arms upon them. I insisted, as best I could, that the Emperors should still wear those arms since they are the real arms of the Empire. . . .   To this the Emperor replied that the matter was still being debated between himself and the people."

It is plain from this account that, in describing the refugee prince as a Palæologus, the Spanish chroniclers were mistaken.   Dates confirm this. According to Pero Tafur, the prince in question had become the spokesman of the oppressed Greek nobles against his father; but that, rather than fight against the latter, he had sought asylum in Castile, whither he had come "at the time when Don Alfonso was reigning, who conquered Toledo, and whom some call Alfonso of the Pierced Hand.   Here the prince was known as Count Don Pedro, and was father of Don Esteban Yllan."   This king, Alfonso VI., was born in 1030, and died in 1109.   At that time the Palæologus family was only rising to prominence, and was far from having ambitions towards the Greek throne.   In any case the King, "married the prince to one of his own legitimate sisters, and left him to govern the kingdom while he went to war. . . .   They called him Don Peryllan, and he it was, they say, who entered Toledo and set up the King there. . . .   He is buried in the chapel of the ancient kings of Toledo, and high up on the roof he is painted on horseback with his standard and arms. . . ."   The capture of Toledo was in 1085; and Count Peryllan was certainly an historical personage. Sandoval records that the King made him governor of the Toledan Muzarabes, who "had always lived as Christians under the Moors."   The fact that Tafur saw his own arms on the buildings of Constantinople confirms the reality of his statements.   But Byzantine heraldry is an obscure subject; and an exhaustive search has failed to trace the identity of the self-exiled Porphyrogenitus. Perhaps some scholar, acquainted with the original histories of the period, may eventually disclose it.

Spain was regarded as the foremost champion of Christendom against the Turks; and thither journeyed a crowd of Greeks and other refugees, of all ranks and professions, who spread themselves throughout the chief towns of the kingdom and became engaged in unceasing propaganda on behalf of their forfeited rights and lost relations.   In Toledo alone there resided the Voivode of Moldavia, an Archbishop from Greater Armenia, the Bishops of Ithaca and Lepanto, Bishop Hieronymos Cocunari, George Cocunari, Governor of Spiro, the monks Nicephorus and Sabbas, the sea-captain Constantine, Eustace and George Œconomos, and many others.   The Bishops were planning the restitution of their sees; the monks, of their monasteries; the captain, of his sailors; the rest, of their wives and children.   The first instance of Greco's befriending a compatriot was in 1582, when he acted as interpreter for Michael Rizo Carcandil, who had been denounced before the Inquisition as a Mussulman.[1]   It was during this case that he described himself as a native of Candia.   Later, in 1603, he and George Manuel vouched their knowledge of the monk Sabbas for legal purposes.   In 1605, Eustace Œconomos made Greco his executor.   Finally, in 1614, two more Greeks, Constantine Phocas and the doctor Demetrius Paramoulis, were with Greco at his death and witnessed his will.

The relationship between the well-established Theotocopoulos

---

[1] The accused, who had been forcibly made a Turk in Athens in his youth, had eventually escaped to Rome and entered the service of another Greek, Demetrius Phocas, who had already one other servant called Nicola.   On arrival in Spain, the latter denounced both his master and fellow, the basis of the charge being, apparently, that they washed too much.   It was the age immediately preceding the expulsion of the Moriscoes, and all strange practices were regarded with suspicion.

family and their less fortunate fellow exiles is also revealed by a long series of documents in the Toledo archives dealing with the case of Thomas Trechello. This unfortunate man, a native of Cyprus, had recently received a royal and papal licence to beg alms for the ransom of his wife and son. Soon after, he fell mortally ill. But before dying, he entrusted his purpose to Manusso Theotocopoulos, supposedly a brother of El Greco (see note on page 171), in the following words: "Item: it is my wish that all the alms received by the said Señor Manusso he shall send and remit to Venice to the Lord Archbishop Gabriel of Philadelphia (Venice), that he may send them to Cyprus to the said city of Leukosia, where they are to be delivered to a priest and preaching monk named Panfenio in the monastery of Zonati in order that he may deliver them to my wife and son, who live in the said city near the said monastery of Zonati, which said wife of mine is called Cibriana, and my son, Hieronymos Thomas." Manusso took the licence and such money as had already been received; but being, as he says in a petition to the Alcade, "sick and infirm—*enferme y empedido*," and not having been able, and not being able, to make use of the licence himself, he begged that it might be extended for as long as possible, in order that the responsibility for collecting the ransom might devolve on the apothecary Pedro Sanchez de Mendoza. An astonishing number of affidavits, including those of George Manuel and Preboste, were required to complete this process. Whether Cibriana and Hieronymos Thomas ever received their liberty is unknown. But the incident is interesting as showing that Greco was neither so lonely an exile as he is generally depicted nor necessarily out of communication with his native island.

During his early youth in Italy, Greco painted not only the Mount Sinai, but also a portrait on copper of Bessarion, the famous Greek Cardinal of the previous century, whose palace in Rome sheltered many of the refugees from Constantinople immediately after the fall. A posthumous likeness of this kind can only have been undertaken by the artist in deference to its associations. Towards the end of his life he was wont to discourse with the Hellenist Antonio Covarubbias, who understood his native tongue, upon the future of Greece—at a time when, in the eyes of the West, Greece no longer existed. The true conceit, faith it may be called, in his race flashed out: the Spaniards, in his opinion, were worse than the Italians; and they were bar-barians.[1] On painting a picture of St. Paul, of which two ver-sions are now at Toledo, he placed in the apostle's hand a paper bearing the legend: " Προς Τίτον τῆς κρητῶν ἐκκλησίας πρῶτον ἐπίσκοπον χειροτονεθέντα—to Titus, ordained first bishop of the church of the Cretans." This, for him, was St. Paul's impor-tance: that he once wrote a letter to the first head of the Cretan church. In an age when it seemed that all hope for his people was extinguished, he was faithful alike to the past and to the future. If he could paint better than anyone else on earth, it was because he was a Greek. He preserved always the signa-ture of his school and tradition, whose style, attached to other names, may still be seen on icons in the Greek churches of Egypt. All the pride of centuries, and all the glories that had become no more than a memory, seem to have revived for one last triumph

---

[1] The authority for these conversations is Meier-Græfe, who has informed the writer that, to the best of his memory, he derived his knowledge of them from Señor Cossio.

in the words : " Δομήνικος Θεοτοκόπουλος κρής ἐποίη —Domenicos Theotocopoulos, Cretan, did it."

And if Greco was a Greek, he was a Byzantine. His mysticism is commonly accepted; and it is commonly identified, also, with the communings of St. Teresa and St. John of the Cross, Spanish contemporaries. "What must a soul concealed in God desire," wrote the former, "but to love, and love again, and being lighted up with love, transmute itself anew to loving?" Greco's soul desired more than that. If the feminine stuff of sixteenth century mysticism comes out in some of his religious pictures, it was because he was painting to order for the Church. But essentially he was not religious, in the restricted sense of the word. "He was a great philosopher," wrote Pacheco, who knew him. His mysticism, in fact, was of a superior type. Just as he knew that reproduction or idealisation of visible object was not only no reproduction, but a degradation, so he knew that reason could help him but little in his quest. Yet his was no subjective, vagrant mentality. On the contrary, he possessed the supreme objectivity of all : the ability to subordinate his intelligence and genius to the understanding of the One Element through man and the beauty of the world. Had William Blake had genius or education, he might have been a great artist; but he could never have painted portraits. Greco painted magnificent portraits. The comparison epitomises the character of Greco's mysticism. It was no part of his philosophy to submerge his individuality and consciousness in direct communion with the External. He was concerned, rather, to reach it through the objects about him. That is art. And that was art to the Byzantines. But for them, the only channel was the narrow Christian story. Greco, their child, set his sails on the ocean.

In the eighth and ninth centuries, the Byzantines discovered a new purpose in art. In the tenth and eleventh, they perfected a corresponding technique. In the eleventh and twelfth, their rulers, scholars, preachers, monks, and common folk, coalesced in a common impulse towards humanisation. In the thirteenth and fourteenth, they communicated the purpose, in the guise of a humanised style of painting, to Italy. The Italians then revived the classical technique of reproduction, which so overwhelmed them that, in the sixteenth, they lost the purpose. But, in the sixteenth, came the last Byzantine, who borrowed of the new freedom, only to further the original aim. Then he died without succession; and not until three centuries later was the aim rediscovered. This is the history of interpretational painting in Europe.

BIBLIOGRAPHY

Note.—This does not include the many general works on Byzantine, Italian, Spanish, and twentieth century art, which have contributed to the opinions expressed in the text.

CHAPTER 2: ICONOCLASM

Arnold, Sir T., *Painting in Islam*, ch. i., Oxford, 1928.

Bevan, E., *Later Greek Religion*, London, 1927.

Bouquet, A. C., *The Real Presence*, Cambridge, 1928.

Bréhier, L., *La querelle des images*, Paris, 1904.
———— *L'art chrétien: son developpement iconographique*, Paris, 1928 (2nd edition).
———— and Battifol, P., *Les Survivances du culte impérial romain*, Paris, 1920.

Clerc, C., *Les théories relatives au culte des images du IIe siècle après J.C.*, Paris, 1915.

Conybeare, F. C., *The Key of Truth: a Manual of the Paulician Church of Armenia*, Oxford, 1898.

Dujardin, E., *The Source of the Jewish Tradition*, trans. by J. McCabe, London, 1911.

Gardner, A., *Theodore of Studium*, London, 1905.

Gfrörer, A., *Byzantinische Geschichten, Vol. III: Der Bildersturm*, Graz, 1873.

Glover, T. R., *Progress in Religion*, London, 1922.

Harnack, A. von, *A History of Dogma*, Vol. IV., trans. by E. B. Speirs and J. Miller, London, 1898.

Lavoix, H., *Les arts musulmans: de l'emploi des figures*, Gazette des Beaux Arts, 1875.

Lombard, A., *Constantin V., Empereur des Romains*, Paris, 1902.

MARIN, L., *Les moines de Constantinople*, Paris, 1897.

MILLET, G., *Les iconoclastes et la croix*, Bulletin de Correspondance Hellénique, Vol. XXXIV.

PARGOIRE, R. P. J., *L'église byzantine de 527 à 847*, Paris, 1905.

SCHWARZLOSE, K., *Der Bilderstreit*, Gotha, 1890.

STRZYGOWSKI, J., *Origin of Christian Church Art*, trans. by O. M. Dalton and H. J. Braunholtz, Oxford, 1923.

TOUGARD, A., *La persécution iconoclaste d'après la correspondance de saint Théodore Studite*, Revue des Questions Historiques, July, 1891.

VASILIEV, A. A., *History of the Byzantine Empire*, Vol. I., pps. 307-324 and 343-352, Madison (U.S.A.), 1928, giving more detailed references.

CHAPTER 3: THE EXPANSION OF ICONOGRAPHY

I. GENERAL

BRÉHIER, L., *L'art chrétien: son developpement iconographique des origines à nos jours*, Paris, 1928 (2nd edition).

DALTON, O. M., *Byzantine Art and Archæology*, Oxford, 1911. Ch. XII. deals with particular themes.
———— *East Christian Art*, Oxford, 1925.

DIEHL, CH., *Manuel d'art byzantin*, Paris, 1926 (2nd edition).

KRUMBACHER, K., *Geschichte der byzantinischen Litteratur*, Munich, 1897, surveying the whole body of Byzantine texts, and having an excellent index. Bibliography 9, *Kunstgeschichte*, p. 1113, particularly sections 4, *Ikonographie und Symbolik*, and 10, *Einfluss der byzantinischen Kunst auf das Abendland*, suggest innumerable problems.

MILLET, G., *Recherches sur l'iconographie de l'Evangile aux XIVᵉ, XVᵉ et XVIᵉ siècles, d'après les monuments de Mistra, de la Macédoine et du Mont Athos*, Paris, 1916, a monumental dictionary of themes and their origins, but confined to the Gospel only.

II. IN THE SPHERE OF CONSTANTINOPLE

ANISIMOV, A. J., *Our Lady of Vladimir,* trans. by Princess N. G. Yaschwill and T. N. Rodzianko, Prague, 1928.

BURY, J. B., *A History of the Eastern Roman Empire, 802-867,* London, 1912.

FORSTER, E. M., *Alexandria: A History and a Guide, Part I., Sect. III., II., Neoplatonism,* Alexandria, 1922.

GHELLINCK, G. DE, *Le mouvement théologique du XIIᵉ siècle,* Paris, 1914.

PSELLOS, M., *Chronographie,* trans., and with valuable introduction, by E. Renauld, Paris, 1926.

VASILIEV, A. A., *History of the Byzantine Empire,* Vol. I., pps. 352-363 and 437-452, Madison (U.S.A.), 1928

ZERVOS, C., *Michel Psellos,* Paris, 1920.

III. IN THE POPULAR SPHERE

BRÉHIER, L., *Le théâtre religieux à Byzance,* Journal des Savants, August and September, 1913.
——— *Les " homélies " du moine Jacques,* Académie des Inscriptions et de Belles Lettres, Fondation Piot, Mémoires, 1920.

JERPHANION, G. DE, *La date des peintures de Toqale Kilissé en Cappadoce,* Revue Archéologique, 1912.
——— *Le rôle de Syrie et de l'Asie Mineure dans la formation de l'iconographie chrétienne,* Beyrut, 1922.
——— *Les églises rupestres de Cappadoce,* text, with plates in two albums, Paris, 1925.

JUGIE, M., *Homélies mariales byzantines,* Patrologia Orientalis, compiled by R. Graffin and F. Nau, Vol. XVI., Paris, 1922.

LA PIANA, G., *La rappresentazioni sacre nella letteratura bizantina dalle origini al secolo XI.,* Grottaferrata, 1912.

IV. In Italy

Bréhier, L., *Les colonies d'orientaux en occident,* Byzantinische Zeitschrift, 1903.

Carrà, C., *Giotto,* London, 1925.

Cecchi, E., *Les peintres siennois,* French trans. by J. Chuzeville, Paris, 1928.

Frothingham, A. L., *Byzantine Artists in Italy,* American Journal of Archæology, Vol. IX., 1894.

Grüneisen, W. de, *Tradizione orientale-bizantina, influssi locale ed inspirazione individuale nel ciclo cristologico della " Maestà " di Duccio,* Siena, 1913.

Mâle, E., *L'art religieux de la fin du moyen âge en France,* Paris, 1922 (2nd edition).

Muntz, E., *Les artistes byzantins dans l'Europe latine du Ve au XVe siècle,* Revue de l'Art Chrétien, 1893.

Muratov, P., *La peinture byzantine,* French trans. by J. Chuzeville, Paris, 1928. The plates are useful, though the author has but the faintest idea of what is and is not Byzantine painting.

Soulier, G., *Les influences orientales dans la peinture toscane,* Paris, 1924.

Thode, H., *Saint François d'Assise et les origines de l'art de la Renaissance en Italie,* Paris, 1904.

Van Marle, R., *La peinture romaine au moyen-âge,* Strasbourg, 1921.

———— *Recherches sur l'iconographie de Giotto et de Duccio,* Strasbourg, 1920.

———— *The Development of the Italian Schools of Painting,* The Hague, 1923-1926.

Wilpert, J., *Die Römischen Mosaiken und Malereien der Kirchlichen Bauten von IV-XIII Jahrhundert,* Freiburg im Breisgau, 1916.

V. Particular Themes

Note.—The origins and precedents of many subjects in Byzantine art are only to be found in the remotest by-ways of archæology and theology. The books given here are mainly valuable for the clues they provide. See also Section I.

CABROL, F., AND LECLERQ, H., *Dictionnaire d'archéologie chrétienne et de liturgie*, A-Li, Paris, 1907-1930.

DENYS OF FOURNA, see Chapter 4.

DIDRON, M., *Christian Iconography*, trans. by E. J. Millington, London, 1851.

DURAND, P., *Etude sur l'Etimacia . . . dans l'iconographie grecque chrétienne*, Chartres, 1867.

JACOBY, A., *Ein bisher unbeachteter apokrypher Bericht über die Taufe Jesu*, Strasbourg, 1902.

JAMES, M. R., *The Apocryphal New Testament*, Oxford, 1924.

MONNIER, T., *La descente aux enfers*, Paris, 1905.

STRZYGOWSKI, J., *Ikonographie der Taufe Christi*, Munich, 1885.

VARIOT, J., *Les évangiles apocryphes*, Paris, 1878.

WALKER, A., *Apocryphal Gospels, Acts, and Revelations*, Edinburgh, 1870.

WILPERT, J., *Die Malereien der Katakomben Roms*, Freiburg im Breisgau, 1903.

CHAPTER 4: THE PAINTINGS OF ATHOS AND MISTRA

CENNINI, CENNINO, *The Book of Art of*, trans. from Italian by C. J. Herringham, London, 1899.

DENYS OF FOURNA, *Guide de la peinture* (usually known as Didron's *Manuel d'iconographie chrétienne*), trans. from Greek by P. Durand, Paris, 1845.
———— *Manuel d'iconographie chrétienne, accompagné de ses sources principales inédites*, with preface and notes by A. Papadopoulo-Kérameus, St. Petersburg, 1909 (all in Greek). The text is fuller than in the above, and there is an efficient index.

MILLET, G., *Inscriptions byzantines de Mistra*, Bulletin de Correspondance Hellénique, 1899.
———— *Monuments byzantins de Mistra*, Paris, 1910.
———— *Monuments de l'Athos, I.: Les peintures*, Paris, 1927.
———— *Rapport sur une mission à Mistra*, Bulletin de Correspondance Hellénique, 1895.
———— *Recherches au Mont Athos*, Bulletin de Correspondance Hellénique, 1905.

MILLET, G., *Recherches sur l'iconographie de l'Evangile . . .* (see previous section).

————, PARGOIRE, J., AND PETIT, L., *Recueil des inscriptions chrétiennes de l'Athos,* Paris, 1904.

TOZER, H. F., *A Byzantine Reformer* (George Gemistos Plethon), Journal of Hellenic Studies, 1886.

———— *Byzantine Satire,* Journal of Hellenic Studies, 1881. This and the above article give the best descriptions extant of the social life of Mistra in the fifteenth century.

CHAPTER 5: I. CRETAN CULTURE AFTER THE FALL OF CONSTANTINOPLE

ARISTARCHI, S. D', *Les Grecs à l'Escurial,* Ὁ ἐν Κωνσταντινουπόλει Ἑλληνικὸς Φιλολογικὸς Σύλλογος, Πεντηκονταετηρὶς 1861-1911, Constantinople, 1913-1921.

FIRMIN-DIDOT, A., *Alde Manuce et l'Hellénisme à Venise,* Paris, 1875.

GEROLA, G., *Monumenti Veneti nell' Isola di Creta,* Vol. III., Venice, 1908.

HESSELING, D. C., *Histoire de la littérature grecque moderne,* ch. i., Paris, 1924.

MARSHALL, F. H., AND MAVROGORDATO, J., *Three Cretan Plays,* Oxford, 1929.

MAVROGORDATO, J., *The Greek Drama in Crete in the Seventeenth Century,* Journal of Hellenic Studies, 1928.

———— *An Unknown Greek Culture,* Die Böttcherstrasse, Bremen, December, 1928.

———— *The Erotokritos,* Oxford, 1929.

PERNOT, H., *Etudes de littérature grecque moderne,* ch. iv., Paris, 1916.

VELUDO, J., Ἑλλήνων Ὀρθοδόξων Ἀποικία ἐν Βενετίᾳ, Venice, 1893.

CHAPTER 5: II. GRECO

BERTAUX, E., *Notes sur le Greco, III.: Le byzantinisme,* Revue de l'Art Ancien et Moderne, 1913.

Calvert, A. F., and Hartley, C. G., *El Greco*, London, 1909.

Cossio, M. B., *El Greco*, Madrid, 1908.
———— *Lo que sabe de la Vida del Greco*, Madrid, 1914.

Mancini, G., *Alcuni considerationi appartenenti alla pittura*, pp. 210-212, British Museum, Harleian MSS. 1672. See also R. Longhi, *Il soggiorno romano del Greco*, L'Arte, 1914.

Mayer, A. L., *Dominico Theotocopuli, El Greco*, Munich, 1926.
———— *Grecos Gotik und seine Beziehungen zur Byzantinischer Kunst*, Kunst und Künstler, 1915.

Meier-Græfe, A. J., *The Spanish Journey*, trans. by J. Holroyd Reece, London, 1926.

Rutter, F., *El Greco*, London, 1930. Mr. Rutter very kindly placed an advance copy of this book at the writer's disposal.

San Roman, F. de B., *El Greco en Toledo*, Madrid, 1910.
———— *De la Vida del Greco (Nueva serie de documentos ineditos)*, Archivo Español de Arte y Arqueologia, Vol. III., 1927.

Villar, E. H. del, *El Greco en España*, Madrid, 1928, with extensive bibliography.

Willümsen, J. F. W., *La jeunesse du peintre El Greco*, Paris, 1927. This book, though æsthetically unreliable, and filled with preposterous attributions, contains useful biographical facts.

Not less valuable than books has been the wisdom of Dr. Tancred Borenius, Mr. John Mavrogordato, and Mr. G. M. Young.

INDEX

Note.—Large categories of names, otherwise removed from the general argument of the book, will be found under "Greco" and "Iconoclasm." Iconographic themes and subjects of pictures are printed in italics.

227

CLASSIFICATION OF PLATES SHOWING DATES, SCHOOLS, AND ARTISTS

CAPPADOCIAN SCHOOL

Late Xth or early XIth century : QARANLEQ KILISSEH, Pl. 45. i.

MACEDONIAN SCHOOL ON MOUNT ATHOS

Early XIVth century : PROTATON, Pls. 11. i, 15. ii, 24. i, 25. i, 39. i, 42. ii, 47, 84. i, 85. i, ii.

C. 1302 : CHILANDARI, Pls. 33. i, 34. ii, 40. ii, 41. ii, 52. ii, 61. i.

1312 : VATOPEDI, Pls. 11. ii, 37. i, 41. i, 50, 55. i.

C. 1312 : VATOPEDI (NARTHEX), Pls. 43. i, 48. i, 58. i.

XIVth or XVth century : CHAPEL OF THE PRODROME, CARYES, Pls. 8. i, ii, 10. i, ii, 24. ii, 28. i, ii, 29. i, ii, 30. i, ii, 67. i, 78. ii.

FLORENTINE SCHOOL

C. 1290-1300 : by a PUPIL OF GIOTTO, Pl. 68. ii.

1305-1306 : by GIOTTO, Pls. 12. iii, 25. ii, 35. ii, 57. i, 75. ii.

SIENESE SCHOOL

1308-1311 : by DUCCIO, Pls. 11. iii, 19. i, 37. ii, 39. ii, 42. i, 43. ii, 48. ii, 53. ii, 55. ii, 59. ii.

C. 1330 : by UGOLINO DA SIENA, Pl. 82. iii.

C. 1350 : by BARNA DA SIENA, Pl. 27. i.

SCHOOLS OF MISTRA

I. Early

Probably 1310-1320 : ST DEMETRIUS', Pls. 13. i, 76. i.

II. Middle

Probably late XIVth century : BRONTOCHEION, Pls. 16. i, 76. ii.

Late XIVth or early XVth century : PERIBLEPTOS, by the finished artist, Pls. 9. ii, 32. ii, 36. ii, 59. i, 68. i, 77. i, 79. i.
by the impressionist artist, Pls. 49. i, 57. ii.

III. Late

C. 1428 : PANTANASSA, Pls. 14. ii, 17, 19. ii, 20, 22, 34. i, 36. i, 60. i, ii, 77. ii, 78. i, 83. i.

CRETAN SCHOOL ON MOUNT ATHOS

1512 : LAVRA REFECTORY, Pls. 72, 74. i, ii, 87. ii.

1535 : LAVRA, by THEOPHANES OF CRETE, Pls. 33. ii, 38. i, 49. ii, 52. i, 53. i, 69. i, ii, 83. i, 83. ii, 85. iii.

1544 : XENOPHONTOS,, by ANTONY, Pls. 13. ii, 21. i, 23. i, 24. iii, 27. ii, iii, 38. ii, 44, 51. i, 54. ii.

1547 : DIONYSIOU, by ZORZI OF CRETE, Pls. 45. ii, 54. i, 63.

Probably 1547 : DIONYSIOU REFECTORY, Pls. 70, 71. i, ii, 75. i.

1555 : ST PAUL'S, Pls. 14. i, 15. i, 18, 23. ii, 31. i, ii, 35. i, 38. iii, 61. ii, 64. ii.

1560 : LAVRA, CHAPEL OF ST NICOLAS, by FRANGOS CATELLANOS OF THEBES, Pl. 64. i.

1563 : XENOPHONTOS, by THEOPHANES, Pls. 51. ii (probably), 62. i.

1568 : DOCHEIARIOU, Pls. 21. ii, 23. iii, 32. i, 58. ii, 86.

XVIth century : DOCHEIARIOU REFECTORY, Pl. 9. i.

1584-1628 : LAVRA, dome, Pl. 12. ii.

1621 : CHILANDARI REFECTORY, Pl. 40. i.

BY EL GRECO

1565 (?) : Pls. 90, 93. i, ii.

1566 (?) : Pl. 84. ii.

1579 : Pl. 46.

Probably 1579-1580 : Pl. 73.

1580-1581 : Pl. 81.

1584-1587 : Pl. 66.

1584-1594 : Pl. 26.

1594-1604 : Pl. 88.

C. 1604 : Pl. 80.

After 1600 (?) : Pl. 94.

1604-1614 : Pl. 12. iv.

VARIOUS

XVIth century : by EMMANUEL TSANPHOURNARI, Pl. 87. i.

Early XVIIth century : ST NICOLAS', MISTRA, Pl. 16. ii.

Probably XVIIth century : CHAPEL OF ST LAZARUS, XENOPHONTOS, MOUNT ATHOS, Pl. 67. ii.

Probably 1701 : PRODROME, CARYES, MOUNT ATHOS, dome, Pl. 12. i.

i

Mosaic of the GOOD SHEPHERD.

Mausoleum of Galla Placidia, Ravenna.

Vth century.

see p. 27.

ii

Mosaic of the DEISIS (Christ between the Virgin and St John the Baptist).

Vatopedi, Mount Athos.

XIth century.

see p. 189.

This theme belongs essentially to the middle period of Byzantine art. In St Mark's at Venice, the evangelist takes the place of the Baptist.

These two mosaics illustrate the difference in the conceptions of Christ before and after the iconoclast controversy. The first reveals the early type of Hellenistic god gracefully posed in a setting of symbolic benevolence; the second, the Supreme Judge, invested with the face and furniture of earthly royalty, and attended by the two chief intercessors on behalf of the world.

Plate 2

i

ii

i

Mosaic of the VIRGIN AND CHILD attended by angels, martyrs, and
   local dignitaries.

Parenzo.

539-543.

see pp. 26, 28.

The earliest surviving instance of the Virgin's occupying the place of honour
   in the apse.

ii

Mosaic of the VIRGIN AND CHILD attended by the archangels.

Chiti, Cyprus.

IXth century.

see pp. 28, 30.

Possibly the earliest surviving example of post-iconoclast decoration.

These two mosaics, like those on Pl. 5, illustrate the static and the rhythmic conceptions of the
human form before and after the iconoclast controversy.

Plate 3

i

ii

i

Ivory of ST JOHN THE BAPTIST.

Chair of Maximian, Ravenna.

VIth century.

see p. 29.

ii

Ivory of ST JOHN THE BAPTIST.

Victoria and Albert Museum, London.

XIth century.

see p. 29.

These two ivories illustrate the coarse Hellenistic naturalism of the pre-iconoclast period compared with the exquisite formalism of the true and later Byzantine genius.

Plate 4

i

ii

i

Mosaic of ST DEMETRIUS between the Prefect
   Leo and a bishop.

St Demetrius', Salonica.

VIIth century.

see pp. 26, 30.

ii

Mosaic of the DESCENT INTO HELL.

St Luke's of Stiris in Phocis, Greece.

XIth century.

see p. 30, also notes to Plate 58.

See note to Plate 3.

Plate 5

i

ii

CHURCH INTERIOR, facing south.

Xenophontos, Mount Athos.

Pavement of *opus alexandrinum*, pillars, and probably
   whole structure, XIth century.

Paintings 1544.

see pp. 79, 114, 151.

This interior, typical of all the Athonite churches except the Protaton at Caryes, shows the charm
and purity of the " Greek cross " plan which developed after the iconoclast controversy (see
p. 75), simultaneously with a more exact and sacramental iconography. The method here
observed of dividing the various scenes into panels by red and white borders is characteristic of the
Cretan School, and was obviously favoured by the lack of uninterrupted wall-space in the Greek
cross plan. The Macedonian school, in general, preferred the long frieze, in which the same figure
appears several times (see Pl. 15. ii). This habit derived from the monkish-didactic illustrators
and is found throughout Cappadocia. With the exception of St. Demetrius', a basilica, the
churches of Mistra incline to the former method. But it is impossible to draw too fine a distinction on this point.

Plate 6

INTERIOR OF CRUCIFORM REFECTORY, facing west, or towards the bottom of the cross.

The Lavra, Mount Athos.

Walls and marble-topped tables probably c. 1000.

Roof and paintings 1512.

see p. 149.

Plate 7

i

GOD : " I AM THAT I AM."

Prodrome, Caryes, Mount Athos.

Macedonian School.

XIVth or XVth century.

see pp. 121, 124 (colour), 193.

Daniel VII, 9 : " whose garment was white as snow, and the hair of his head like the pure wool."   See also Exodus III, 14.

ii

THE HOLY GHOST.

Prodrome, Caryes, Mount Athos.

Macedonian School.

XIVth or XVth century.

see pp. 121, 124 (colour).

For the propriety of depicting God and the Holy Ghost, see p. 68.   They here form part of the Trinity, the third person being implied by the altar beneath them.   This theme is unknown before the XIVth century.   Compare Pl. 9. ii, where Christ is actually portrayed in the robes and office of a priest.   Compare also Pl. 26.   The inscription in the present instance seems to have been designed either by the composition or by a desire to confute the Latin *filioque* : " The All-Holy Ghost proceeding from the Father and abiding in the Son."   For the significance of the two Auras, see note to Pl. 31.

Plate 8

i

ii

i

GOD, as seen by St John the Evangelist.

Docheiariou Refectory, Mount Athos.

Cretan School.

XVIth century.

see p. 160 (colour).   Compare Pl. 71. ii.

ii

TRINITY.

Peribleptos, Mistra.

Middle School of Mistra, by the more finished
of the two Peribleptos artists (see p. 135).

Late XIVth or early XVth century.

see p. 193, note to Pl. 8.   Compare Pl. 26.

A procession of angels, depicted on the side-walls
of the apse, defiles past the altar bearing the
adjuncts of the Liturgy (see Pl. 77. i).

Plate 9

ii

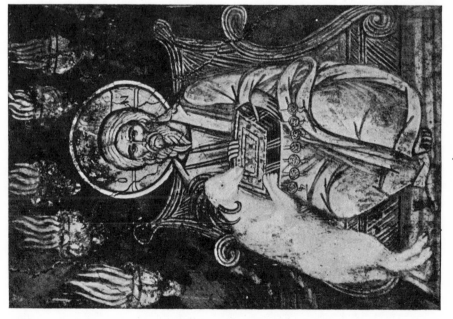

i

i

NOAH, bearing the ark.

Prodrome, Caryes, Mount Athos.

Macedonian School.

XIVth or XVth century.

see p. 122 (colour).

Noah is earliest depicted in the Roman catacombs, standing in
the ark.

ii

JONAH.

Prodrome, Caryes, Mount Athos.

Macedonian School.

XIVth or XVth century.

see p. 121 (colour).

The earliest known representation of Jonah is sculptured on
a IIIrd century sarcophagus at Arles. The theme was
popular in early Christian iconography as typifying the three
days' entombment and the Resurrection—a parallel developed
by Tertullian and St Augustine. Despite the fact that
Denys of Fourna includes the whole Jonah cycle in his
manual, neither this scene (a single one) nor its fellows are
found elsewhere on Athos or at Mistra.

Plate 10

i

ii

i

CHRIST, addressing the woman of Samaria.
    Protaton, Mount Athos.

Macedonian School.

Early XIVth century.

see p. 114 (colour).

ii

CHRIST, explaining the Washing of Feet.

Vatopedi, Mount Athos.

Macedonian School.

1312.

iii

CHRIST, appearing preparatory
    to the Ascension.

Siena.

By Duccio.

1308-1311.

see p. 102.

These three paintings illustrate the identity of inspiration in Greek and Italian art at the opening
of the XIVth century. The face in fig. iii finds analogy in that of fig. i; while Duccio's method
of linear lighting, employed by him in the post-Crucifixion scenes of the Maesta, may be seen in
fig. ii. For the resemblance between Duccio's apostles and those in fig. ii, see Pls. 43. ii, 48. ii.
None the less, it is important to note the increased grace and gentleness of the Italian's conception.

Plate 11

i

ii

iii

i

CHRIST PANTOCRATOR.

Prodrome, Caryes, Mount Athos.

Probably 1701 (see p. 119).

see pp. 81, 192.

The circular inscription reads:
"Know and behold that I am and
there is no God but me. I made
the earth and man on it, and
with my hand I established the
heaven."

ii

CHRIST PANTOCRATOR.

The Lavra, Mount Athos.

Cretan School.

Between 1584 and 1628; perhaps a
restoration of the 1535 original.

see pp. 81, 192.

iii

Medallion of CHRIST.

Ceiling of the Arena Chapel, Padua.

by Giotto.

1305-1306.

see p. 103.

iv

Portrait of CHRIST.

Casa Greco, Toledo.

by El Greco.

1604-1614.

see p. 192.

The single iconographic tradition of these four paintings is obvious. The Christ Pantocrator, Ruler of the World, though first appearing in the Vth century at St Paul's outside the Walls, Rome, did not come to occupy the central cupola of every Byzantine church till after the iconoclast controversy and the evolution of the Greek cross plan. It is common to both the Macedonian and Cretan Schools; but on account of its dome's vulnerability to earthquakes and weather, has been the first composition to disappear in ruined churches, and the first to be wholly repainted during the repair of others.

Plate 12

i

ii

iii

iv

i

VIRGIN AND CHILD, erect.

St Demetrius', Mistra.

Early school of Mistra, showing monkish-didactic influence.

Probably 1310-1320.

see pp. 81, 131 (colour), 203.

ii

VIRGIN AND CHILD: "MISTRESS OF THE ANGELS."

Xenophontos, Mount Athos.

Cretan School, by Antony.

1544.

see p. 81.

The Virgin is seated on the throne and cushion of Byzantine royalty. The Archangels wear the uniform of ushers to the Byzantine court.

It is impossible to enumerate here the various types of Virgin, usually based on the oldest and sacredest icons of Eastern Christendom, which have been perpetuated in Orthodox iconography. Denys of Fourna gives sixteen. Not till after the iconoclast controversy did the Virgin universally displace Christ in the vault of the main apse, eventually exchanging her rôle of intercessor for that of queen (see note to Pl. 3. i).

Plate 13

i

ii

i

VIRGIN AND CHILD.

St Paul's, Mount Athos.

Cretan School.

1555.

ii

VIRGIN AND CHILD, the Virgin suppliant.

Pantanassa, Mistra.

Late School of Mistra.

c. 1428.

see p. 138.

The uplifted arms derive from the female suppliant of late pagan funerary monuments and the earliest Christian iconography.

Plate 14

i

ii

i

PRESENTATION OF THE VIRGIN : the priest receives her, aged three, from Joachim and Anna, attended by Hebrew maidens ; (above) she receives food from an angel.

St Paul's, Mount Athos.

Cretan School.

1555.

ii

PRESENTATION OF THE VIRGIN : she arrives with Joachim and Anna, and is followed to the priest by Hebrew maidens bearing lighted candles.

Protaton, Mount Athos.

Macedonian School.

Early XIVth century.

The vindication, at the Council of Ephesus in 431, of Mary's claim to the title of Theotokos (God-bearer) gave impetus to her cult. By the VIth century, the iconography of her conception and childhood, from Joachim's first bemoanment of his sterility to her betrothal with Joseph, had already been expanded into nine scenes, including Nativity and Presentation, and deriving their details from the IInd century Protevangelium of James the Less and the other " Infancy Gospels." These may be seen on the pillars (VIth century) of the ciborium at St Mark's. How clearly they tended to derive from the corresponding scenes of Christ's infancy is illustrated at Daphni (c. 1100), where Joachim lifts his daughter to the priest despite her three years. A later cycle, of which traces remain in the Brontocheion at Mistra, rounded off her history. But scenes from this, with the exception of the ubiquitous Dormition (Pls. 65, 67. i, ii, 68. i, 69. i, ii), are less common.

Plate 15

i

ii

i

ZACHARIAS the priest.

Brontocheion, Mistra.

Middle School of Mistra.

Probably late XIVth century.

see pp. 132-3 (colour).

The written scroll, in Byzantine iconography, denotes its holder's actual words. Zacharias utters : " Christ, fulfilling the words of salvation of the prophets, was born of thee, O Virgin." The Greek, which forms an iambic and a half, is probably taken from a Byzantine hymn paraphrasing Luke II. 69, 70 : " And hath raised up an horn of salvation for us in the house of his servant David ; as he spake by the mouth of his holy prophets, . . ." Thus, perhaps, will the future archæologist, discovering, " The King of Love my shepherd is, his goodness faileth never " inscribed on some Anglican window-pane, resolve his perplexity in Psalm XXIII. 1 : " The Lord is my shepherd ; I shall not want."

ii

ANGEL OF ANNUNCIATION.

St Nicolas', Mistra.

Early XVIIth century.

see p. 161 (colour), note to Pl. 17.

Plate 16

i

ii

ANGEL OF ANNUNCIATION.

Pantanassa, Mistra.

Late School of Mistra.

c. 1428.

see pp. 141-2 (colour), 203.

Above, as is customary, David sings : " Hearken, O daughter, and consider, and incline thine ear." (Psalm XLV. 10.)

The Annunciation is early found in the IInd century cemetery of Priscilla at Rome. Its iconography was considerably expanded by James the Less and the Pseudo-Matthew. Hence the fountain in the foreground, at which Mary had come to fill her pitcher. Note the quail drinking ; also the palatial background, with porphyry pillars, emblematic of royalty.

Plate 17

NATIVITY.

St Paul's, Mount Athos.

Cretan School.

1555.

see pp. 157-8 (colour).

This scene (see also Pls. 19. i, 21. i, ii), is first known to have been portrayed in the Roman catacombs of the IVth century. It probably existed also in the church of the Nativity at Bethlehem (nave IVth century, chancel VIth), since this building was spared by the Persians in 615, on their finding its façade embellished with a large picture of the Magi clothed in Persian national dress. The present composition, of which the earliest example is found on a VIth century paten in the British Museum, has become disordered with a wealth of incident. Mary rests on a large cushion. On the authority of the Pseudo-Matthew, the birth takes place in a cave, which the party only exchanged for a stable on the third day. Nevertheless his ox and ass (first found on a Roman sarcophagus of 343) are present, and Duccio (Pl. 19. i) builds the stable in the cave. Above, the star is in the centre; the angel appears to the shepherds; the Magi arrive (see also Pl. 20). Below, Joseph in the corner observes the standing still of creation according to James the Less; though in Pl. 20 a shepherd blows a horn, and in Pl. 21. ii, another plays a pipe. In the opposite corner, the midwife Zelomi pours water for the infant's bath; while her crony Salome tests its heat. It is often asserted that the apocryphal gospels provide authority for this bath. They do not. The earliest known literary reference is by Symeon Metaphrastes towards the end of the Xth century. The incident itself is found depicted in the IVth century cemetery of St Valentine in Rome.

The story of Salome, and of how the hand that doubted the virgin birth was withered and then cured, is told by James the Less and the Pseudo-Matthew. From the time of St Jerome (died 420), who angrily affirmed that Mary *et mater et obstetrix fuit*, it has continued to arouse disgust in the squeamish. Yet it is not difficult to imagine the surprise, even querulousness, of a sophisticated society suddenly asked to reform itself on account of a series of events which began with, and could be disregarded with, a virgin birth. The necessity for countering this querulousness was recognised by St Clement of Alexandria (died c. 215). And it was doubtless for this reason that the incident was subsequently included in the rigid scheme of Byzantine iconography as a perpetual reminder of the available corroborative evidence.

Plate 18

i

NATIVITY.

Kaiser Friedrich Museum, Berlin.

by Duccio.

1308-1311.

see p. 102.

ii

NATIVITY : GOATHERD AND KIDS.

Pantanassa, Mistra.

Late School of Mistra.

c. 1428.

see p. 144.

See note to Pl. 18.

Plate 19

Photo Hanfstaengl

i

ii

NATIVITY : ARRIVAL OF THE MAGI.

Pantanassa, Mistra.

Late School of Mistra.

c. 1428.

see p. 144 (colour), note to Pl. 18.

Plate 20

i

NATIVITY.

Xenophontos, Mount Athos.

Cretan School, by Antony.

1544.

The star, placed at the top of a vault, does duty
for the Baptism also.   See Pl. 27. ii, iii.

ii

NATIVITY.

Docheiariou, Mount Athos.

Cretan School.

1568.

See note to Pl. 18.

Plate 21

i

ii

PRESENTATION OF CHRIST.

Pantanassa, Mistra.

Late School of Mistra.

c. 1428.

see p. 142 (colour).

This scene was probably first portrayed during the IVth or Vth century, in the church erected on the site of Solomon's temple at Jerusalem. Variations in its iconography are rare, save that, in the Macedonian School, Symeon sometimes holds the child. The altar, with its canopy and cone, is based on that of St Sophia. Behind Mary stands Joseph bearing "a pair of turtle doves or two young pigeons," and in between them Anna, daughter of Phanuel (Luke II. 36), who prophesies: "This child has made heaven and earth secure." This utterance, prescribed also by Denys of Fourna, can perhaps be identified with the Pseudo-Matthew's version: "In him is the redemption of the world."

Plate 22

i

PRESENTATION OF CHRIST.

Xenophontos, Mount Athos.

Cretan School, by Antony.

1544.

ii

PRESENTATION OF CHRIST.

St Paul's, Mount Athos.

Cretan School.

1555.

see p. 157 (colour).

iii

PRESENTATION OF CHRIST.

Docheiariou, Mount Athos.

Cretan School.

1568.

See note to Pl. 22.

Plate 23

i

ii

iii

i

SLEEPING CHRIST.
Protaton, Mount Athos.
Macedonian School.
Early XIVth century.
see p. 114 (colour).

ii

SLEEPING CHRIST.
Prodrome, Caryes, Mount Athos.
Macedonian School.
XIVth or XVth century.
see pp. 121, 124.

iii

SLEEPING CHRIST.
Xenophontos, Mount Athos.
Cretan School, by Antony.
1544.
see p. 152.

The literary origin of this theme has yet to be discovered.

Plate 24

i

ii

iii

i

BAPTISM OF CHRIST.

Protaton, Mount Athos.

Macedonian School.

Early XIVth century.

see p. 193.

Of the allegorical figures at the bottom, that on Christ's right represents the Jordan, that on his left, the Sea. Denys of Fourna prescribes only the former. But David sang: "When Israel went out of Egypt . . . Judah was his sanctuary. The sea saw it and fled; Jordan was driven back" (Ps. CXIV). And Habakkuk: "Was the Lord displeased against the rivers ? . . . and was thy wrath against the sea. . . ?" (III. 8). The figures borrow the character of Hellenic demi-gods. The earlier of them to appear in Christian iconography is Jordan, crowned with reeds, in the Vth century Orthodox Baptistery at Ravenna. Sometimes Jordan empties an urn. See Pl. 27. ii, where the Sea, as happens elsewhere, usurps his two steeds.

ii

BAPTISM OF CHRIST.

Arena Chapel, Padua.

by Giotto.

1305-1306.

see p. 103.

The Baptism scene (see also Pls. 26, 27. i, ii) is first found in the IInd or IIIrd century cemetery of Callixtus at Rome. Here, as in nearly all the catacomb examples, Christ takes the form of a Hellenistic child. In the baptisteries at Ravenna (Vth and VIth centuries) he has grown up, but is still beardless. The familiar Syrian type first appears in the VIth century cemetery of Ponzianus at Rome and in the Syrian gospels of Rabula at Florence (586).

The introduction of one or more angels into the scene first occurs on the Monza flasks and on the chair of Maximian at Ravenna, both of the VIth century. It is probable, therefore, that this innovation was due to the extensive definition of the angels' ranks and functions undertaken by Denys the Areopagite at the end of the IVth. Their ministrations were presumably suggested by those prescribed for deacons at church baptisms.

Plate 25

i

ii

BAPTISM OF CHRIST.

Prado, Madrid.

by El Greco.

1584-1598.

see pp. 192-3, note to Pl. 8.

This composition derives from two themes in Byzantine iconography: the Baptism (Pls. 25. i, 27. ii); and the Trinity (Pls. 8. i, ii, 9. ii). The date is conjectural, but cannot well be later, as Greco's other Baptism in the Hospital de Tavera, the last picture he painted, is entirely different. In this, God, seated three-quarter-face in a corner and holding an orb, has been moved from his frontal, Byzantine position. The angels below, on the other hand, resume their traditional ministrations with a towel (see note to Pl. 25), which are omitted in the present picture.

Plate 26

i

BAPTISM OF CHRIST.

San Gimignano, Italy.

by Barna da Siena.

Middle of XIVth century.

The artist is progressing from Duccio to Fra Angelico. But the essential features of the composition remain.

ii

BAPTISM OF CHRIST.

Xenophontos, Mount Athos.

Cretan School, by Antony.

1544.

see pp. 193, 204, note to Pl. 25. i.

Christ crushes four scarlet serpents. See Ps. LXXIV. 13 : "thou brakest the heads of the Dragons in the waters." This theme came to be enlarged on in Greek church ritual and is first known to have been illustrated in the Chloudov Psalter (IXth century). The marble raft which enables Christ to perform the operation conveniently is unknown before the XIVth century. Byzantine art is sinking into ineptitude.

iii

STAR.

Xenophontos, Mount Athos.

Cretan School, by Antony.

1544.

see p. 204, note to Pl. 21. i.

Plate 27

Photo Alinari

i

ii

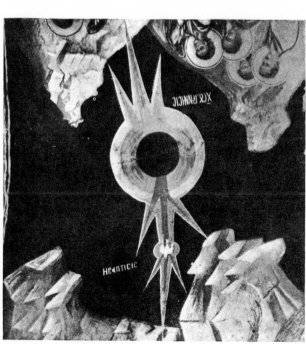

iii

i

DEATH OF JOHN THE BAPTIST, in three scenes :—

" John the Prodrome reproaching Herod ; "

" Herod's Supper ; "

" The Prodrome's Execution."

Above : Samuel, Aaron.

Below : SS Cosmas, Panteleimon, Damian, Theodore Tiron, Theodore Stratilates, Demetrius.

Prodrome, Caryes, Mount Athos.

Macedonian School.

XIVth or XVth century.

see pp. 123, 124 (colour).

The books in the niche give scale to this minute chapel.

ii

" JOHN THE PRODROME GUIDED BY THE HOLY ANGEL IN THE DESERT."

Prodrome, Caryes, Mount Athos.

Macedonian School.

XIVth or XVth century.

see pp. 120, 122-3 (colour).

Luke I. 80 and the Pseudo-Matthew combine to justify this scene.

The cycle of the Prodrome (see also Pls. 29. i, ii, 30. i, ii) is first depicted in the VIth century gospel of Sinope at Paris. His cult had already been developed in Palestine, where churches marked his birthplace and the scene of the Baptism. The incidents of the angel in the desert, the preaching of repentance, and the meeting with Christ, are contained in the Xth century church of Toqale Kilisseh in Cappadocia. In the present instance, the costumes and positions of certain figures are unavoidably reminiscent of the later Middle Ages or early Renascence in the West, an impression which is confirmed by the tasselled baldochino above Herod (Pls. 28. i, 30. ii). It is remotely possible that this can be explained by the presence on the Holy Mountain of an Amalfitan monastery, which only lost its independence as a ruling house in 1393. In any case the iconography of these scenes is totally distinct from that of the corresponding ones which recur, at rare intervals, elsewhere on the Mountain, and also from that prescribed by Denys of Fourna.

Plate 28

i

ii

i

"JOHN THE PRODROME PREACHING BAPTISM AND REPENTANCE."

Prodrome, Caryes, Mount Athos.

Macedonian School.

XIVth or XVth century.

see pp. 120, 123 (colour).

ii

"JOHN THE PRODROME SHOWING CHRIST TO THE MULTITUDE."

Prodrome, Caryes, Mount Athos.

Macedonian School.

XIVth or XVth century.

see p. 123 (colour).

See note to Pl. 28.

Plate 29

i

ii

i

"THE PRODROME'S EXECUTION."

Prodrome, Caryes, Mount Athos.

Macedonian School.

XIVth or XVth century.

see pp. 120, 124 (colour), 125.

ii

"HEROD'S SUPPER."

Prodrome, Caryes, Mount Athos.

Macedonian School.

XIVth or XVth century.

see pp. 120, 121, 124 (colour), 125.

This unusual scene is found in the gospel of Sinope (VIth century) and in the Baptistery of St Mark's (XIVth century). The former shows a Hellenistic banquet, at which the guests recline; a servitor brings the head. In the latter Salome dances with the head and there is only one other guest beside Herodias at the table.

See note to Pl. 28.

Plate 30

i

ii

i

CHRIST TRANSFIGURED.

St Paul's, Mount Athos.

Cretan School.

1555.

see pp. 156-7 (colour), 204.

ii

TRANSFIGURATION.

St Paul's, Mount Athos.

Cretan School.

1555.

see pp. 156-7 (colour), 204, 207.

Transfigurations, both of the VIth century, are found in St Apollinare in Classe, Ravenna, and at the monastery of St Catherine, Mount Sinai. The former is purely symbolic and lacks a human figure. The latter, lying within the orbit of early Syrian realism, depicts Christ in an aura as in the present compositions (see also Pls. 32. i, ii, iii, 33. i, ii). The triple aura, which is seen here and also on Pls. 8. i, ii, 62. i, ii, and 75. i, was the outcome of Hezychast speculation in the XIVth century, the uncreated light being held to emanate simultaneously from the three persons of the Trinity.

Plate 31

i

ii

i

TRANSFIGURATION.

Docheiariou, Mount Athos.

Cretan School.

1568.

ii

CHRIST TRANSFIGURED.

Peribleptos, Mistra.

Middle School of Mistra, by the more finished
of the two Peribleptos artists (see p. 135).

Late XIVth or early XVth century.

see p. 136.

iii

TRANSFIGURATION.

Dionysiou, Mount Athos.

Cretan School, by Zorzi of Crete.

1547.

see pp. 125, 154.

See note to Pl. 31.

Plate 32

i

ii

iii

i

TRANSFIGURATION.
Chilandari, Mount Athos.
Macedonian School.
c. 1302.
see p. 115.

ii

TRANSFIGURATION.
The Lavra, Mount Athos.
Cretan School, by Theophanes of Crete.
1535.
see p. 151 (colour).

See note to Pl. 31.

Plate 33

i

ii

i

RAISING OF LAZARUS.

Pantanassa, Mistra.

Late School of Mistra.

c. 1428.

see pp. 108, 139-141 (colour). Compare Pl. 1 (frontispiece) for detail.

This is the finest of all the paintings at Mistra and Mount Athos.

ii

RAISING OF LAZARUS.

Chilandari, Mount Athos.

Macedonian School.

c. 1302.

see p. 115.

This scene, though depicted in the Roman cemetery of Callixtus (IInd or IIIrd century), is first found in its present form in the VIth century gospel of Rossano. It attained greater prominence after the iconoclast controversy, and was further emphasised, in the XIVth or XVth centuries, by the expansion of the Passion theme (it is from the raising of Lazarus that St John dates Caiaphas' plot). In the present group (see also Pl. 35. i, ii), only Pl. 35. i, reproduces the " cave " ; the others depict a sarcophagus ; though a cave may be implied by the entrance in the mountain above the apostles' heads in the top picture here.

Plate 34

i

ii

i

RAISING OF LAZARUS.

St Paul's, Mount Athos.

Cretan School.

1555.

see pp. 155-6 (colour).

ii

RAISING OF LAZARUS.

Arena Chapel, Padua.

by Giotto.

1305-1306.

see p. 103.

Giotto's strict adherence to Byzantine iconography is noticeable in the positions of Christ, Lazarus, Mary and Martha, and the bearers of the marbled lid.

See note to Pl. 34.

Plate 35

i

ii

i

ENTRY INTO JERUSALEM.

Pantanassa, Mistra.

Late School of Mistra.

c. 1428.

see pp. 108, 142-3 (colour).

Note the child and fountain on the right.

ii

ENTRY INTO JERUSALEM.

Peribleptos, Mistra.

Middle School of Mistra, by the more finished of the
two Peribleptos artists (see p. 135).

Late XIVth or early XVth century.

see pp. 108, 135.

This scene (see also Pls. 37. i, ii, 38. i, ii, iii) is unknown before the VIth century, when it appears in the gospels of Rossano and on the chair of Maximian at Ravenna. The little figures facetiously removing their clothes at the bottom are definitely children and are so labelled at Chilandari (Mount Athos) and by Denys of Fourna. In Duccio's painting (Pl. 37. ii) the fact is self-evident. But Giotto reproduces their attitudes more faithfully in the Arena Chapel at Padua. Why they are children is unknown. The extraordinary clothes of the multitude issuing from Jerusalem can probably be explained by later Byzantine fashions.

The Entry into Jerusalem marks the first scene in the great Passion cycle whose expansion began after the affirmation of Christ's proper humanity at the Council of Chalcedon in 451. According to Denys of Fourna, the cycle really starts later, with Judas' pact, continuing through twenty-two scenes to the Descent into Hell. But the prominence which the Entry always receives in Byzantine churches, while many of the subsequent scenes are omitted, shows what its significance was thought to be in actual practice.

Plate 36

i

ii

i

ENTRY INTO JERUSALEM.

Vatopedi, Mount Athos.

Macedonian School.

1312.

see pp. 117-8 (colour).

ii

ENTRY INTO JERUSALEM.

Siena.

by Duccio.

1308-1311.

see p. 102.

Duccio, in accordance with Western practice, depicts the ass and the colt of St Matthew.

The figure in the tree (see also Pl. 38. i, ii) was probably originally suggested by St Luke's story of Zacchæus in the sycamore at Jericho, during the journey to Jerusalem. Owing to his being " of little stature," he was transformed into a child cutting branches, as depicted here ; so Denys of Fourna describes him.

See also note to Pl. 36.

Plate 37

ii

i

i

ENTRY INTO JERUSALEM.

The Lavra, Mount Athos.

Cretan School, by Theophanes of Crete.

1535.

ii

ENTRY INTO JERUSALEM.

Xenophontos, Mount Athos.

Cretan School, by Antony.

1544.

see pp. 152 (colour), 207.

iii

ENTRY INTO JERUSALEM.

St Paul's, Mount Athos.

Cretan School.

1555.

see p. 158.

See notes to Pls. 36 and 37.

Plate 38

i

ii

iii

i

LAST SUPPER.

Protaton, Mount Athos.

Macedonian School.

Early XIVth century.

see p. 114 (colour).

ii

LAST SUPPER.

Siena.

by Duccio.

1308-1311.

see pp. 102, 113.

This scene (see also Pl. 40. i, ii) must not be confused, as it is in some books, with the Eucharistic, non-historical suppers depicted in the Roman catacombs. Its first appearance is not till the VIth century, in St Apollinare Nuovo at Ravenna and the gospels of Rossano. In the former, it takes the form of a Hellenistic banquet, the partakers reclining; in the latter, it is combined with the Washing of Feet. Denys of Fourna, unlike St John, places it after the Washing of Feet.

Plate 39

i

Photo Anderson

ii

i

LAST SUPPER.

Chilandari (Refectory), Mount Athos.

Cretan School.

1621.

see p. 161.

This fine composition is unfortunately distorted by
the camera. It is frequently found in the apse of
monastic refectories, above the chief seat.

ii

LAST SUPPER.

Chilandari, Mount Athos.

Macedonian School.

c. 1302.

see p. 115.

See note to Pl. 39.

Plate 40

i

ii

i

WASHING OF FEET.

Vatopedi, Mount Athos.

Macedonian School.

1312.

see p. 118 (colour).

For the adjoining scene, where Christ explains the
Washing of Feet, see Pl. 11. ii.

ii

WASHING OF FEET.

Chilandari, Mount Athos.

Macedonian School.

c. 1302.

see p. 115.

The two chief actors in this scene, Christ and Peter, are depicted on a IVth or Vth century bas-
relief in the Lateran Museum. The composition is further developed in the VIth century gospels
of Rossano. In all cases (see also Pl. 42. i, ii) St Peter points to his head in token of the words :
" Lord, not my feet only, but also my hands and my head." In the top picture, and also in
Pl. 42. ii, note the background of Christian Jerusalem. This derives from the Patriarch's customary
imitation of the ceremony, whence the illustrators probably took their first inspiration. Duccio
(Pl. 42. i) preserves the biblical interior.

Plate 41

i

ii

i

WASHING OF FEET.

Siena.

by Duccio.

1308-1311.

see pp. 102, 113.

ii

WASHING OF FEET.

Protaton, Mount Athos.

Macedonian School.

Early XIVth century.

see p. 114 (colour).

The remarkable resemblance between these two paintings culminates in the sandals, which are often mistaken, at first sight, for black beetles.

See also note to Pl. 41.

Plate 42

Photo Anderson

i

ii

i

GARDEN OF OLIVES.

Vatopedi (Narthex), Mount Athos.

Macedonian School.

c. 1312.

see p. 119.

The artist here, and in Pls. 48. i, and 58. i, is to be distinguished from him who decorated the nave (Pls. 11. i, 37. i, 50, 55. i). Their dates are substantially the same. The light sky (see also Pl. 48. i) is a unique innovation.

ii

GARDEN OF OLIVES

Siena.

by Duccio.

1308-1311.

see pp. 102, 119.

The three sleeping apostles, Peter, James and John, are first represented in the VIth century, on the columns of the ciborium in St Mark's, and in the gospels of Rossano. In the present pictures, note the still valid difference between the Greek and the North Italian olive.

Plate 43

i

Photo Anderson

ii

GARDEN OF OLIVES.

Xenophontos, Mount Athos.

Cretan School, by Antony.

1544.

see p. 207.

Inept as much of this painting may be, its connection
with Greco is plain.

Plate 44

i

BETRAYAL.

Qaranleq Kilisseh, Cappadocia.

Cappadocian School.

Late Xth or XIth century.

see pp. 106, 188.

ii

BETRAYAL.

Dionysiou, Mount Athos.

Cretan School, by Zorzi of Crete.

1547.

see pp. 125, 188.

This incident is first depicted on a IVth century sarcophagus discovered near the Porta Maggiore, Rome. Here, the actors are reduced to three : Judas implants the kiss ; the captain of the band draws his sword. In the VIth century it became general, and is found on the columns of the ciborium in St Mark's, in St Apollinare Nuovo at Ravenna, and in the gospels of Rossano. The present composition, based on the account of St John, who mentions " lanterns and torches and weapons," combines the three separate incidents of Kiss, Arrest, and Peter's Attack on Malchus (see also Pls. 47, 48. i, ii).

The dramatic intensity of feeling aroused by the Betrayal among the Byzantines is expressed by Nicolas Messarites (born 1163) in his description of the VIth century mosaics in the church of the Holy Apostles at Constantinople : " Who are these torch-bearers, worthy of darkness, respiring bloody fire against the Light of the World ? Who are these that brandish cudgels against him who led Israel from out the midst of the Egyptians ? . . . . Who are the men that bear these spears ? Who their captain ? Who their general ? "

Plate 45

i

ii

DIVESTMENT OF CHRIST.

Cathedral Sacristy, Toledo.

by El Greco.

1579.

see pp. 178-9 (colour), 181, 188, 209.

The subject is an unusual one; and Greco, casting about in his mind for a precedent composition, evidently bethought himself of the Byzantine Betrayal. The chief points of resemblance are :—

1. The composition of the hinder group : the frontal position of Christ ; the three-quarter faces on either side of him ; the profiles behind ; the weapons ; and the general pattern of light and shade.

2. The bending figure in the foreground, a substitute for Peter and Malchus.

3. The leering faces on either side of Christ, which appear in all Greco's Divestments and seem to derive from those of Judas and the Captain (see particularly Pl. 47).

4. The outstretched bare arms and withdrawn head of the man who performs the Divestment, analogous with the pose of the Captain in Pls. 45. ii, and 47.

Plate 46

Detail of the BETRAYAL.

Protaton, Mount Athos.

Macedonian School.

Early XIVth century.

see p. 188, notes to Pls. 45, 46.

Plate 47

i

BETRAYAL.

Vatopedi (Narthex), Mount Athos.

Macedonian School.

c. 1312.

see pp. 119 (colour), 188, note to Pl. 43. i.

ii

BETRAYAL.

Siena.

by Duccio.

1308-1311.

see pp. 102, 113, 119.

See also notes to Pls. 45 and 46.

Plate 48

i

ii

Photo. Anderson

i

IMPOSITION OF CHRIST ON THE CROSS.

Peribleptos, Mistra.

Middle School of Mistra, by the more impressionist
of the two Peribleptos artists (see p. 135).

Late XIVth or early XVth century.

see p. 105.

ii

IMPOSITION OF CHRIST ON THE CROSS.

The Lavra, Mount Athos.

Cretan School, by Theophanes of Crete.

1535.

see p. 105.

This rare scene was only evolved in the XIIIth and XIVth centuries, simultaneously with the
general expansion of the Passion theme in literature and art. Its iconography never became fixed.
In the Protaton (Mount Athos, early XIVth century) Christ mounts a single ladder with his back
to the beholder. Denys of Fourna prescribes a recumbent posture for both Christ and the Cross
during the nailing.

Plate 49

i

ii

CRUCIFIXION.

Vatopedi, Mount Athos.

Macedonian School.

1312.

see p. 117-8 (colour).

Crucifixion remained a form of official execution up to the time of Constantine. Till then, and for two centuries more, Christian artists were unwilling to depict Christ is such degrading circumstances. None the less he is so found on a IInd or IIIrd century gem from Constanza, and on a Vth century ivory, both in the British Museum. In the VIth century the scene appears on the Monza flasks and in the Syrian gospel of Rabula ; Choricius (527-565) describes a mosaic of it in a church at Gaza. But it is not found at Rome or Ravenna, nor in the gospels of Rossano and Sinope. While on the pillars of the ciborium in St Mark's, though the whole body of actors, thieves, Virgin, and St John, is represented, on the cross is only a lamb in a medallion. In the VIIth century, Christ on the cross, the Virgin, and St John, appear in Santa Maria Antiqua at Rome. Christ wears a long robe, as he does in the gospel of Rabula. And the whole painting is of undoubtedly Syrian or Palestinian origin.

From these facts it may be inferred that the Hellenistic tradition, surviving in the centres of the Empire, shrank from the emotional crudity of the scene ; and that the introduction of the Crucifixion into Christian iconography was due to the Syrian illustrators. Even when its depiction became general, after the iconoclast controversy, its note was one of triumph rather than of suffering. Yet there is suffering at Daphni (XIth century). And there, as at Toqale Kilisseh (late Xth century), the Virgin gazes upward, instead of towards the beholder in the formal manner of Santa Maria Antiqua. This insistence on suffering, to mark the climax of one Passion and the first hint of another, was not fully developed till the XIIIth and XIVth centuries. But in literature, it began as early as the Gospel of Nicodemus (2nd Greek version, IVth century or later), and on a higher level of invention than that of monkish illustrators anxious to convey only historical facts. The Virgin faints on hearing the news ; then hurries to Golgotha crying : " Bend down, O cross, that I may bid farewell to my son like a mother." The words later put into her mouth by Romanus the Melodious (491-518 or 713-716) may also be quoted, as a parallel to the gigantic sorrow of the scene at Vatopedi : " I am borne down, my son, borne down with love. Truly I cannot endure to see myself in my room and you on the wood, myself in my house and you in your grave. Let me come with you. I am healed by the very sight of you."

Such was the sentiment expanded in the IXth century by George of Nicomedia, who talked of a " sorrow beyond words," and ultimately communicated, through a further succession of writers, to the Pseudo-Bonaventure and the forerunners of the Italian Renascence.

Plate 50

i

CRUCIFIXION.

Xenophontos, Mount Athos.

Cretan School, by Antony.

1544.

see pp. 152 (colour), 207.

The sun and moon (see also Pls. 50, 52. i), veiled to express the darkness that ensued from the sixth to the ninth hour, are found in the VIth century on the Monza flasks and in the VIIth in Santa Maria Antiqua. In the Gospel of Nicodemus it is related that " Pilate sent for the Jews and said unto them : Did ye see that which came to pass ? But they said : There was an eclipse of the sun after the accustomed sort."

ii

CRUCIFIXION.

Xenophontos, Mount Athos.

Cretan School, probably by Theophanes.

Probably 1563.

see p. 151, note to Pl. 52. i.

Though this painting and the one above are contained in the nave of the same church, they are not both by the same artist. Theophanes decorated the narthex of the church in 1563.

The skull below the cross (see also Pls. 50, 52. i) is that of Adam. St Jerome records the tradition that he was buried on Golgotha, " the place of a skull."

See also note to Pl. 50.

Plate 51

i

ii

i

CRUCIFIXION.

The Lavra, Mount Athos.

Cretan School, by Theophanes of Crete.

1535.

see p. 103.

This, like Pl. 51. ii, is an example of the separate type of
"narrative" Crucifixion. The three crucifixions together
first appear in the gospel of Rabula (586), where all three
figures wear long tunics. The thieves here are labelled the
Holy Just and the Unjust: an angel ministers to the one;
a devil torments the other. Their positions are prescribed
by Denys of Fourna, who says that the Just (Dysmas) was old,
and the Unjust (Gestas) young. According to one text of
the gospel of Nicodemus, Dysmas was crucified on Christ's
right, and Gestas on his left.

ii

CRUCIFIXION.

Chilandari, Mount Athos.

Macedonian School.

c. 1302.

see p. 115.

See also notes to Pls. 50, 51. i, ii.

Plate 52

i

ii

i

DEPOSITION OF CHRIST FROM THE CROSS.

The Lavra, Mount Athos.

Cretan School, by Theophanes of Crete.

1535.

ii

DEPOSITION OF CHRIST FROM THE CROSS.

Siena.

by Duccio.

1308-1311.

see p. 102.

Joseph of Arimathæa stands on the ladder ; the Virgin receives the body ; St John weeps by its side ; Nicodemus extracts the nails.

This scene first occurs in the late Xth century at Toqale Kilisseh in Cappadocia. By the XIVth the iconography had changed : in the Peribleptos at Mistra, Joseph is on the ladder instead of on the ground, and the Virgin kisses the face instead of the hands. St John (XIX. 39) gives authority for the presence of Nicodemus. According to one version of the Gospel of Nicodemus (IVth century or later), it was the Virgin who persuaded Joseph of Arimathæa to demand the body. George of Nicomedia (IXth century) emphasises her part in the actual operation, saying that "she herself alone was anxious to perform the deposition from the cross." Hence derived the account of the Pseudo-Bonaventure.

Plate 53

i

Photo Anderson

ii

i

DEPOSITION OF CHRIST FROM THE CROSS.

Dionysiou, Mount Athos.

Cretan School, by Zorzi of Crete.

1547.

ii

DEPOSITION OF CHRIST FROM THE CROSS.

Xenophontos, Mount Athos.

Cretan School, by Antony.

1544.

See note to Pl. 53.

Plate 54

i

ii

i

LAMENTATION OVER THE BODY OF CHRIST.

Vatopedi, Mount Athos.

Macedonian School.

1312.

see p. 106.

ii

BURIAL OF, AND LAMENTATION OVER, THE BODY OF CHRIST.

Siena.

by Duccio.

1308-1311.

see p. 106.

Early examples of the women introducing the mummy into the tomb are frequent. But the scene in the top picture, and in Pls. 56 and 57. i, that of embalmment (John XIX. 40) and lamentation, is first found in Cappadocia in the Xth or XIth century, and was not translated to Greece till the XIIIth or XIVth. On its reaching Italy, artists like Duccio, mistaking the marble slab on which the body rests for a tomb, and probably unfamiliar with this method of preparing the body, transformed it into an actual burial scene ; hence the absence of the cross in the top picture and in Pl. 57. i—though Giotto is careful to omit both slab and tomb. The Byzantine theme became the prototype of the Italian *Pieta*. The Gospel of Nicodemus (2nd Greek version) records that Joseph of Arimathæa and Nicodemus " along with the mother of God and Mary Magdalene and Salome (see note to Pl. 18), along with John, and the rest of the women, did what was customary with the body with white linen. . ." The figure with the arms upraised, a permanent feature of the scene, and borrowed by Duccio and Giotto, is Mary Magdalene, who, on the same authority, declared that she would " go alone to Rome, to the Cæsar," that the world might know what had been done. Nicetas Choniates (XIIth century) records that the church of the Pantocrator in Constantinople possessed the " red stone, of a man's length," formerly at Ephesus, " on which it is said that Christ was enshrouded ; " and that the Emperor Manuel Commenus had carried it up from the port of the Buceleon on his back.

See also note to Pl. 56.

Plate 55

i

ii

LAMENTATION OVER THE BODY OF CHRIST.

Xenophontos, Mount Athos.

Cretan School, by Antony.

1544.

see pp. 106, 153, 207.

The intensity of grief here depicted, the climax of the Passion of the Virgin, finds precedent in the Gospel of Nicodemus (2nd Greek version), and in the works of George of Nicomedia (IXth century). In the first the Virgin cries : " How am I not to lament thee, my son ? How should I not tear my face with my nails ? This is that, my son, which Symeon the elder foretold to me when I brought thee, an infant of forty days old, into the temple. . . Who shall put a stop to my tears, my sweetest son ? No one at all except thyself alone, if, as thou saidst, thou shalt rise again in three days." The second writes : " And when they had stretched the divine body on the ground, she flung herself upon it, to bathe it with scalding tears. And in a gentle voice she spoke words of emotion : 'Behold, Lord, the foretold mystery is accomplished. Behold, thine incarnation is finished. I kiss the mouth and moveless lips of him who has created the whole visible world. I kiss the closed eyes of him who has given sight to the blind.' "

In the year 1200, a Russian pilgrim to Constantinople recorded that the tears of the Virgin, " white as drops of wax," were preserved in the church of the Pharos.

See also note to Pl. 55.

Plate 56

i

LAMENTATION OVER, OR BURIAL OF, THE BODY OF CHRIST.

Arena Chapel, Padua.

by Giotto.

1305-1306.

see p. 106, notes to Pls. 55, 56.

ii

Detail from the BURIAL OF CHRIST.

Peribleptos, Mistra.

Middle School of Mistra, by the more impressionist of the two Peribleptos artists (see p. 135).

Late XIVth or early XVth century.

see pp. 100, 137 (colour), 201.

This scene, as distinct from the Lamentation, though prescribed by Denys of Fourna, is unknown on Mount Athos and is only found this once at Mistra.

Plate 57

i

ii

i

DESCENT INTO HELL.

Vatopedi (Narthex), Mount Athos.

Macedonian School.

c. 1312.

see p. 119 (colour), note to Pl. 43. i.

Only, one out of the three texts of the Descent mentions Christ
setting up his cross in Hell. In this respect, and in the
absence of an aura, this picture differs from all those of
Mistra and Mount Athos save that in the Protaton.

ii

DESCENT INTO HELL.

Docheiariou, Mount Athos.

Cretan School.

1568.

This scene is typical. The actors from Christ's right to left
are: Jonah, Isaiah, Jeremiah, two Just Kings, David, John
the Baptist, Adam, Christ treading the gates of Hell, Eve,
and others accounted righteous under the old dispensation.
Below the gates, an angel chains Beelzebub, and broken locks
go flying.

This theme is first depicted on the VIth century columns of the ciborium in St Mark's. Its
iconography can only be understood by reading the three accounts of it, which, though probably
older, have become attached to the Gospel of Nicodemus. As a subject in Orthodox decoration
it superseded the Resurrection.

These three accounts are in themselves masterpieces of inspired writing. Apart from its dramatic
value, the subject was one of incalculable importance ; for by it, in one gesture, the Christian system
embraces all that has gone before it. The origin of the legend, and of its inclusion in Christian
dogma, is notoriously obscure. Possibly it derived from Egypt. Certainly it was of Eastern
origin, since it is found in the earliest creeds, of Sirmium (359 ; composed by Mark the Syrian),
of Nike (359), and of Constantinople (360). In the so-called Nicene creed (381) it does not appear.
But in the following century it was brought into prominence by the Nestorians' accusing the
Orthodox of Apollinarianism, a heresy which denied the soul of Christ. The Orthodox replied
that since Christ descended into Hell, and they admitted the fact, he must have had a soul. Hence
the insistence on this theme, to the exclusion of others more important, in the creed of St Athanasius. In the liturgy of St Basil it was further emphasised. Finally, in the Byzantine dramatic
homilies, it was utilised as the final act and failure of a plot which the devil had been maturing,
ever since Christ's presence on earth had been revealed to him at the Baptism.

Plate 58

i

ii

i

THE MARYS AT THE TOMB.

Peribleptos, Mistra.

Middle School of Mistra, by the more finished of the two Peribleptos artists (see p. 135).

Late XIVth or early XVth century.

St Matthew mentions the Marys only. St Mark is the authority for the " sweet spices " which they carry.

ii

THE MARYS AND SALOME AT THE TOMB.

Siena.

by Duccio.

1308-1311.

see p. 102.

St Mark mentions Salome (see note to Pl. 18).

These two pictures provide one of the most striking illustrations of the identity of inspiration in Greek and Italian art in the XIVth century.

This theme, indicative of the Resurrection (Denys of Fourna prescribes this as well; but it is unknown at Mistra or Mount Athos), is first found in the VIth century on the Monza flasks and in St Apollinare Nuovo. From these examples, it is plain that the original artists were inspired by the ceremonies held at the Holy Sepulchre in Christian Jerusalem, which have been described, with their setting of buildings, by various pilgrims. In Byzantine art of the middle period, the incident disappeared; though it is found at Monreale (1147-1189). It was preserved in Cappadocia, and by the didactic illustrators.

Plate 59

i

ii

Photo Anderson

i

GROUP WATCHING THE ASCENSION.

Pantanassa, Mistra.

Late School of Mistra.

c. 1428.

see 143 (colour), 203.

The angel on the Virgin's right says: " Ye men of Galilee, why stand ye gazing up into heaven ? " (Acts I. 11).

ii

GROUP WATCHING THE ASCENSION.

Pantanassa, Mistra.

Late School of Mistra.

c. 1428.

see p. 143 (colour).

These two groups face one another on the walls of the chancel. The trees behind each are painted with great charm and regard for species. On the vault between them, not here illustrated, Christ is seated in an aura upheld by four angels.

This latter composition (see Pl. 61. i), seems to be a later development, being first found in the churches of Qaranleq and Tchareqle Kilisseh in Cappadocia (Xth or XIth century). The earliest known example of the theme is on the Vth century doors of St Sabina in Rome, where a Hellenistic Christ is snatched diagonally into heaven by a hand. The symmetrical type with two angels only (see Pls. 61. ii, 62. i, ii) is first found in the VIth century, on the pillars of the ciborium in St Mark's, in the gospel of Rabula, and on the Monza flasks. In the two latter cases, the Virgin is " suppliant," as in the lower picture.

Plate 60

i

ii

i

ASCENSION.
Chilandari, Mount Athos.
Macedonian School.
c. 1302.
see pp. 115-6 (colour).

ii

ASCENSION.
St Paul's, Mount Athos.
Cretan School.
1555.

See also note to Pl. 60.

Plate 61

i

ii

i

ASCENSION.

Xenophontos (Narthex), Mount Athos.

Cretan School, by Theophanes.

1563.

see p. 151.

ii

ASCENSION.

Xenophontos, Mount Athos.

Cretan School, by Antony.

1544.

See also note to Pls. 31 and 60.

Plate 62

ii

i

PENTECOST.

Dionysiou, Mount Athos.

Cretan School, by Zorzi of Crete.

1547.

see pp. 125, 153.

On one of the Monza flasks (VIth century), the Pentecost is associated with the Ascension, a dove descending from Christ's aura on to the head of an apostle. As a separate theme, it appears in the Syrian gospel of Rabula (586), and was also to be seen in the church of the Holy Apostles at Constantinople (decorated under Justinian). The latter provided the prototype for the present pictures (see also Pl. 64. i, ii), the apostles being seated. In the former, the Virgin appears in the centre and all are standing ; while thirteen flamelets descend and a dove hovers in the sky. It is impossible not to remark on the astonishing resemblance between this composition and the Pentecost by El Greco in the Prado, in which all reappear standing, the Virgin in the centre, with the dove above her, and similar flamelets descending. Greco, it is true, introduces the two other Marys. But the likeness between the two compositions is so strong, that Greco must almost certainly have had in mind some example of the Syrian type of Pentecost, transmitted to Crete through the didactic illustrators.

The figure of the " Cosmos " below (see also Pl. 64. i) seems to be a development of the XIVth century. The figure holds a cloth in which are twelve scrolls signifying the preaching of the Gospel in twelve different languages.

Plate 63

i

PENTECOST.

The Lavra (Chapel of St Nicolas), Mount Athos.

Cretan School, by Frangos Catellanos of Thebes.

1560.

see p. 159 (colour).

The background of buildings derives from the traditional embellishments of the site of the Holy Sepulchre.

ii

PENTECOST.

St Paul's, Mount Athos.

Cretan School.

1555.

See also note to Pl. 63.

Plate 64

i

ii

DORMITION OF THE VIRGIN.

Xenophontos, Mount Athos.

Cretan School, by Antony.

1544.

see pp. 106, 152 (colour), 153, 189, 207.

This scene (see also Pls. 67. i, ii, 68. i, 69. i, ii) appears to be unknown before the Xth century, when it was painted at Toqale Kilisseh in Cappadocia.

The numerous and divergent MSS of the Dormition in Greek, Latin, Syriac, Coptic, and Arabic, have never been critically edited as a whole, and never collated with the accounts of those VIIth and VIIIth century writers who made use of older authorities. Consequently it is difficult even to guess at what date, and under what auspices, the legend first evolved. The best known account is that falsely ascribed to Melito Bishop of Sardis. Though the Council of Ephesus in 431 had sealed the Church's approbation of the Virgin cult, this work was nevertheless condemned by Pope Gelasius I (492-496). And it was not until the reign of the Emperor Maurice (582-602) that the feast of the Dormition was officially instituted. In the first half of the VIIIth century, St John Damascene wrote three homilies on the subject, whose popularity was ensured by their violence of language. The present scene is based on the second of them. According to Denys of Fourna, the saint and his friend·the poet Cosmas should appear in person in the top corners of the picture, each uttering appropriate quotations from his own works. This may be seen at the Lavra, Mount Athos.

Both in composition and feeling, the scene evolved is the crowning achievement of Byzantine iconography, giving fullest play to the pattern of line and light on which the Byzantine artist depended for the success or failure of his effects. Above the rigid, horizontal body, a vertical Christ, assisted by an ethereal symmetry of angels, receives his mother's soul in the guise of a little child. In the sky, on either side, the apostles arrive by cloud, sometimes singly, sometimes in parties of six as here, summoned from the dead or from distant lands (St Thomas, from India, was late). Having come to ground, they cluster round the body in attitudes of sorrow, and among them, recognisable by their cross-bedizened Byzantine vestments, stand Denys the Areopagite, Timothy of Ephesus, and Hierotheus, whom Denys describes as his teacher. St Peter swings a censer. Below the bier, an angel severs the hands of the Jew (variously named Jephonias, Juphia, and Reuben) who tried to upset it. The hands cleave to the bier; their owner dances in agony till they are restored.

Plate 65

BURIAL OF COUNT ORGAZ (lower half, lifesize) :
Mourners, Officiating Clergy, SS Stephen and Augustine, and
George Manuel Theotocopoulos.

Santo Tomé, Toledo.

by El Greco.

1584-1587.

see pp. 189, 207, 212-4.

The relation between this Burial and the Byzantine Dormitions (see p. 189) becomes more striking when it is remembered how radically Greco's composition differs from any other in Renascence or High Renascence painting.

Mr Rutter, in his recent book, has at last given certainty to the tradition that the page in the foreground is El Greco's son. This son, George Manuel, was born in 1578. And on a paper protruding from the page's pocket are the words "Domenicos Theotocopoulos did it, 1578." This date cannot celebrate the completion of the picture, as Greco did not receive his first contract for it (afterwards duplicated) till six years later. But referring to the birth of his son, the facetious note of the signature finds analogy in the legend attached to the view of Toledo on Pl. 94 (see p. 198). It has been suggested that the artist wrote 1578 in mistake for 1587. Under the Byzantine system of numeration which he employed, this would have been impossible.

In richness of technique and quality of brushwork, the lower half of the Count Orgaz is probably the most accomplished piece of painting known to man. The ripe philosophy expressed in this gallery of human beings is not to be compared with the ecstatic vernal beauty of the St Maurice. Appreciation of the latter must always depend on individual taste and individual colour sense. But in the Count Orgaz, whose colour is of a wintry sadness, the virtues conventionally sought by West European artists from the XVth to the XVIIIth centuries attain their zenith. And few are those who have seen the picture who deny it.

It is a mistake to regard the difference in manner between the St Maurice and the Count Orgaz as implying a logical and continuous process of development. Greco had two manners : East and West European. He used them, consciously, as occasion demanded. The East European manner of the St Maurice having met with disapproval, it was now for Greco to show that he could beat the West European artists at their own game. This he set out to do, and did.

Plate 66

i

DORMITION OF THE VIRGIN.

Prodrome, Caryes, Mount Athos.

Macedonian School.

XIVth or XVth century.

see pp. 106, 120, 122 (colour), 189.

The fourth Bishop (see also Pl. 68. i) is probably James of Jerusalem. Above Christ's head, the Virgin ascends to heaven in an aura (see also Pl. 68. i). In the accounts already referred to (see note to Pl. 65), she enjoyed burial and resurrection in the manner of Christ, leaving an exquisitely sweet smell behind her in the tomb. In the Vth century, an insertion was made into Eusebius' History to the effect that "in the year A.D. 48 Mary the Virgin was taken up into heaven."

ii

DORMITION OF THE VIRGIN.

Xenophontos (Chapel of St Lazarus), Mount Athos.

School of Asia Minor.

XVIIth century (?).

see pp. 106, 189.

This curious painting is clearly the work of a monk recruited in Asia Minor, where the old Cappadocian style flourished until the middle of the XIXth century.

See also note to Pl. 65.

Plate 67

i

ii

i

DORMITION OF THE VIRGIN.

Peribleptos, Mistra.

Middle School of Mistra, by the more finished of the two Peribleptos artists (see p. 135).

Late XIVth or early XVth century.

see pp. 106, 189, notes to Pls. 65, 67. i.

ii

DEATH OF ST FRANCIS.

Upper Church, Assisi.

by a pupil of Giotto.

c. 1290-1300.

The derivation of this picture from the Byzantine Dormition is self-evident.

Plate 68

i

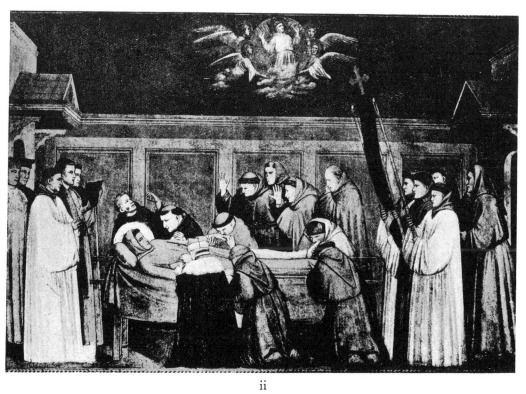

ii

i

DORMITION OF THE VIRGIN : MOURNING WOMEN.

The Lavra, Mount Athos.

Cretan School, by Theophanes of Crete.

1535.

see p. 151.

ii

DORMITION OF THE VIRGIN : MOURNING APOSTLES.

The Lavra, Mount Athos.

Cretan School, by Theophanes of Crete.

1535.

see p. 151.

This scene at the Lavra, owing to its long wall-space, is expanded to its fullest extent. The present extracts from it show Theophanes' ability as a draughtsman, which restoration has not concealed.

See also note to Pl. 65.

LAST JUDGEMENT : HELL.

The Lavra (Refectory), Mount Athos.

Cretan School.

1512.

see pp. 150, 191.

This Last Judgement (see also Pl. 74. i, ii), covering three walls of a transept, is unusually elaborate. The end and centre wall is that with the window. For an analysis of the general plan, see note to Pl. 75.

The conception of a Last Judgement was so far developed by Antiquity that Juvenal and Lucretius could laugh at it. Christ was careful to conceal details and date (Mark XIII. 32). But St Paul pronounced definitely that " we must all appear before the judgement seat of Christ " (2 Cor. V. 10). The river of fire, originating in Daniel (VII. 10), was first mentioned in this context by Commodianus of Gaza in the IIIrd century. The majority of details is taken from the Apocalypse of Mary (IXth century), which was itself based on the Apocalypse of Paul (late IVth century). In these works, the damned are classified and tortured according to the prejudices of the author ; they include, in the former, those who lay late on Sunday and those who did not rise at the entry of a priest. The authenticity of the latter is derided by St Augustine. And Sozomen (Vth century) says : " The book now circulated as the Apocalypse of Paul . . . is commended by most monks," hinting also that it was composed by heretics. It is significant that the Apocalypse of Mary and the Damnation scenes appear in the Byzantine sphere simultaneously.

The theme of the soul's judgement is frequently represented in the Roman catacombs, where the figures never number more than four or five. The schematic panorama of the Middle Ages is first foreshadowed in a clay medallion (probably Vth century) in the Barberini Library at Rome. Here Christ, accompanied by six apostles, sits in judgement over a crowd of suppliants hemmed in by gates. In the VIth century, the Hellenistic tradition of Ravenna presents a youthful Christ separating rams and ewes in St Apollinare Nuovo. But the contemporary MS of Cosmas Indicopleustes in the Vatican shows a bearded Christ in an aura above two rows of suppliants ; and a fresco at Baouit in Egypt (same date) depicts the tormenting demon. Evidently, the menace of the theme was of Asiatic or African origin. In its present form, it is known to have been developed as early as the IXth century (see below), and was first placed on the West walls of churches, as at Torcello (XIIth century) or at St Demetrius' at Mistra (probably 1310-1320). Later it was banished to refectories.

From the present composition it is possible to suspect an undercurrent, perhaps subconscious, of quiet scepticism on the part of the XVIth century artist. In the Athonite monasteries, the division between the educated and uneducated monks is clearly maintained. Pictures of the Last Judgement were doubtless thought by the former to benefit the latter. And possibly not without reason. For Cedrenus (late XIth century) records that in the middle of the IXth century such a picture by the monk Methodius so appalled King Boris of Bulgaria that he and his whole people were converted to Christianity.

Plate 69

ii

i

APOCALYPSE : THE FOUR HORSEMEN.

Dionysiou (Refectory), Mount Athos.

Cretan School.

Probably 1547.

see p. 154.

Revelation VI. 2-8 : " And I saw, and behold a white horse :
and he that sat on him had a bow ; and a crown was given
unto him : and he went forth conquering, and to conquer.
. . . And there went out another horse that was red :
and power was given to him that sat thereon to take peace
from the earth, and that they should kill one another : and
there was given unto him a great sword. . . . And I
beheld, and lo a black horse ; and he that sat on him had a pair
of balances in his hand. And I heard a voice in the midst of
the four beasts say, A measure of wheat for a penny, and three
measures of barley for a penny ; and see thou hurt not the oil
and the wine. . . . And I looked, and behold a pale
horse : and his name that sat on him was Death, and Hell
followed with him. And power was given unto them over
the fourth part of the earth, to kill with sword, and with
hunger, and with death, and with the beasts of the earth."

The artist (see also Pl. 71. i, ii) has here risen to his context.
Denys of Fourna makes the pale horse green.

One of the earliest representations of the Apocalypse is the Vth century mosaic of St Paul's outside
the Walls, Rome, where the four and twenty elders (see Pl. 71. ii) proffer their crowns to Christ
Pantocrator. Denys of Fourna prescribes altogether twenty-four scenes.

Plate 70

i

APOCALYPSE: THE EARTHQUAKE.

Dionysiou (Refectory), Mount Athos.

Cretan School.

Probably 1547.

see p. 154.

Revelation VI. 12-17: " And lo, there was a great earthquake ; and the sun became black as sackcloth of hair, and the moon became as blood ; and the stars of heaven fell unto the earth, even as a fig tree casteth her untimely figs, when she is shaken of a mighty wind."

ii

APOCALYPSE: THE FOUR AND TWENTY ELDERS.

Dionysiou (Refectory), Mount Athos.

Cretan School.

Probably 1547.

see p. 154, Pl. 9. i.

Revelation IV.

See also note to Pl. 70.

Plate 71

ii

i

Plate 72

DREAM OF PHILIP II.

Escurial, Madrid.

by El Greco.

Probably 1579-1580.

see p. 191.

This was evidently intended as a small sketch for a larger composition, and was probably done while Greco was at the Escurial engaged on the St Maurice. The artist had in mind no dream, but a Last Judgement, in which the King was to appear among the elect. But to have called the picture a Judgement would have been to affront the royal majesty. For the analogies of the Undying Worm and the Choir of Pious Kings see Pl. 74. i, ii.

Plate 73

i

LAST JUDGEMENT: CHOIRS OF HOLY WOMEN, HERMITS, BISHOPS, AND PIOUS KINGS.

The Lavra (Refectory), Mount Athos.

Cretan School.

1512.

see pp. 150, 192.

ii

LAST JUDGEMENT: THE UNDYING WORM.

The Lavra (Refectory), Mount Athos.

Cretan School.

1512.

see pp. 150, 191.

See also notes to Pls. 72 and 75.

Plate 74

i

ii

i

LAST JUDGEMENT.

Dionysiou (Refectory), Mount Athos.

Cretan School.

Probably 1547.

see p. 154.

ii

LAST JUDGEMENT.

Arena Chapel, Padua.

by Giotto.

1305-1306.

see p. 103.

Giotto does his best to transform the Byzantine multiplicity of incident into an artistic unity, tempered with a certain degree of benevolence. The cross is a simplification of the Hetimasia (see top picture and Pl. 76. i).

The plan of a Byzantine Last Judgement (see also Pl. 72 and note) is as follows :—

Top row : Angels, Six Apostles, Virgin, Christ in Glory with the River of Fire issuing from his feet, St John the Baptist, Angels, Six Apostles. The Virgin and St John the Baptist appear as intercessors under the new and the old dispensations. See Deisis on Pl. 2. i.

Middle row : On Christ's right, Choirs of Patriarchs and Prophets, Bishops, Martyrs, and Hermits, Pious Kings, and Holy Women (see also Pl. 74. i). Hetimasia (see Pl. 76. i). On Christ's left, Weighing of Souls (in top picture, below Hetimasia), River of Fire, Damned in Torment, Devils.

Bottom row : Right, the Righteous seek admission through the Gate of Paradise. Left, Hell again, the Undying Worm, Classes of Sinners (see Pl. 72, 74. ii).

Plate 75

i

ii

i

HETIMASIA or PREPARATION OF THE THRONE.

St Demetrius', Mistra.

Early School of Mistra.

Probably 1310-1320.

see p. 131.

Psalm IX. 7 runs : " But the Lord shall endure for ever : he hath prepared his throne for judgment." Psalm LXXXIX. has similar references. Ephraim the Syrian (died 387) also mentions the Preparation of the Throne. Apart from these authorities, the origin of the theme is obscure. It first appears in both baptisteries at Ravenna (Vth and VIth centuries), and was probably the official substitute devised by early Byzantine art for the too-realistic Last Judgement. Certainly it symbolised the Last Judgement ; this is proved by its later inclusion in the general scheme of that event (see Pl. 75. i). In the XIIth century, it reappears at Torcello, Palermo, and Monreale. It is also found in St Sophia at Constantinople. The earlier type consists of a draped throne surmounted by a cross only. Later, the lance and the reed with a sponge were added, together with the book, dove, and footstool, and the figures of Adam and Eve prostrated in front (see Pl. 75. i). The present example is remarkable for its fine composition of angels, and also for the fact that it appears in a church where the Last Judgement is depicted quite separately. It is placed, as was customary, in one of the Eastern apses.

ii

ANGELS, WREATH, AND CHRYSOBUL.

Brontocheion, Mistra.

Middle School of Mistra.

Probably late XIVth century.

see p. 133.

See also note to Pl. 77.

Plate 76

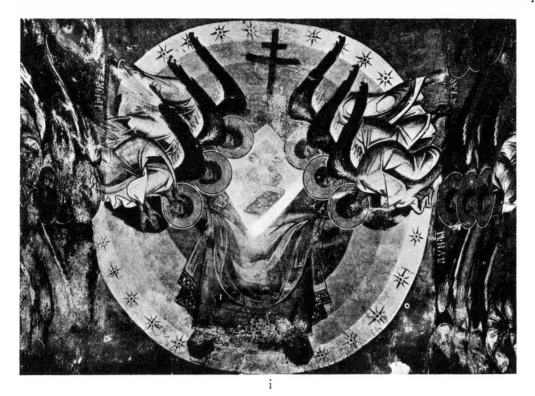

i

ii

i

DIVINE LITURGY: ASSISTANT ANGELS.

Peribleptos, Mistra.

Middle School of Mistra, by the more finished of the two Peribleptos artists (see p. 135).

Late XIVth or early XVth century.

see pp. 80, 135-6 (colour).

Angels in procession defile before the Celebrant Christ on Pl. IX. ii, bearing the furniture of Holy Communion. Depictions of Christ, in the robes of a priest, dispensing communion to the apostles, are found as early as the VIth century. But the present conception appears to be without precedent.

ii

CHERUBIM.

Pantanassa, Mistra.

Late School of Mistra.

c. 1428.

This six-winged creature occupies a small pendentive in one of the upper galleries, and recalls his prototypes on the four great pendentives of St Sophia at Constantinople.

References to angels are found throughout the Bible from Genesis onward. Christian artists of the first four centuries could therefore have known that they had wings, were clothed in white or shining raiment, and formed the court of God, their function being to act as occasional intermediaries between him and earth, and to replace the Antique hypothesis of demons. Yet the painters of the Roman catacombs depict them without wings, possibly for fear of that very resemblance to pagan figures of Victory which they afterwards attained. And at the second council of Nicæa in 787, when certain reforms were introduced into ecclesiastical art, it was necessary to forbid their investiture with the purple of Imperial ushers—a prohibition which was generally disregarded. The final definition of their characteristics, ranks, and symbols of authority, was the work of the so-called Denys the Areopagite, who wrote at the end of the Vth century. In the VIth, they are found fully developed at Ravenna, and on the pillars of the ciborium in St Mark's, where both the present types, the bowed procession and the six-winged cherubim, find precedent.

Plate 77

i

ii

i

ONE OF THE " SEVENTY APOSTLES."

Pantanassa, Mistra.

Late School of Mistra.

c. 1428.

Denys of Fourna gives the names of these earliest Christians, with particulars as to their ages and beards. The present example illustrates how the toga survived as the dress of those who had no other uniform.

ii

ST MARK.

Prodrome, Caryes, Mount Athos.

Macedonian School.

XIVth or XVth century.

The evangelist writes the first words of his own gospel, as is customary with all four. This habit of depicting the author at work is first found in the gospels of Rossano (VIth century), and was of Hellenistic origin.

Plate 78

i

ii

ST JOHN CHRYSOSTOM.

Peribleptos, Mistra.

Middle School of Mistra, by the more finished of the two Peribleptos artists (see p. 135).

Late XIVth or early XVth century.

see pp. 81, 136, 194, note to Pl. 80.

The great bishop of the IVth century brings up the rear of the procession of angels on Pl. 77. i, and utters : " God, our God, who (gives) the divine bread, the Lord and God, the nourishment of the whole world." He wears the magnificent vestments appropriate to his rank under the Empire.

Plate 79

ST BERNADINO.

Casa Greco, Toledo.

by El Greco.

c. 1604.

see p. 194.

By comparing this with Pl. 79, it is easy to discover that Greco's habit of elongating the human figure was not due to astigmatism. ⸱ St Bernadino's robe is a supreme example of how a uniform expanse of dull colour can be made to arouse interest simply by the quality of the paint.

Plate 80

ST MAURICE AND THE THEBAN LEGION : St Maurice
explains the dilemma to his Captains ; the Legion lines up
for Execution ; Heaven prepares a Reception.

Escurial, Madrid.

by El Greco.

1580-1581.

see pp. 19-20 (colour), 189-191, 209, 210-212 (colour), note to
Pl. 66. Compare the uniforms with those on Pl. 82. i, ii, iii.

Meier-Graefe has remarked that only Signorelli and Michael Angelo have " trafficked in such
masses of naked bodies ". From Michael Angelo Greco doubtless learnt two lessons: not to
allow the bodies to be naked ; and not to scuplture them, but to paint them, creating their
form and anatomy by contrasts of colour. Velasquez based his *Las Lanzas* very largely on the
scene in the background. But the blue which dominates his great picture is only Titian's blue
again ; and he rejects decisively the gift of pure colour which Greco brought to Western
Europe.

Plate 81

i

SS THEODORE STRATILATES AND
   THEODORE TIRON.

The Lavra, Mount Athos.

Cretan School, by Theophanes of Crete.

1535.

see pp. 81, 190.

The two Theodores were martyred at
   the beginning of the IVth century. The
   first was a general; the second a poor
   recruit.

ii

BYZANTINE SOLDIER, from the Victory
   of Heraclius.

Arezzo.

by Piero della Francesca.

c. 1440.

see p. 191.

iii

ROAD TO CALVARY.

National Gallery, London.

by Ugolino da Siena.

c. 1330.

see p. 191.

These three pictures illustrate both the traditional and the actual uniform of the Romano-Byzantine
soldier. Hence that of St Maurice and his Captains on Pl. 81.

Plate 82

i

ii

iii

i

HEAD OF A BISHOP.

Pantanassa, Mistra.

Late School of Mistra.

c. 1428.

see p. 144 (colour), 209.

ii

HEAD OF A SERVANT, from the Supper at Emmaus.

The Lavra, Mount Athos.

Cretan School, by Theophanes of Crete.

1535.

see p. 151.

The hair is red.

Plate 83

i

ii

i

ST EUTHYMIUS.
Protaton, Mount Athos.
Macedonian School.
Early XIVth century.
see pp. 114, 194.

ii

ST JEROME, as a Cardinal.
National Gallery, London.
by El Greco.
1566 (?).
see p. 194.

Several versions of this picture exist. In the present only, which is agreed to be the earliest, appears the following inscription : "L. Cornaro Aet. suae 100. 1566." On the other hand, a picture described as "St Jerome as a Cardinal" is found in Greco's inventories. The Cornaro inscription was probably added later. Yet Cornaro was never a Cardinal; and it is therefore difficult to believe that the addition was made without some definite reason, if it were to be obviously false to all who saw it. It is by no means improbable that Greco was in Venice by 1566; and that, having seen the famous centenarian, he used him as a model for St Jerome, at the same time allowing the fact to be known. St Jerome was never a Cardinal either. But he was at least secretary to a Pope in 383.

Whoever Greco's picture may represent, it is clear that he is here following the traditional type of Byzantine eremite, with his long beard indicative of great age (St Euthymius lived to within four years of 100) and the curious tippet-like garment in which the eremitic saint is always depicted. In posture of head, structure of nose, position and expression of the eyes, and particularly in the hollow shadow which gives each face its shape, the pictures are singularly alike.

Plate 84

ii

i

i

ST DAVID OF SALONICA.

Protaton, Mount Athos.

Macedonian School.

Early XIVth century.

see p. 114.

ii

ST JOHN THE BAPTIST

Protaton, Mount Athos.

Macedonian School.

Early XIVth century.

see p. 114.

iii

EXALTATION OF THE CROSS : detail.

The Lavra, Mount Athos.

Cretan School, by Theophanes of Crete.

1535.

see p. 151.

For other examples of Theophanes' sculptural formalism, see Pl. 69. i, ii.

The scene here depicted is not to be confused with the Invention. Macarios, Patriarch of Jerusalem, performs the Exaltation from an ambo, beneath which stands the Empress Helena. Unfortunately, recent research has eliminated her from any part in the proceedings. But it is generally admitted that the Cross was discovered while Constantine still reigned, about 335. As early as 347, Cyril of Jerusalem remarks that chips of it are scattered all over the earth. In 385, the pilgrim Etheria makes first mention of the ceremony of Exaltation. But not until the VIth century is September 14th recorded as the date of the actual feast. In 615, the Cross was carried off by the Persians. The Empire had lost its Palladium. And its recapture by Heraclius thirteen years later was celebrated in Jerusalem and Constantinople with such emotion and ceremony as to bequeath the feast to the Orthodox Church in perpetuity.

Plate 85

i

ii

iii

DEATH OF ST EPHRAIM THE SYRIAN.

Docheiariou, Mount Athos.

Cretan School.

1568.

see pp. 150, 160, 196.   Compare Pl. 87. i, ii.

St Ephraim was the most popular of the early hermits.   Having
taken service as a bath-keeper in Edessa, he was rebuked by
a hermit for thus mingling with the worldly, and thenceforth
gave himself to study and contemplation.   He died about 373.

The present picture and that on Pl. 87. i find exact parallel in the Description of the Death of St
Ephraim attributed to Mark Eugenikos in the first half of the XIVth century, though probably
the work of his brother John.   The latter wrote numerous Descriptions, whose literary form is
based on those of Philostratos (IIIrd century).   The best known is that of Trebizond.   Others
depict Corinth, the island of Imbros, and Petrina in the Peloponnese ; and others again describe
actual pictures, whose subjects are an imaginary landscape filled with hounds and birds, a young
and princely couple in a pleasure-garden, the Virgin, and St John Chrysostom.   It seems probable
that the Description of the Death of St Ephraim was also based on a picture.   For the incidents of
this Description, and of the two Deaths here reproduced, are repeated with the utmost precision
in the Death of St Athanasius of Athos on Pl. 87. ii.   Actually, therefore, both author and painters
can have been concerned with nothing more definite than a typical eremite's death, into which has
been introduced a parenthesis of scenes from his eremitic life.   Such a convention is a late one,
and in art examples of it do not appear to have survived from before the XVIth century: only one
other is found on Athos (Dionysiou, 1547), and none at Mistra.   Its popularity may have been
increased by the account of the Eugenikoi.   But it cannot have originated with them.

Their Descriptions, however, show, as does the humanistic detail of the Pantanassa at Mistra
(see pp. 138-44), that the Byzantines of the XIVth and early XVth centuries were advancing, like
the contemporary Italians, towards a new appreciation of the out-of-doors.   This fact is important.
For Greco, despite all his greatness as a colourist and technician, achieved nothing more intellectually
remarkable than his interpretation of landscape.   For him, the countryside was not merely delicious,
or picturesque, or threatening, or pastorally anecdotal, or a setting for the chase, as with previous,
contemporary, and subsequent artists.   In his view, rather, it must be treated like any other province of the artist's material, like a sitter or a great occasion, as a dramatic unity, to express not the
seasonal vagaries of different climates, but the divinity of the whole visible world.   He needed
neither crags nor tempests, neither starry carpets nor autumnal erubescence ; he was content,
instead, with the view from his window, or the view *of* his window.   Nothing illustrates more
clearly how impervious he was to the influence and fashion of the High Renascence.   By his
interpretation of landscape, he was not only the precursor of modern painters, but was the first to
discover to the world, though not unfortunately to communicate, an emotion which has since
inspired many of its finest passages in literature and music.

Such an achievement can only be attributed to the born greatness of its parent.   Nevertheless,
the following plates (87-94) offer a commentary on it which is not without interest.   The present
picture and Pl. 87. i, ii, together with the Descriptions of the Eugenikoi and occasional details at
Mistra, show how far or how little had landscape been developed by the Byzantines.   Pls. 88 and 89
show that even in his old age Greco could still compose an ecclesiastical landscape-formula after
the habit of the Byzantines.   Pls. 90-93 show how in his youth he actually executed a Byzantine
ecclesiastical landscape-formula in an impressionist and would-be secular manner.   Lastly, Pl. 94
shows the real mind of the developed artist in a quiet view of Toledo on a rainy day.

Plate 86

i

DEATH OF ST EPHRAIM THE SYRIAN.

Vatican.

by Emmanuel Tsanphournari.

XVIth century.

see p. 197.

It is recorded on the frame that this picture was brought from Greece by Squarcione (1394-1474). This is false, as Tsanphournari is known to have worked in Venice in the XVIth century. His work appears to have retained its Byzantine character more closely than that of other Greek painters in the same town.

ii

DEATH OF ST ATHANASIUS OF ATHOS.

The Lavra (Refectory), Mount Athos.

Cretan School.

1512.

see pp. 149-50, 196.

St Athanasius founded the Lavra, and is depicted within its walls.

See also note to Pl. 86.

Plate 87

Photo Anderson

i

ii

ALLEGORIA DE LA VIDA DE LOS CAMALDULENSES.

Instituto de Valencia de Don Juan, Madrid.

by El Greco.

1594-1604 (?).

see p. 196, note to Pl. 86.

The Camaldolensian community, a branch of the Benedictine
order, was founded about the year 1000 by St Romuald, who
wished to revive the eremitic ideal.   The monks were to have
each his separate house, but a common church.   Camaldoli
is near Arezzo.   And the community, still in separate houses,
may be visited to this day by those whose strength is equal to
their curiosity.

In the present picture, SS Benedict and Romuald stand on either side of a tablet inscribed with
verses on the eremitic life.   Above, appears a view of the original foundation, which Greco
must presumably have derived from some such contemporary print as that on Pl. 89.

Plate 88

Engraving of the CAMALDOLENSIAN COMMUNITY, (detail).

British Museum.

c. 1600.

see p. 196, notes to Pls. 86, 88.

Plate 89

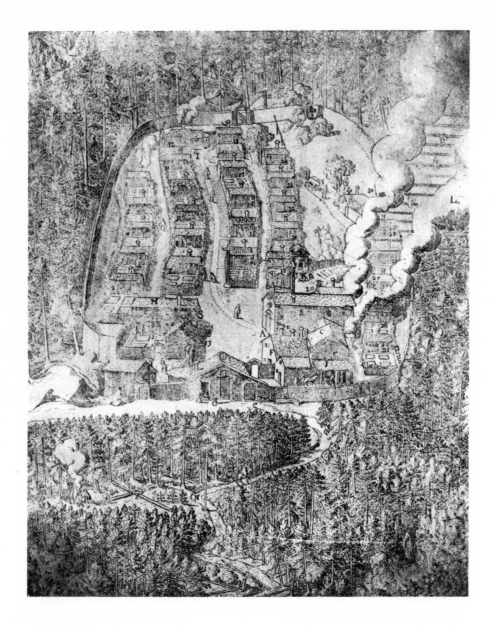

MOUNT SINAI.

Baron F. Hatvany, Budapest.

by El Greco.

1565 (?).

see pp. 195-6, note to Pl. 86.

This picture derives from the same landscape-formula as the prints on Pls. 91 and 92. Note particularly the winding steps up the central peak, the inverted perspective of the monastery, the church and tower within, the tree at the near corner, the extra wall to guard the gate, the turbaned horde appearing above the corner of the hill, the cemetery in the foreground, the similar enclosures in the background, the arriving visitors (in the prints they are the archbishop and suite; but here the dismounted traveller kisses the abbot's hand), the unsaddled horse, the camels, and, in the right-hand corner, the Nile—all of which are to be found in one or other of the prints.

Plate 90

Note to Plate 91

Woodcut of MOUNT SINAI.
from the Monastery Library.
October 5th, 1688.
see p. 195, note to Pl. 86.

This woodcut was printed at Lvov in Poland and has been hand-coloured. Landscape-formulas of this kind date from very early times, as may be seen on Mount Athos. They were circulated in the countries of Orthodox Christendom, that the faithful might gain some idea of the holy places such as Jerusalem and Athos. It is significant that the small inscription in the corner is in Russian. The monastery of St Catherine was founded under Justinian, received a charter from Mahomet, and is the seat of an autocephalous Church.

Plate 91

Engraving of MOUNT SINAI.

from the Monastery Library.

1736.

see p. 195, notes to Pls. 86, 90, 91.

This picture was evidently destined for extensive foreign circula-
tion. At the top is an appeal to the princes of the West in
Latin; below, though here omitted, a key to the numbers in
Greek, Latin, and Russian. The following inscription
appears in Italian : " Recuperato dal Sig. Michel Forro da
Nausa 1736." This is duplicated in Greek.

Plate 92

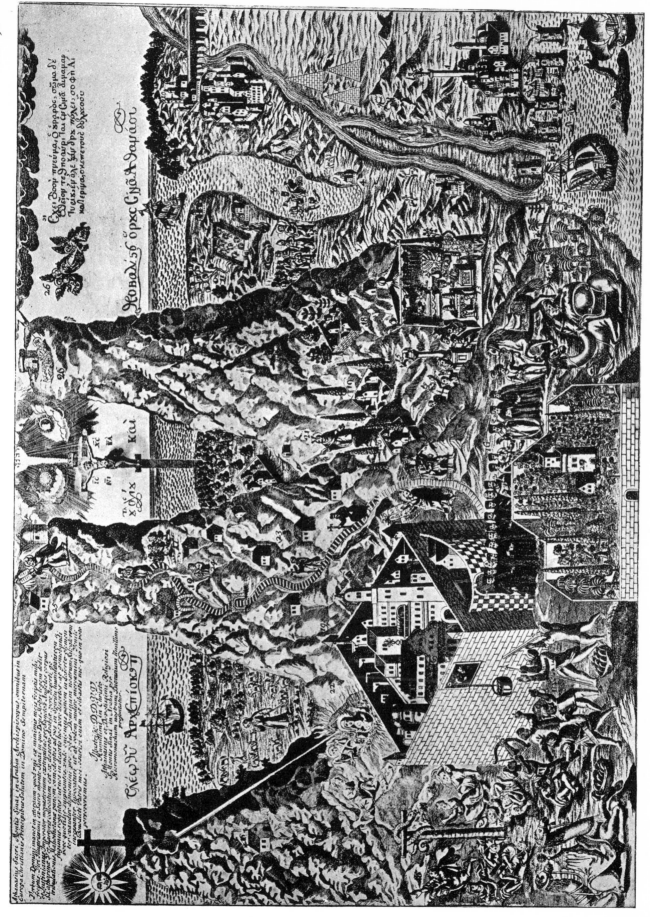

i

MOUNT SINAI : detail of the monastery.

Baron F. Hatvany, Budapest.

by El Greco.

1565 (?).

see pp. 195-6, notes to Pls. 86, 90.

ii

MOUNT SINAI : detail of arriving pilgrims.

Baron F. Hatvany, Budapest.

by El Greco.

1565 (?).

see pp. 195-6, notes to Pls. 86, 90.

Plate 93

i

ii

TOLEDO.

Casa Greco, Toledo.

by El Greco.

after 1600 (?).

see pp. 194, 197–8 (colour), 202, note to Pl. 86.

The photograph gives an entirely erroneous impression of dark-ness and storm. Actually, the picture is very light in tone and suggests nothing more sinister than a cloudy afternoon.

Plate 94